Real Cookin' For Real People

Kathy Thornton

authorHOUSE®

AuthorHouse™
1663 Liberty Drive, Suite 200
Bloomington, IN 47403
www.authorhouse.com
Phone: 1-800-839-8640

First published by AuthorHouse 7/28/2008

ISBN: 978-1-4343-5097-8 (sc)

Printed in the United States of America
Bloomington, Indiana

This book is printed on acid-free paper.

Introduction

For years it was a game at our house to try new recipes. Then we would vote for either a keeper or a loser. As the recipe file grew I began to think about putting together a cookbook. My girls got married and really started wanting a cookbook so they wouldn't have to call me every time they wanted a recipe.

This cookbook is filled with tried and true recipes. Some have been given to me by dear friends and family, found in magazines or cookbooks and others just put together with what I had in the house! We love good food, but we also love to have family and friends around us to enjoy this food. The more we love you the more we want to cook something up for you!

In this book you will find everything from comfort food to very elegant company dishes. Through trial and error I have put this cookbook together with all my favorite foods. Because of our love for food you will find something for every taste. Find a recipe, prepare it and enjoy!

Kathy Thornton

Table of Contents

APPETIZERS, RELISHES & BEVERAGES   1

BREADS & MUFFINS   41

BREAKFAST   73

CAKES   99

CANDY   153

COOKIES, BROWNIES & BARS   175

DESSERTS   215

MAIN DISHES & CASSEROLES   253

PIES   335

SALADS   365

SOUPS, SAUCES & GRAVIES   391

VEGETABLES & SIDE DISHES   417

MISC. & HELPFUL HINTS   443

INDEX   461

APPETIZERS, RELISHES & BEVERAGES

SALSA

3 regular cans diced tomatoes, or can use fresh
1/2 onion
1/4 to 1/2 C. sliced jalapeno peppers
1/2 bundle cilantro
2-1/2 tsp. garlic powder
1 tsp. salt
1 tsp. cumin
1 Tbs. sugar

In food processor, chop well the onion, peppers and cilantro. Add the tomatoes, chop. Add the rest of the ingredients and mix well. Serve with tortillas chips. Makes a little over a quart.

CORN SALSA

2 C. corn
1/2 red pepper, chopped
1/4 red onion, chopped fine
1/4 C. cilantro, chopped
1/2 tsp. salt
1 Tbs. lime juice

Mix all the ingredients in a bowl and serve with any Mexican food. May use as a dip for tortilla chips, too.

SIMPLE GUACAMOLE

2 med. avocados, peeled and mashed
1 Tbs. lemon juice
1/4 C. salsa
1/8-1/4 tsp. salt

Sprinkle lemon juice over avocados. Add salsa and salt. Smash and mix together.

TEX-MEX DIP

2 C. sour cream
1 C. salsa

Mix together and serve with tortilla chips.

MEXICAN CREAM CHEESE DIP

1- 8 oz. pkg. cream cheese
1 C. salsa

Mix together and serve with tortilla chips.

TACO DIP

1 can refried beans
1 can chopped green chilies
1-1/2 lbs. ground beef, cooked and drained
1 jar salsa
1/2 C. shredded Cheddar cheese
1/2 C. shredded Mozzarella cheese
sour cream
green onions
tomatoes

Layer the first 6 ingredients in a large pie plate. Microwave on high 5 minutes. Spread the sour cream on top. Sprinkle onions and tomatoes. Serve with tortilla chips.

CHEESE DIP

1 lb. processed cheese
1 can Mexican style tomatoes
1 lb. hamburger, browned and drained

Mix all together and heat on stove top or microwave until cheese is melted. Serve with tortilla chips. Can also add a can of pork 'n beans.

LAYERED TACO DIP

2 cans refried beans
1/2 C. sliced jalapeno peppers
2 avocados, mashed with a small amount of lemon juice
1/2 C. mayonnaise or salad dressing
1/2 C. sour cream mixed with 1 pkg. taco seasoning
2 bunches green onions, chopped
3 med. tomatoes, chopped
1/2 jar salsa
2 C. shredded cheese

Make layers in order given. Refrigerate. Serve with tortilla chips.

CHEESE BALL

3- 8 oz. pkg. cream cheese
4 pkg. pressed beef
1 Tbs. A-1 sauce
1 Tbs. Accent
1 Tbs. Worcestershire sauce
1/2 C. green onions, chopped

Reserve nine pieces of the beef to wrap around the cheese ball. Chop the rest and mix all the ingredients together. Make into a ball. Wrap with the beef slices. Serve with crackers.

CREAM CHEESE BALL

3- 8 oz. pkg. cream cheese
2-3 Tbs. mayonnaise
2 Tbs. Parmesan cheese
6 slices, bacon, fried crisp and crumbled
1/2 C. green onions, chopped
3 Tbs. Worcestershire sauce

Mix together and pat into a ball. Refrigerate. Serve with crackers.

SMOKEY CHEESE BALL

2-8 oz. pkg. cream cheese
1-10 oz. pkg. shredded Cheddar cheese
2 dashes liquid smoke
1 pkg. shredded beef (or can use crisp fried bacon.)
2 tsp. mayonnaise
1/2 tsp. garlic powder
chopped pecans

Combine together and shape into a ball. Roll in chopped pecans.

DILLY DIP

1 C. sour cream
1 C. mayonnaise
1 Tbs. dill weed
1/4 C. chopped onion
2 Tbs. parsley flakes
2-3 tsp. seasoned salt

Mix together and serve with crackers and vegetables.

CREAMY SPINACH DIP

1- 8 oz. cream cheese
1 tsp. garlic powder
1 pkg. (9 oz.) frozen creamed spinach, thawed
2 C. diced Swiss cheese
2 unsliced round loaves (1 Lb. each) Italian or French bread

Beat cream cheese and garlic powder until smooth. Stir in spinach and Swiss cheese. Cover and microwave on high for 5-8 minutes or until cheese is melted, stirring occasionally. Cut a 4" circle in the center of one loaf of bread. Remove bread, leaving 1" at the bottom. Cut the removed bread and the second loaf into 1-1/2 " cubes. Spoon hot spinach dip into the bread shell. Serve with bread cubes.

SPINACH DIP

1 pkg. dry vegetable soup mix
1/2 C. sour cream
1 C. mayonnaise
1-10 oz. pkg. frozen chopped spinach, thawed
1 can water chestnuts, drained
1/2 C. onions, chopped

Press spinach into a colander to remove all the liquid. Squeeze hard. Blend together soup mix, sour cream and mayonnaise. Fold in Spinach, water chestnuts and onions. Best if allowed to refrigerate for several hours. Serve with crackers, vegetables or chips.

HOT CRAB DIP

8 oz. pkg. cream cheese
1/2 C. crab meat (6 oz. can, drained)
1 Tbs. milk
2 Tbs. onion, chopped
1/2 tsp. horseradish
1/4 tsp. salt
1/4 tsp. pepper
1/3 C. slivered almonds

Mix all but the almonds together. Bake at 375 for 15 minutes. Top with almonds. Serve with crackers.

CHICKEN ALMOND SPREAD

1 C. chopped cooked chicken
1 C. finely chopped almonds
8 Tbs. cream
salt and pepper to taste

Mix chicken with almonds and cream. Season to taste and make into sandwiches.

DIJON CHEESE SPREAD

1 pkg. (8 oz.) cream cheese
1 C. shredded sharp cheddar cheese
1 Tbs. Dijon mustard
3 Tbs. real bacon bits
3 Tbs. green onions, sliced

Beat cream cheese and cheese with mixer until well blended. Stir in mustard, bacon and 2 Tbs. onions. Put in a serving bowl and refrigerate several hours. Let stand at room temp 30 minutes before serving and sprinkle with the rest of the onions. Serve with crackers.

REUBEN SPREAD

2-1/2 C. cubed, cooked corn beef
1 jar (16 oz.) sauerkraut, rinsed and well drained
2 C. (8 oz.) shredded Swiss cheese
2 C. shredded Cheddar cheese
1 C. mayonnaise

Put all the ingredients in a slow cooker and mix well. Cover and cook on low for 3 hours, stirring occasionally. Serve warm with snack rye bread.

QUESADILLA

1/4 C. water
1 large tomato, diced
1/2 onion, chopped
1/2 C. jalapeno peppers, sliced
6 strips, bacon, cooked and crumbled
1 lb. shredded Monterey Jack and Colby cheese
sour cream
salsa
guacamole

Cut chicken in small squares. Fry in pan, then add the water and seasoning mix. Cook just a few minutes. Set aside. Place any varieties of the ingredients listed and place in a quesadilla maker and bake. Or can put in a skillet and cook one side then flip to the other. Serve with sour cream, salsa and guacamole.

POTATO AND CHEESE QUESADILLA

2 C. corn
1/2 red bell pepper, finely chopped
1/4 red onion, finely chopped
1/4 C. chopped cilantro
1/2 tsp. salt
1 Tbs. lime juice
pepper
1 medium baking potato, peeled and cut into 1/4" cubes
1/2 C. chicken broth
1 C. shredded Monterey Jack cheese

To make the salsa, combine the corn, pepper, onion, cilantro and salt in a bowl. Mix in the lime juice and set a side. Heavily spray a nonstick skillet with cooking spray. Over med-high heat, add the potato, stirring to coat it with the spray. Cook until potato is well browned in spots, about 2 minutes, stirring several times. Pour in the broth. Cook, stirring often, until potatoes are almost soft and almost all the liquid has been absorbed. Season to taste with pepper. Cover a tortilla with some of the potato. Sprinkle cheese over that. Place in quesadilla maker and bake according to directions. Or can put in a skillet sprayed with nonstick spray.

CHICKEN QUESADILLAS

3 boneless skinless chicken breasts
1 pkg. fajita seasoning mix
1/4 C. water
1 large tomato, diced
1/2 onion, chopped
1/2 C. jalapeno peppers, sliced
6 strips, bacon, cooked and crumbled
1 lb. shredded Monterey Jack and Colby cheese
sour cream
salsa
guacamole

Cut chicken in small squares. Fry in pan, then add the water and seasoning mix. Cook just a few minutes. Set aside. Place any varieties of the ingredients listed and place in a quesadilla maker and bake. Or can put in a skillet and cook one side then flip to the other. Serve with sour cream, salsa, and guacamole.

MEXICAN EGG ROLLS

2 Tbs. oil
1-1/2 lbs. chicken breast, finely chopped
2-1/2 C. onion, chopped
1-2 Tbs. prepared dry chili mix
4 oz. green chopped chilies
1 C. grated Cheddar cheese
1 C. grated Monterey Jack cheese
1/2 C. finely chopped cilantro
1/2 jalapeno chili, seeded and finely chopped
3 Tbs. picante sauce
1 tsp. salt
1 lb. egg roll wrappers (16 in pkg.)

Heat the oil in a skillet. Add the chicken and onions, stir well, then add the chili powder and stir again. Cook and stir until chicken is done. Remove from heat and add everything but the wrappers. Mix well. On a lightly floured surface, put 1 wrapper down and place 1/4 cup filling in and wrap according to directions on pkg. Deep fry 3 minutes. Drain.

SERVE WITH SPICY GUACAMOLE SAUCE

1 avocado, peeled, seeded and chopped
1 C. sour cream
1/2 C. picante sauce
1/3 C. finely chopped cilantro
1/2 finely chopped jalapeno
Mash all together or put in a food processor until smooth. Chill.

EGG ROLLS

1/2 C. onions, finely chopped
1/4 C. water chestnuts, chopped
1/4 C. bean sprouts (or you can use shredded cabbage)
1 C. cooked shrimp or ham
1 Tbs. green onion tops
1 Tbs. soy sauce
1/2 tsp. monosodium glutamate
1/4 tsp. pepper
3-inch square egg roll wrapper

Mix all the ingredients except the wrappers. Place 1 tablespoon mixture in centers of each wrapper. Roll up, fold edges in. Seal by dipping finger in water and moistening edges. Fry in deep, hot fat for 2-3 minutes or until golden brown. Drain on paper towels.

WON TONS

1/2 lb. ground pork
6 water chestnuts, chopped fine
1/2 tsp. salt
1 green onion stalk, chopped
1 tsp. MSG
1 tsp. soy sauce
1 pkg. won ton wrappers

Combine all the ingredients and place 1/2 tsp. in each wrapper. Dampen edges to fold. Fry in deep fat fryer until golden brown. Drain on paper towel.

STUFFED MUSHROOMS

20 medium mushrooms
3 Tbs. butter
2 Tbs. onion, finely chopped
2 Tbs. red peppers, finely chopped
14 snack crackers, finely crushed
2 Tbs. grated Parmesan cheese
1/2 tsp. Italian seasoning

Remove stems from mushrooms. Finely chop enough of the stems to measure 1/4 cup. Set aside. Melt butter. Add chopped mushroom stems, onions and peppers. Cook and stir until vegetables are tender. Stir in cracker crumbs, cheese and seasoning. Spoon crumb mixture evenly into mushroom caps. Place on ungreased baking sheet. Bake at 400 for 15 minutes.

Mushrooms can be stuffed several hours in advance. Cover and chill until ready to serve. Uncover and bake at 400 for 20 minutes, or until heated through.

FANCY CRESCENTS

1 tub (8 oz) chive & onion cream cheese spread
3 slices bacon, cooked and crumbled
2 cans refrigerated crescent dinner rolls

Mix cheese spread and bacon. Separate the rolls into triangles. Cut each triangle in half lengthwise. Spread each triangle with 1 heaping teaspoon of cheese mixture. Roll up, starting at the shortest side and rolling to opposite point. Place, point side down, onto an ungreased baking sheet. Bake at 375 for 12-15 minutes.

For a sweet version, use the strawberry cream cheese and pecans, almonds or walnuts in place of the bacon.

CREAM CHEESE BITES

8 oz. cream cheese
2 Tbs. mayonnaise
3 Tbs. minced greed onion
1 egg, beaten
1 box snack crackers

Microwave cream cheese 30 seconds. Mix in mayo and stir until smooth. Mix in onion and egg. Lay out crackers on a baking sheet. Spread cream cheese mixture on top. Mound slightly in center. Use about 2 teaspoons of mixture. Place 3 inches below broiler and turn on HIGH. Broil until cheese starts to turn golden. About 90 seconds. Let cool and place on serving platter.

MOZZARELLA CRACKERS

1 (8 oz) pkg. cream cheese
60 snack crackers
1 C. spaghetti sauce

Cut cream cheese crosswise into 15 slices. Then cut each slice crosswise in half. Top each of the crackers with 1 cheese slice. Cover with another cracker. Place on a baking sheet. Bake at 325 for 8 minutes or until cheese starts to melt. Serve with spaghetti sauce as a dip.

KOLETTE'S VEGGIE PIZZA

2-8 oz. pkg. cream cheese
3/4 C. mayonnaise
1 pkg. ranch dressing mix
baked pizza crust
shredded carrots
cauliflower
broccoli
green onions
radishes
peppers
tomatoes
shredded cheese

Mix the cream cheese, mayonnaise and ranch mix. Spread on crust. Top with any of the vegetables you want. Sprinkle cheese on top. Cut into squares and serve.

PIZZA ENGLISH MUFFINS

2 lbs. ground beef
1-1/2 lb. sausage
1 small onion, chopped
1 can tomato paste (6 oz.)
1 tsp. garlic salt
1 tsp. oregano
1/2 tsp. cayenne pepper
3 pkg. (12 oz. ea.) English muffins, split
3 C. shredded Mozzarella cheese
2 C. shredded Cheddar cheese
2 C. shredded Swiss cheese

Cook the beef, sausage and onion until meat is no longer pink. Drain. Stir in tomato paste, garlic salt, oregano and cayenne. Spread over the cut side of the muffins. Place on baking sheets. Combine cheeses and sprinkle over meat mixture. Bake at 350 for 15-20 minutes.

ANTIPASTO

1/2 lb. salami or pepperoni, cut into bite sized pieces
1/2 lb. provolone or mozzarella cheese, cut into bite size pieces
10-15 cherry tomatoes, halved
4-8 peperoncini peppers
1 medium red onion, sliced thin and chopped
15 oz. can black olives, drained
8 oz. can mushrooms, quartered
5.75 oz. jar green olives, drained
1 tsp. Italian seasoning

Mix all together. Cover with dressing and put in air tight container and refrigerate. Chill at least 1 hour before serving.

DRESSING:

1/4 C. white vinegar
3 Tbs. water
2 tsp. sugar
1 tsp. lemon juice
1 tsp. garlic salt
1 tsp. onion salt
1 tsp. pepper
1 tsp. parsley flakes
1/4 tsp. basil
1/4 tsp. oregano
1/4 tsp. thyme
1/2 C. good olive oil

In a bottle or cruet, shake all the ingredients together, except oil, until well blended and salt have dissolved. Add the oil and shake well. Pour over the above mixture and refrigerate.

PICKLE BITES

1 jar whole baby kosher dill pickles
1- 8 oz. pkg. cream cheese
1 pkg. thin sliced beef

Drain pickles. Form cream cheese around each pickle. Wrap each covered pickle with a slice of the beef. Slice into 1/2 inch slices. Place flat on a serving plate. Cover with plastic wrap and refrigerate until ready to serve. Can also use 2-3 green onions in place of the pickle.

CRISPY CEREAL MIX

7 C. crispy cereal squares (corn on one side and rice on the other)
1 C. mixed nuts
1 C. pretzels
3 Tbs. margarine, melted
1/4 tsp. garlic salt
1/4 tsp. onion salt
2 tsp. lemon juice
4 tsp. Worcestershire sauce

Combine the cereal, nuts and pretzels in a 9X13 pan. Set aside. Stir together the rest of the ingredients. Gently stir into the cereal mixture until evenly coated. Bake at 250 for 45 minutes. Stir occasionally. Spread on paper towels to cool.

CRUNCHY TRAIL MIX

1 pkg. chocolate coated candies (melts in your mouth)
1 pkg. peanut butter coated candies
1 can chow Mein noodles (3 oz.)
1-1/4 C. peanuts
1-1/4 C. raisins

Combine all ingredients. Store in an air tight container.

PUMPKIN SEEDS

1 C. seeds from freshly cut pumpkin, washed and dried
2 Tbs. vegetable oil
1-2 Tbs. ranch dressing mix

In a skillet, sauté seeds in oil for 5 minutes, or until lightly browned. Using a slotted spoon, transfer seeds to an ungreased cookie sheet. Sprinkle with the dressing. Mix and stir to coat. Spread in a single layer. Bake at 325 for 10-15 minutes. Store in an air tight container.

FRUIT FILLED QUESADILLA

flour tortillas
2 tsp. melted margarine
powdered sugar or cinnamon sugar
1 can pie filling, any flavor
12 oz. cream cheese

Lightly brush one side of tortilla with margarine. Spread tortilla with a thin layer of cream cheese. Spread about 1/4 C. pie filling on one half of the tortilla. Fold in half, pressing edges to seal. In a large skillet on medium heat, cook tortilla until lightly browned, about 4 minutes. Turn and brown other side. Dust with powdered sugar.

APPLE CHEESE QUESADILLA

1 flour tortilla
1 apple, sliced
1/4 C. shredded cheese, any type

Place a layer of apple slices on half the tortilla. Sprinkle with cheese. Fold in half. Microwave for 15-20 seconds, until cheese melts.

CANDY BAR QUESADILLA

3 flour tortillas
2 Tbs. margarine melted
3 bars milk chocolate candy
vanilla ice cream

Brush both sides of the tortillas with margarine. Place one down in a quesadilla maker or on a cookie sheet. Place half of a candy bar on each tortilla. Place another tortilla on top. (Brush with margarine). Bake according to directions with quesadilla maker. Or fold over the ones on the cookie sheet. Bake at 450 for 4-6 minutes. Top with a scoop of ice cream.

PEANUT BUTTER CHOCOLATE QUESADILLA

flour tortillas
1/4 C. creamy peanut butter
1/4 C. marshmallow cream
2 small bananas, sliced
1/2 C. semi-sweet chocolate chips

Lightly coat each tortilla with nonstick cooking spray. Spread 1 Tbs. peanut butter and marshmallow cream on half of each tortilla. Arrange 1/4 of the banana slices and 2 Tbs. chocolate chips over marshmallow cream. Fold over to over filling. Heat a nonstick skillet over medium heat for 1 minute. Add two quesadillas. Cook 1-2 minutes or until tortillas are golden brown and crisp, turning once. Or if you have a quesadilla maker, spread the fillings over one tortilla, top with another and bake in maker.

STRAWBERRY PIZZA

1 refrigerator sugar cookie dough, rolled out to size of pizza pan. Bake as directed.
8 oz. cream cheese
1 C. powdered sugar
1 C. whipped topping
1 qt. strawberries

Cream together cream cheese, sugar and whipped topping. Spread over cooled cookie crust. Top with strawberries. And any other fruit you would like. Kiwi....mandarin oranges....bananas...peaches...etc.

PECAN TARTS

1 C. flour
3 oz. cream cheese
1 stick margarine
3/4 C. brown sugar
dash of salt
2/3 C. pecans
2 Tbs. margarine, melted
1 egg
1 tsp. vanilla

For the pastry, mix the flour, cream cheese, and 1 stick of margarine. Press into tart pan, making miniature pie shells. For the filling, mix the brown sugar, salt, pecans, margarine, egg and vanilla. Pour into shells. Bake at 350 for 20-25 minutes.

MINIATURE CHERRY CHEESECAKES

6 oz. cream cheese
3/4 C. sugar
1 tsp. vanilla
2 eggs
vanilla wafers
cherry pie filling

Whip together the cream cheese, sugar, vanilla and eggs. Place a wafer in a foil baking cup. Pour mixture on top. Bake at 350 for 20 minutes. Cool. Put pie filling on top. Refrigerate.

RED HOT APPLESAUCE HEARTS

1/4 C. red hot candies
1 C. boiling water
1 pkg. (3 oz.) strawberry gelatin
2-1/2 C. applesauce

Dissolve candies in water. Stir in gelatin until dissolved. Fold in applesauce. Pour into 12 oiled 1/3 c. individual molds. Or a 4-cup heart shaped mold, or a 1 qt. bowl. Chill for at least 3 hours.

SPICY RED APPLESAUCE

1-25 oz. applesauce
3 oz. cinnamon hearts or red hot candies

Put 1/2 C. applesauce in a pan over low heat. Add candies, stir to dissolve. Remove from heat and let cool. Stir in the rest of the applesauce and refrigerate.

VALENTINE CUTOUTS

2 pkg. cherry or raspberry gelatin
1-1/2 C. boiling water
1 C. milk
1 pkg. vanilla instant pudding

Dissolve gelatin in water. Set aside for 30 minutes. In a small bowl whisk the milk and pudding until smooth. About 1 minute. Quickly pour into gelatin. Whisk until well blended. Pour into an oiled cookie sheet. Chill until set. Cut into cubes or use a heart shaped cookie cutter.

COOKIE DOUGH CHEESE BALL

1- 8 oz. pkg. cream cheese
1/2 C. butter
1/4 tsp. vanilla
3/4 C. powdered sugar
2 Tbs. brown sugar
3/4 C. miniature semi-sweet chocolate chips
3/4 C. finely chopped pecans
graham crackers

Beat cream cheese, butter and vanilla until fluffy. Gradually add the sugars. Beat just until combined. Stir in chocolate chips. Cover and refrigerate for 2 hours. Wrap cream cheese mixture in plastic wrap and form into a ball. Refrigerate for 1 hour. Just before serving roll in pecans. Serve with graham crackers.

KIDS GELATIN

4 envelopes unflavored gelatin
3 pkg. gelatin, any flavor
4 C. boiling water

Mix gelatins. Pour water over and mix well. Pour into a 9X13 pan. Refrigerate until solid. Cut into squares. Need not be refrigerated after reaching solid state.

FRESH FRUIT DIP

1 C. marshmallow cream
2/3 C. sour cream
1/3 C. mayonnaise
assorted fruit

Combine the first 3 ingredients and whisk until smooth. Refrigerate until serving. Serve with fruit.

FRUIT DIP

1-1/2 C. milk
1 pkg. instant vanilla pudding
1 C. cherry vanilla yogurt
1 carton whipped topping
assorted fruit

Combine milk and pudding. Mix well. Let stand 2-3 minutes. Add yogurt. Mix well. Fold in whipped topping. Refrigerate.

QUICK FRUIT DIP

1 jar marshmallow cream
1-8 oz. pkg. cream cheese

Mix with electric mixer until well blended and creamy.

APPLE DIP

1- 8 oz. pkg. cream cheese
3/4 C. brown sugar
1/4 C. sugar
1 tsp. vanilla

Beat all ingredients with mixer until smooth.

CHOCOLATE CREAM FRUIT DIP

1- 8 oz. cream cheese
1/4 C. chocolate syrup
1 7 oz. jar marshmallow cream
apple wedges, strawberries, banana chunks

Beat cream cheese and chocolate syrup together. Fold in marshmallow cream. Cover and refrigerate until serving. Serve with fruit.

CHOCOLATE CARAMEL FONDUE

1 can sweetened condensed milk
1 jar (12 oz.) caramel ice cream topping
3 sq. (1 oz. ea.) unsweetened chocolate
assorted fresh fruit or pretzels

Combine milk, caramel topping and chocolate. Cook over low heat until chocolate is melted.

PICKLED BEETS

2 C. sugar
2 C. water
2 C. vinegar
1 tsp. whole cloves
1 tsp. allspice
1 tsp. cinnamon
1 gallon beets, unpeeled and leaving a 3" stem

Cook beets until soft. Peel and stem. Cut into slices or wedges. Cook the above ingredients until they boil. Add the beets and simmer. Put into jars and let seal. Do not need to pressure.

RED PICKLES

1 gallon large cucumbers
1 C. lime
water to cover
2 tsp. red food coloring
1 tsp. alum
1 C. vinegar

Clean seeds out of center of cucumbers. Slice into rings. Add lime and enough water to cover the cucumbers. Add 1 tsp. food coloring. Let set 24 hours. Drain. Rinse the cucumbers and let stand in cold water for 3 hours. Drain. Mix 1 tsp. food coloring, alum and vinegar, plus enough water to cover cucumbers. Simmer for 2 hours. Drain.

RED HOT SYRUP:

2 C. vinegar
2 C. water
7 C. sugar
1 C. red hot candies
4 sticks cinnamon

While cucumbers simmer, make red hot syrup by mixing all the ingredients and heat until red hots dissolve. Pour over the pickles and let stand overnight. The next morning, heat and can.

DILL JAR

1/2 C. pickling salt
6 C. water
1 pint vinegar
1 hot chili pepper, whole
1 clove garlic, whole

Combine and put in a gallon jar. Then add any combination of vegetables.

cucumbers, sliced
baby carrots, whole
celery, cut in 3" pieces
cauliflower, broken in pieces
green beans, blanched first
onions, very small ones.

Do not have to keep refrigerated, but can if you want.

ZUCCHINI RELISH

10 C. zucchini, chopped fine
4 C. onion, chopped fine
5 Tbs. salt
2 green peppers, chopped fine
2 red peppers, chopped fine
2-1/4 C. vinegar
6 C. sugar
1 Tbs. nutmeg
1 Tbs. dry mustard
1 Tbs. cornstarch
2 tsp. celery seed
1/2 tsp. pepper

Mix together the zucchini, onion and salt. Let stand over night in the refrigerator, in a crock or in granite. Drain, rinse in cold water. Drain again. Mix the rest of the ingredients and add to the zucchini. Cook on low for 30 minutes. Put in jars and seal. Makes 6 pints.

SWEET TOMATO RELISH

4 C. green tomatoes
1 sweet red pepper
1 green pepper
2 onions
3-4 tart apples
2-1/2 C. sugar
2-1/2 C. vinegar
1 tsp. salt
1 tsp. mustard seed
2 tsp. celery seed

In food processor, chop the tomatoes and then drain the extra juice off. Put the peppers, onion and apples in the processor and chop fine. Mix with the tomatoes. Add the rest of the ingredients. Boil 10 minutes. Scald jars and put the relish in and seal the jars.

CHOW CHOW

1 gallon cabbage, shredded
1 gallon green tomatoes, chopped fine
1 pint onions, chopped fine
6 large bell peppers, chopped fine
1/2 C. hot peppers, chopped fine
1/2 C. sugar
3 qt. vinegar
1 tsp. dry mustard
1 tsp. ginger
2 tsp. salt
2 tsp. cinnamon
1 tsp. garlic powder

Cook all the ingredients together until tender. Pour into sterilized jars and seal.

PICCALILLI

1 qt. green tomatoes
1/2 green pepper
1 hot pepper
1 onion
1/2 head of cabbage
1/2 C. vinegar
1/4 tsp. celery seed
1/2 tsp. pickling spices
1 tsp. salt

Chop all the vegetables very fine. With a food processor works great. Add the spices and cook over medium heat to a rolling boil for 5 minutes. Fill pint jars and process in a canner.

CORN RELISH

1-1/2 C. corn, fresh or frozen
1 small red pepper, chopped fine
1/4 C. red onion, chopped fine
3 Tbs. vinegar
1/4 tsp. dill seed
3 Tbs. honey
1/2 tsp. dry mustard
1 tsp. salt
1 tsp. pepper

Combine all the ingredients. Makes 2 quarts. You can make a bigger batch and can them. Good with hamburgers and hot dogs. You can also add some jalapeno peppers to give it a spicy taste and serve with tortillas chips.

TEA

1 family size tea bag
3/4 C. sugar
3 qt. water

Put the sugar and 1/3 of the water in a pitcher. If using a tea maker or coffee maker put the tea bag in and let brew. Stir well. Fill the rest of the pitcher with cold water or ice cubes. Stir well. If not using a tea maker, put the tea bag in some water and microwave 5 minutes and then let set for 5 minutes. Add to the sugar water in the pitcher. Stir well. Fill pitcher to the top with cold water or ice cubes. Stir well. Cut the sugar to 1/2 C. for 2 qt. pitcher.

RASPBERRY TEA

4 qt. water
1-1/2 C. sugar
1 pkg. (12 oz.) frozen unsweetened raspberries
10 individual tea bags
1/4 C. lemon juice

Bring water to a boil. Remove form heat. Stir in sugar until dissolved. Add the raspberries, tea bags and lemon juice. Cover and steep for 3 minutes. Strain. Discard berries and tea bags. Cool. Serve over ice.

SHERBET PUNCH

1/2 gallon sherbet, any flavor you want
2 qt. ginger ale

Scoop sherbet into a punch bowl. Slowly pour in the ginger ale. Serve. Replenish the sherbet and ginger ale as needed.

EASY PUNCH

4 qt. white grape juice
2 qt. bottle 7-up
food coloring of your choice

Mix together and serve. You can freeze 1 quart of this and use it in the punch bowl to assure coldness.

SUNSET COOLER

6 C. crushed ice
6 C. orange juice
1/2-3/4 C. strawberry syrup

Combine all the ingredients in a pitcher and mix well.

CREAMY ORANGE DRINK

1 C. orange juice
1 C. water
2 egg whites
3/4 tsp. vanilla
1/4 C. sugar
1 heaping C. ice

Combine all the ingredients in a blender. Set on high for 15-30 seconds.

FRUIT SMOOTHIE

2 C. milk
1 Tbs. honey
1 banana, peeled and cut in 2" pieces
1/2 pint strawberries
1/2 tsp. vanilla
1-2 C. crushed ice

Put all the ingredients in a blender and puree until smooth.

RED HOT PUNCH

3 Tbs. red hot candies
1/2 C. warm water
1/4 C. sugar
6 C. white grape juice
1 qt. ginger ale

Cook candy, water and sugar over low heat, stirring constantly until candy is dissolved. Strain and cool. Combine the rest of the ingredients. Chill.

New found recipes

New found recipes

New found recipes

New found recipes

New found recipes

New found recipes

New found recipes

BREADS
&
MUFFINS

CINNAMON ROLLS

1 pkg. yeast
1 C. warm milk
1/3 C. sugar
1/2 C. melted margarine
1 tsp. salt
2 eggs
4 C. flour

Dissolve yeast in milk. Add the rest of the ingredients. Knead into a ball. Let rise until double. Roll out to about 1/4" thick.

Spread with filling.

FILLING:

1 C. brown sugar
1/4 C. margarine
3 Tbs. cinnamon

Mix together and microwave until margarine is melted. Spread on dough. Roll up and slice into 1" slices. Put on a greased pan. Let rise until double. Bake at 400 for 10 minutes.

ICING:

1/2 C. margarine
1-1/2 C. powdered sugar
1 oz. cream cheese

Beat all ingredients together until fluffy. Spread lots of the icing on rolls while hot.

SKY HIGH BISCUITS

3 C. flour
4-1/2 tsp. baking powder
2 Tbs. sugar
1/2 tsp. salt
3/4 tsp. cream of tartar
3/4 C. margarine
1 egg, beaten
1 C. milk

Combine the dry ingredients. Cut in the margarine until it resembles cornmeal. Add the egg and milk, stirring quickly and briefly. Knead lightly on a floured surface. Pat gently into a 1" thickness. Cut into round biscuits. Place in a square pan. Put close together. Bake at 450 for 12-15 minutes.

BRENDA'S BATTER BREAD

1 C. milk, scalded
3 Tbs. sugar
1 tsp. salt
1/4 C. shortening
1 C. warm water
2 pkg. yeast
4-1/2 C. flour

Blend milk, sugar, salt and shortening and cool to lukewarm. Mix together water and yeast. Add to milk mixture. Stir in flour. Beat 2 minutes. Cover and let rise until double, about 40 minutes. Stir down and beat 30 seconds. Turn into a greased 1-1/2 qt. casserole or square pan. Bake at 375 for 1 hour. You can also use muffin pans and bake 20 minutes.

PERFECT DINNER ROLLS

1 C. warm water
2 pkg. yeast
1/2 C. margarine, melted
1/2 C. sugar
3 eggs
1 tsp. salt
4-1/2 C. flour

Combine the water and yeast. Let stand until foamy. About 5 minutes. Stir in margarine, sugar, eggs and salt. Beat in flour, 1 cup at a time, until the dough is too stiff to mix. Cover and refrigerate 2 hours or up to 4 days. Grease a 9X13 pan. Turn dough out onto a floured surface. Divide dough into 24 equal size pieces. Roll each piece into a ball. Place in even rows in pan. Cover and let rise until double. About 1 hour. Bake at 375 for 15-20 minutes. Brush with warm margarine if desired.

BREAD MACHINE WHITE BREAD

1-1/2 tsp. yeast
2 C. plus 2 Tbs. flour
1 tsp. salt
1 Tbs. sugar
1 Tbs. dry powdered milk
1 Tbs. shortening or sweet butter
1 C. less 1 tbs. warm water

Put all the ingredients in your bread machine at stated by the manufacturer and bake as directed.

BREAD MACHINE GARLIC BREAD

1 C. warm water
1 Tbs. margarine, softened
1 Tbs. instant dry milk powder
1 Tbs. sugar
1-1/2 tsp. salt
4-1/2 tsp. dried parsley flakes
2 tsp. garlic powder
3 C. flour
2 tsp. yeast

Put all the ingredients in your bread machine as stated by the manufacturer and bake as directed.

CHEESE BREAD

5-1/2 C. flour, divided
2 Tbs. sugar
2 pkg. quick rise yeast
1-1/2 tsp. salt
1/2 tsp. pepper
2 C. water
2 Tbs. margarine
3/4 C. plus 2 Tbs. shredded Cheddar cheese, divided
1/4 C. finely chopped onion

Combine 2-1/2 c. flour, sugar, yeast, salt and pepper. Heat water and margarine to 120-130 degrees. Add to the dry ingredients. Beat just until moistened. Stir in 3/4 C. cheese, onion and remaining flour. Beat until smooth. Turn onto a lightly floured surface. Shape into a ball. Place in a greased 2 qt. baking dish. Cover and let rise in a warm place until double. About 20 minutes. Bake at 350 for 40-45 minutes. Sprinkle with remaining cheese. Bake 5 minutes longer.

QUICK ONION BREAD

1-1/2 C. biscuit/baking mix
2 Tbs. dried, minced onion
1/2 C. milk
1/3 C. water
1 egg, slightly beaten
1/2-1 tsp. hot pepper sauce
2 Tbs. margarine, melted

Combine the first 6 ingredients. (Mixture will be lumpy). Transfer to a greased 9" pie plate. Drizzle margarine over top. Bake at 400 for 18-22 minutes. Cool 10 minutes.

COTTAGE CHEESE MUFFINS

1 egg
1 C. milk
1/4 C. butter, melted
1 Tbs. chopped fresh dill or 1 tsp. dried dill
3/4 C. small curd cottage cheese
2 C. flour
1 Tbs. sugar
2-1/2 tsp. baking powder
1/2 tsp. baking soda
1/2 tsp. salt

Whisk together the egg, milk, butter and dill. Add the cottage cheese and blend well. Add the dry ingredients and stir just until blended. Spoon into greased muffin tins. Bake at 375 for 20 minutes.

CHILI CHEESE MUFFINS

3/4 C. flour
3/4 C. cornmeal
2 tsp. baking powder
1/2 tsp. baking soda
1/2 tsp. salt
1-1/2 tsp. chili powder
3/4 C. sour cream
2 eggs
1/4 C. butter, melted
1/4 C. green chilies, peeled and diced
1/2 C. grated Cheddar cheese

Whisk together the sour cream, eggs, and butter until smooth. Stir in the chilies and cheese. Mix together the dry ingredients and add to the mixture. Spoon into greased muffin tins. Bake at 400 for 15 minutes.

CORN FRITTERS

1 can corn
milk
1-1/2 C. flour
3 tsp. baking powder
3/4 tsp. salt
1 egg, beaten

Drain corn, reserving liquid. Add enough milk to the liquid to measure 1 cup. Sift dry ingredients. Combine egg, milk mixture and corn. Add to the dry ingredients. Mix just until moistened. Drop by teaspoon into deep hot fat for 3-4 minutes or until golden brown.

ZUCCHINI FRITTERS

1/2 C. milk
1 egg, slightly beaten
1 C. flour
1-1/2 tsp. baking powder
1/2 of 1-ounce pkg. ranch style dip mix
2 C. shredded zucchini

Combine milk and egg. Stir together dry ingredients and add to the egg mixture. Fold in zucchini. Drop by teaspoon into deep fat fryer. Fry until golden brown. Turn once. Drain on paper towels.

ZUCCHINI WEDGES

1/2 onion chopped
1/4 C. margarine
2-1/2 C. biscuit/baking mix
1 Tbs. minced parsley
1/2 tsp. basil
1/2 tsp. thyme
3 eggs, beaten
1/4 C. milk
1-1/2 C. shredded zucchini
1 C. shredded Cheddar cheese
3/4 C. chopped almonds, toasted

Sauté the onion in the margarine until tender. Combine the dry ingredients. Add the eggs and milk. Fold in zucchini, cheese and almonds. Pour into a greased 9 inch round pan. Bake at 400 for 25-30 minutes. Cut into wedges.

ZUCCHINI BREAD

3 eggs
1 C. oil
2 C. sugar
2 C. zucchini, peeled and grated
3 C. flour
1 tsp. baking soda
1 tsp. salt
3 tsp. cinnamon
1/4 tsp. baking powder
2 tsp. vanilla
1/2 C. chopped nuts

Mix oil, sugar and zucchini. Add the rest of the ingredients and mix well. Divide into 2 greased loaf pans. Bake at 325 for 1 hour.

BANANA NUT BREAD

1/2 C. shortening
1 -1/2 C. sugar
2 eggs
1/2 tsp. vanilla
2 C. flour
1 tsp. baking soda
3/4 tsp. salt
1/2 C. milk
1 C. mashed ripe bananas
1/2 C. chopped walnuts

Cream shortening and sugar. Add eggs, one at a time, mixing well. Add vanilla. Add dry ingredients (sifted together) alternately with the milk and bananas. Stir in nuts. Bake in greased and floured pans (1-large loaf or 2 small loaf pans.) Bake at 350 for 1 hour or when toothpick inserted in center comes out clean.

STRAWBERRIES 'N' CREAM BREAD

1/2 C. margarine
3/4 C. sugar
2 eggs
1/2 C. sour cream
1 tsp. vanilla
1-3/4 C. flour
1/2 tsp. baking powder
1/2 tsp. baking soda
1/2 tsp. salt
1/4 tsp. cinnamon
3/4 C. strawberries, chopped
1/2 C. walnuts, chopped

Cream margarine and sugar until fluffy. Beat in eggs, one at a time. Add sour cream and vanilla. Mix well. Combine dry ingredients. Stir into the creamed mixture just until moistened. Fold in the strawberries and nuts. Pour into a greased loaf pan. Bake at 350 for 60-70 minutes. Serve with strawberry spread.

STRAWBERRY SPREAD:

1-8 oz. pkg. cream cheese
1 Tbs. powdered sugar
1/2 C. strawberries, smashed

Beat cream cheese and sugar until smooth. Add the strawberries. Mix well. Serve with bread, bagels, muffins or toast.

MONKEY BREAD

1 C. milk
1 C. margarine
4 Tbs. sugar
1 tsp. salt
1 pkg. yeast
3-2/3 C. flour
1 tsp. cinnamon
3/4 C. sugar

Combine milk, 1/2 c. margarine, sugar and salt in a pan. Heat until margarine is melted. Cool. Stir in yeast. Place flour in a large bowl. Make a well in flour and pour in liquid mixture. Stir until well blended. Cover and let rise until double. About 1-1/2 hours. Turn dough on a floured surface. Roll to about 1/4" thick. Cut into 2" squares. Melt the remaining margarine. Dip each square into the margarine. Mix the cinnamon and sugar. Dip the squares in it. Layer in a greased bundt pan. Let rise about 40 minutes. Bake at 375 for 35-40 minutes. Dump onto a plate and cool.

QUICK MONKEY BREAD

3/4 C. sugar
1 tsp. cinnamon
4 cans refrigerator biscuits
1 C. brown sugar
3/4 C. margarine
1-1/2 tsp. cinnamon
1 C. nuts, chopped

Mix sugar and 1 tsp. cinnamon. Cut biscuits in quarters. Dip in cinnamon and sugar mixture. Place in greased bundt pan. Mix brown sugar, margarine and 1-1/2 tsp. cinnamon in saucepan. Bring to a boil. Add nuts. Pour mixture over biscuits. Bake at 350 for 34-40 minutes. Dump onto a plate and cool.

CHOCOLATE STREUSEL COFFEE CAKE

1/2 C. butter
1/2 C. shortening
1-1/2 C. sugar
5 eggs
1 Tsp. vanilla
3 C. flour
2 tsp. baking powder
1 tsp. baking soda
1 C. sour cream
1 tsp. cinnamon
1/2 C. sugar
2 sq. baking chocolate, grated

Cream butter, shortening and sugar. Add the eggs, one at a time, beating well after each one. Add vanilla. Sift dry ingredients and add alternately with the sour cream. Beat well. Mix together the cinnamon, sugar and chocolate. Put half the batter in a greased 10" tube pan. Sprinkle half the streusel over batter. Pour the rest of the batter on top and sprinkle the rest of the streusel on top of that. Run a knife around to marbleize. Bake at 350 for 55 minutes. Turn upside down on plate.

CHERRY COFFEE CAKE

1 stick butter
1 C. sugar
2 eggs
1 C. sour cream
2 C. flour
1 tsp. baking powder
1 tsp. baking soda
1/4 tsp. salt
1 tsp. vanilla
1/2 C. cherry preserves

Beat together the butter and sugar. Add the eggs, one at a time and beat well. Add sour cream and mix well. Mix together the dry ingredients and add to the batter. Stir in vanilla and cherry preserves. Spread into two 8 inch greased square cake pans. Bake at 350 for 20-30 minutes.

BRAIDED COFFEE CAKE

3 C. flour, divided
1/4 C. sugar
1 pkg. quick rise yeast
1/2 tsp. salt
1/2 C. milk
1/2 C. margarine
1/4 C. water
1 egg

Combine 2 C. flour, sugar, yeast and salt. In a pan heat milk, margarine and water to 120-130 degrees. Add to the dry ingredients. Beat just until moistened. Add the egg and remaining flour. Beat until smooth. Shape into a ball. Do not knead. Cover and let rise for 10 minutes. Roll dough into an 11X14 rectangle on a large greased baking sheet. Spread filling down center third of the rectangle. (If using cream cheese filling, spread the cream cheese first, then top with jam.) On each long side, cut 1-inch strips, about 3 inches into center. Start at one end, fold alternating strips at an angle across the filling. Pinch ends to seal. Cover and let rise in a warm place until double. About 45 minutes. Bake at 375 for 20-25 minutes.

FRUITY CREAM CHEESE FILLING:

2 pkg. (3 oz. ea.) cream cheese
1/4 c. sugar
1 Tbs. margarine
1 tsp. lemon juice
1/4 C. strawberry jam or preserves of your choice

Beat cream cheese, sugar, margarine and lemon juice until smooth.

CHOCOLATE LOVER'S FILLING:

3/4 C. semi-sweet chocolate chips
1/3 C. evaporated milk
2 Tbs. sugar
1/2 C. chopped pecans
1 tsp. vanilla
1/4 tsp. cinnamon

Combine chocolate chips, milk and sugar. Cook and stir until chocolate is melted. Stir in pecans, vanilla and cinnamon.

RHUBARB MUFFINS

2 C. flour
3/4 C. sugar
1-1/2 tsp. baking powder
1 tsp. salt
3/4 C. nuts, chopped
1 egg
1/4 C. oil
3/4 C. orange juice
1-1/4 finely chopped rhubarb

Combine flour, sugar, baking powder, salt and nuts. In another bowl combine egg, oil and juice. Add to dry ingredients. Stir just until moistened. Stir in rhubarb. Fill 12 lightly greased muffin cups almost to the top. Bake at 375 for 25-30 minutes.

PEANUT BANANA MUFFINS

1-1/2 C. flour
1/2 C. sugar
1 tsp. baking powder
1/2 tsp. baking soda
1/2 tsp. salt
1 egg
1/2 C. margarine, melted
1-1/2 C. mashed ripe bananas
3/4 C. peanut butter chips

Combine flour, sugar, baking powder, soda and salt. In another bowl, combine the egg, margarine and bananas. Stir into dry ingredients just until moistened. Fold in chips. Fill greased or paper lined muffin tins three-fourths full. Bake at 375 for 18-22 minutes. Cool 5 minutes before removing from pan.

STRAWBERRY MUFFINS

1-1/4 C. flour
2-1/2 tsp. baking powder
1/2 tsp. salt
1 C. oatmeal
1/2 C. sugar
1 C. milk
1/2 C. margarine, melted
1 egg, beaten
1 tsp. vanilla
1 C. chopped strawberries

Mix together the flour, baking powder, salt, oatmeal and sugar. In another bowl, combine the milk, margarine, egg and vanilla. Stir milk into dry mixture just until moistened. Stir in the strawberries. Spoon batter into muffin cups. Bake at 425 for 15-18 minutes.

BLUEBERRY CREAM MUFFINS

4 C. flour
1 C. sugar
6 tsp. baking powder
1 tsp. salt
2 eggs
2 C. milk
1/2 C. margarine, melted
2 C. fresh or frozen blueberries (do not thaw) or any fruit of your choice

Combine flour, sugar, baking powder and salt. In another bowl, beat eggs, milk and margarine, Stir into dry ingredients, just until moistened. Fold in the berries. Spoon about 2 tablespoonfuls into greased muffin cups.

FILLING:

1-8 oz. pkg. cream cheese
1 egg
1/3 C. sugar
dash of salt

Beat cream cheese, egg, sugar and salt. Place about 1 Tbs. in the center of each muffin cup (do not spread). Top with remaining batter. Bake at 375 for 18-20 minutes. Cool 10 minutes before removing from pan.

CHERRY MUFFINS

2 C. flour
2 tsp. baking powder
1 tsp. baking soda
1/2 tsp. salt
1 C. tart cherries, chopped
2/3 C. sugar
1/3 C. butter, melted
2 eggs
1/2 tsp. lemon juice
1/2 tsp. almond flavoring

Mix together the flour, baking powder, baking soda and salt. To the cherries, Add the sugar, butter, eggs, lemon juice and almond flavoring. Mix and add the dry ingredients. Stir just until blended. Spoon into greased muffin tins. Bake at 375 for 20 minutes.

GRIDDLE SCONES

1 C. flour
1/2 tsp. cream of tartar
1/4 tsp. salt
1 tsp. sugar
1/2 tsp. baking soda
1/2 tsp. cinnamon
2 Tbs. milk
2 Tbs. shortening

Stir together flour, cream of tartar, salt, sugar, baking soda and cinnamon. Add milk and stir until well mixed. Turn the batter out onto a floured surface and knead a few times. Pat into a circle about 6 inches around. Cut dough into 8 wedges. Melt the shortening on a griddle. When shortening is hot, lower the heat to medium and place the scones on the griddle. Cook until the first side is golden brown. Turn and cook the other side. Scone should not be doughy. It should look like a biscuit. Serve with butter, jelly and or apple butter.

FEATHER LIGHT SCONES

3 C. flour
3 tsp. baking powder
1/2 tsp. baking soda
1/2 tsp. salt
1 C. margarine
1 egg
1 C. vanilla yogurt
1/2 tsp. vanilla
1 tsp. milk
sugar

Combine flour, baking powder, soda and salt. Cut in margarine until mixture resembles coarse crumbs. Stir in egg, yogurt and vanilla just until combined. Turn onto a floured surface. Knead 6-8 times. Roll into a 9" circle. Cut into eight wedges. Place on an ungreased baking sheet. Brush tops with milk. Sprinkle with sugar. (Or a mixture of cinnamon and sugar.) Bake at 425 for 12-15 minutes or until golden brown.

CORUM'S ORANGE SCONES
WITH ORANGE BUTTER

2 C. flour
5 Tbs. sugar
2-1/2 tsp. baking powder
2 tsp. grated orange peel
1/3 C. margarine
1/2 C. mandarin oranges in light syrup, drained
1/4 C. milk
1 egg, slightly beaten
1 Tbs. sugar

Combine flour, 5 Tbs. sugar, baking powder and orange peel. Cut in margarine until mixture resembles coarse crumbs. Add orange segments, milk and egg. Stir just until mixture leaves the sides of the bowl and soft dough forms. Turn dough onto floured surface. Knead lightly 10 times. On greased cookie sheet, roll or pat into 6" circle. Sprinkle with 1 Tbs. sugar. Cut into 8 wedges, separating slightly. Bake at 400 for 15-20 minutes, or until golden brown.

ORANGE BUTTER:

1/2 C. butter, softened
2 Tbs. orange marmalade

Beat butter in a small bowl until light and fluffy. Stir in marmalade. Serve with warm scones.

FUNNEL CAKES

2 eggs, lightly beaten
1-1/2 C. milk
1/4 C. brown sugar
2 C. flour
1-1/2 tsp. baking powder
1/4 tsp. salt
powdered sugar

Combine eggs, milk and brown sugar. Combine flour, baking powder and salt, add to the egg mixture. Beat until smooth. In an electric skillet or deep fat fryer, heat oil to 375. Cover bottom of a funnel spout with finger, ladle 1/2 c. batter into funnel. Holding funnel several inches above skillet, release finger and move funnel in a spiral motion until all the batter is released. Fry for 2 minutes on each side. Drain on paper towels. Dust with powdered sugar. Repeat with the remaining batter.

SOPAIPILLAS

1-1/2 C. milk
1 Tbs. margarine
1 pkg. yeast
1/4 C. very warm water
4 C. flour
1-1/2 tsp. salt
1 tsp. baking powder

Heat milk and margarine just until margarine is melted. Let cool to lukewarm. Sprinkle yeast over very warm water in one cup measure. Stir to dissolve. Let stand until bubbly, about 10 minutes. Sift four, salt and baking powder into a large bowl. Make a well in the center. Combine cooled milk mixture with the dissolved yeast. Add about 1-1/4 cup of the liquid to the flour. Work liquid into dough, adding more if needed to make a soft dough. Turn out onto a floured surface. Knead 15-20 times. Invert bowl over dough. Let rest 10 minutes. Roll out 1/4 of the dough at a time on a lightly floured surface to 1/4 " thickness. Cut into squares or triangles. Fry these in hot oil a few at a time. They should puff out and become hollow very soon after being dropped in oil. Drain on paper towels. Serve with honey.

APPLE FRITTERS

1 C. flour
1 tsp. salt
1/4 C. sugar
1-1/2 tsp. baking powder
1/3 C. milk
1 egg
1 C. finely chopped apples
1/2 C. powdered sugar

Mix dry ingredients together. Add milk and eggs. Beat until smooth. Add apples. Drop by teaspoon into hot grease. Fry 2-3 minutes. Roll in powdered sugar.

LONG JOHNS

1/2 C. shortening
1 C. canned milk
3 pkg. yeast
1/2 C. warm water
1 C. boiling water
8-1/2 to 9 C. flour
2 tsp. salt
1/2 C. sugar
1/2 tsp. nutmeg
2 eggs, beaten

Combine shortening and boiling water. Stir in milk, dissolve yeast in warm water. When shortening is lukewarm, stir in yeast mixture. Add remaining ingredients, adding just enough flour to knead well. Knead on lightly floured surface about 5 minutes. Let rest 10 minutes. Roll out 1/4 inch thick. Cut into strips 1X6 inches long. Cover with a tea towel and let rise 1 hour. Deep fry at 375 until light golden brown on both sides, slip the raised side into hot grease first, then turn. This gives the flat side a chance to raise and cook. Drain on paper towel and frost with following frosting.

FROSTING:

1/4 C. margarine
1/2 C. brown sugar
2 Tbs. heavy cream
powdered sugar
vanilla or maple flavoring

Boil margarine, sugar and cream 3 minutes. Add flavorings. Stir in powdered sugar to make spreading consistency.

GARLIC BUTTER

1 C. butter, softened
1 Tbs. minced garlic
1/4 C. grated Parmesan cheese
1 Tbs. garlic salt
1 tsp. Italian seasoning
1/2 tsp. pepper
1/4 tsp. paprika

Combine all the ingredients until smooth.

STRAWBERRY BUTTER

1/2 C. butter, softened
1/3 C. powdered sugar
1 TBS. strawberry preserves

Combine all the ingredients and beat at medium speed until smooth. Refrigerate. Serve with pancakes, waffles or French toast.

New found recipes

New found recipes

New found recipes

New found recipes

New found recipes

New found recipes

New found recipes

New found recipes

BREAKFAST

SKY HIGH BISCUITS

3 C. flour
4-1/2 tsp. baking powder
2 Tbs. sugar
1/2 tsp. salt
3/4 tsp. cream of tartar
3/4 C. margarine
1 egg, beaten
1 C. milk

Combine the dry ingredients. Cut in the margarine until it resembles cornmeal. Add the egg and milk, stirring quickly and briefly. Knead lightly on a floured surface. Pat gently into a 1" thickness. Cut into round biscuits. Place in a square pan. Put close together. Bake at 450 for 12-15 minutes.

SAUSAGE GRAVY

1 lb. sausage
1/3 C. flour
2-3 C. milk

Brown sausage. Sprinkle flour over and stir. Add milk. Bring to a boil and stir until thick. May add more milk if too thick. May also use hamburger in place of sausage. If using hamburger, season with salt, pepper and garlic powder. Serve over biscuits or toast.

BACON IN THE OVEN

1 lb. bacon

Place the bacon in strips on a sheet cake pan. You can get the whole lb. on this by squeezing them very close together. Bake at 400 for 10 minutes. Turn the bacon over and bake another 10 minutes. Drain on paper towels. This makes the bacon nice and crispy and no splatter mess on the stove!

BREAKFAST BURRITOS

1 Tbs. margarine
8 eggs, beaten
1/4 tsp. pepper
2 C. diced Canadian bacon
6 (8 inch) flour tortillas
6 oz. (1-1/2 C.) shredded Cheddar cheese

Melt margarine in a large skillet. Add eggs, pepper and bacon. Cook and stir about 5 minutes or until eggs are set. Spoon egg mixture evenly onto each tortilla. top with 1 Tbs. cheese. Roll up tortilla tightly. Place seam side down in an ungreased 9X13 pan. Sprinkle with remaining cheese. Bake at 400 for 10-15 minutes or until cheese is melted. Serve with sour cream and salsa.

TEXAS BRUNCH

1 lb. sausage, browned & drained
6 eggs, beaten
1-17 oz. can cream style corn
1-4 oz. can chopped green chilies
1 C. shredded Cheddar cheese
1 C. shredded Monterey Jack cheese
2 Tbs. quick cooking grits
1 Tbs. Worcestershire sauce
dash of pepper

Combine all ingredients and pour into a greased square pan. Bake at 325 for 45 minutes. Let stand 10 minutes before cutting. Serve with salsa and sour cream.

HAM & EGG SKILLET

3 uncooked potatoes, cooked and diced
1 Tbs. margarine
1/4 C. onion, chopped
1/4 C. green pepper, chopped.
1 C. cubed ham
3 eggs, beaten
1 C. shredded Cheddar cheese
salt and pepper to taste

In a skillet sauté potatoes in margarine until tender and golden brown. Add the onion and green pepper. Sauté until tender. Add the ham, eggs, cheese, salt and pepper. Cook until eggs are completely set, stirring occasionally.

HEARTY EGG SCRAMBLE

1/3 C. chopped green onion
1/4 C. chopped green pepper
1/4 C. margarine
2 medium potatoes, peeled, cooked and cubed
1-1/2 C. julienne fully cooked ham
6 eggs
2 Tbs. water
dash of pepper

Cook onion and green pepper in margarine until tender. Add potatoes and ham. Cook and stir for 5 minutes. Beat eggs, water and pepper. Pour over ham mixture. Cook, stirring occasionally until eggs are set.

FARMERS BREAKFAST

6 bacon strips, diced
2 Tbs. diced onion
3 medium potatoes, cooked and cubed
6 eggs, beaten
salt and pepper to taste
1/2 C. shredded Cheddar cheese

Cook bacon until crisp. Remove to paper towel to drain. In drippings, sauté onion and potatoes until potatoes are browned. Pour eggs into skillet. Cook and stir gently until eggs are set and cooked to desired doneness. Season with salt and pepper. Sprinkle cheese and bacon on top. Let stand for 2-3 minutes or until cheese melts.

WAKE-UP CASSEROLE

8 frozen hash brown patties
4 C. shredded Cheddar cheese
1 lb. cooked, cubed ham
7 eggs
1 C. milk
1/2 tsp. salt
1/2 tsp. ground mustard

Place hash browns in a single layer in a greased 9X13 pan. Sprinkle with cheese and ham. Beat eggs, milk, salt and mustard. Pour over ham. Cover and bake at 350 for 1 hour. Uncover and bake 15 minutes or until knife inserted in the center comes out clean.

BREAKFAST BAKE

4-1/2 C. seasoned croutons
2 C. shredded Cheddar cheese
1 med. onion
1/4 C. chopped sweet red pepper
1/4 C. chopped green pepper
1 can (4-1/2 oz.) sliced mushrooms
8 eggs
4 C. milk
1 tsp. salt
1 tsp. ground mustard
1/8 tsp. pepper
8 bacon slices, cooked and crumbled

Sprinkle croutons, cheese, onion, peppers and mushrooms into a greased 9X13 pan. In a bowl, combine the eggs, milk, salt and pepper. Slowly pour over vegetables. Sprinkle with bacon. Bake at 350 for 45-50 minutes.

BREAKFAST CASSEROLE

1 lb. sliced bacon or sausage
1 small onion, chopped
6 eggs, lightly beaten
4 C. frozen shredded hash browns, thawed
2 C. shredded Cheddar cheese
1-1/2 C. small curd cottage cheese
1-1/4 C. shredded Swiss cheese

Cook bacon or sausage and onion until bacon is crisp or sausage is browned. Drain. In a bowl combine the rest of the ingredients. Stir in bacon mixture. Pour into a greased 9X13 pan. Bake uncovered for 35-40 minutes. Let stand 10 minutes before cutting.

LOCO MOCO

2 C. instant brown rice (uncooked)
4 eggs
smoked sausage

Cook rice according to package. Fry or scramble the eggs. Slice the sausage at an angle and fry until hot. Place the rice in a large bowl. Top with an egg and cover with a couple slices of the smoked sausage. You can make some white gravy and cover all with it. Also, can use a hamburger patty in place of the sausage and cover all in brown gravy.

POTATO AND EGG CASSEROLE

One box scalloped potato mix
2 Tbs. margarine
6 eggs
1 C. cream corn
1/2 lb. crab meat
2 Tbs. flour
2 green onions, chopped
1/4 tsp. salt
1/8 tsp. nutmeg
1/4 tsp. cayenne pepper

Cook potatoes as directed on box with the milk and margarine. Bake at 450 in a square pan. Combine the rest of the ingredients. Pour over the potatoes. Reduce heat to 350 and bake for 45 minutes.

SCRAMBLED EGG MUFFINS

1/2 lb. pork sausage, browned and drained
12 eggs, beaten
1/2 C. onion, chopped
1/4 C. green pepper, chopped
1/2 tsp. salt
1/4 tsp. pepper
1/4 tsp. garlic powder
1/2 C. shredded Cheddar cheese

Mix all together and put 1/3 cupful into greased muffin cups. Bake at 350 for 20-25 minutes or until knife comes out clean.

HEARTY QUICHE

5 eggs
3/4 C, milk
1/4 tsp. pepper
4 oz. Havarti cheese, shredded
1 pkg. (3 oz) cream cheese, cubes
3/4 C. frozen California blend vegetables, thawed and patted dry
1 medium plum tomato, thinly sliced
1/3 C. butter
1 tsp. minced garlic
12 slices French bread (1 inch thick)

Whisk eggs, milk and pepper together. Stir in cheeses and vegetables. Pour into a greased 9 inch pie plate. Top with tomato slices. Bake at 375 for 30-35 minutes. Or until knife inserted near center comes out clean. Let stand 5 minutes. Combine butter and garlic. Spread both sides of each slice of bread. Broil 3-4 inches for the heat for 1-2 minutes on each side. Serve with quiche.

CRUSTLESS QUICHE

1/2 C. butter
1/2 C. flour
1-1/2 C. milk
1 tsp. baking powder
1 tsp. salt
2-1/2 C. small curd cottage cheese
1 tsp. Dijon style mustard
9 eggs
11 oz. cream cheese
3/4 lb. Jarlsberg cheese, grated
1/3 C. freshly grated Parmesan cheese

Melt butter, add flour and stir just until mixture bubbles. Slowly add milk, stirring constantly until thickened. Set aside to cool. Stir baking powder, mustard and salt into cottage cheese. Beat eggs well, then beat in softened cream cheese and cottage cheese mixture. Slowly beat in cream sauce, then mix in the cheeses. Pour into 2 buttered 10 inch pie plates. Bake at 350 for 45 minutes or until puffed and browned. Cut into wedges.

OMELET

2 eggs
2 Tbs. water
1 Tbs. margarine
salt
pepper
1/2 C. of any of the following:
chives
corn
cilantro
cheese
bacon bits
olives
ham
onions
jalapenos
tomatoes
mushrooms

Whisk the eggs and water together. Season with salt and pepper. In a 10" skillet, melt the margarine. Pour in egg mixture. Cook over medium heat, continually pushing egg toward center until set. Place filling on one side. Fold over and serve. inserted in center comes out clean.

FRENCH TOAST BAKE

12 slices bread, cubed
1-8 oz. pkg. cream cheese, cubed
8 eggs
1 C. milk
1/2 C. maple syrup

Arrange half the bread in a greased 2 qt. baking dish. Top with cream cheese and remaining bread. Whisk eggs, milk and syrup. Pour over bread. Cover and refrigerate over night. Remove from the refrigerator 30 minutes before baking. Bake at 350 for 30 minutes. Uncover and bake an additional 25 minutes. Serve with maple syrup.

FRENCH TOAST

1 egg
2 Tbs. milk
1/4 tsp. vanilla
1/4 tsp. cinnamon
2 slices bread

Combine the egg, milk, vanilla and cinnamon with a whisk. Soak bread in the mixture one slice at a time. Spray a nonstick skillet with cooking spray. Transfer the bread into skillet. Cook over medium heat until crispy, about 2 minutes. Flip and cook the other side. To serve, top with margarine, syrup and any fruit you wish.

BAKED FRUIT FRENCH TOAST

1/2 C. margarine
1 C. brown sugar
1/2 C. maple syrup
1 loaf sliced bread
1/2 C. margarine, softened
2 C. fruit, canned or fresh (well drained if canned) and sliced thin
8 eggs, well beaten
3/4 C. sugar
2 tsp. cinnamon
2 C. heavy cream
2 tsp. vanilla
1/2 C. margarine, melted
powdered sugar

Heat together, 1/2 C. margarine, brown sugar and syrup in the microwave for 2-1/2 minutes. Grease a 9X13 pan and pour syrup mixture in the bottom. Lay out 12 slices of bread. Spread margarine on a slice and top with fruit. Spread margarine on second slice and place on top of the fruit. Repeat this for the rest of the bread and fruit. Cut these in half and place in pan. Do not overlap. Press down. Beat together the eggs, sugar and cinnamon. Add to cream and vanilla. Pour over bread. Cover and let stand 20 minutes. (You can refrigerate overnight). Pour melted margarine over top. Bake at 350 for 45 minutes. Sprinkle with powdered sugar and maple syrup.

PANCAKES

1-1/4 C. flour
1 egg
1-1/4 C. buttermilk
1/4 C. sugar
1 heaping tsp. baking powder
1 tsp. baking soda
1/4 C. oil
1 tsp. vanilla
pinch of salt

With a mixer, combine all the ingredients until smooth. Pour batter by spoonfuls into hot pan that has been sprayed with a nonstick spray. When edges appear to harden, flip the pancake. They should be golden brown. Makes 10 pancakes.

COTTAGE CHEESE PANCAKES

1 egg
1-1/2 C. buttermilk
1/2 C. cottage cheese
1-1/2 C. flour
2 tsp. baking powder
1/2 tsp. baking soda

Beat the egg lightly. Stir in the milk and cottage cheese. Sift together the rest of the ingredients and then sift into the egg batter. Stir lightly just enough to combine. Pour onto a greased griddle or skillet. Takes about 2-4 minutes per side. Serve with butter, syrup, jelly and or peanut butter.

POTATO & CHEESE QUESADILLAS

2 C. corn
1/2 red bell pepper, finely chopped
1/4 red onion, finely chopped
1/4 C. chopped cilantro
1/2 tsp. salt
1 Tbs. lime juice
1 medium baking potato, peeled and cut into 1/4" cubes
1/2 C. chicken broth
1 C. shredded Monterey Jack cheese

To make the salsa, combine the corn, pepper, onion, cilantro and salt in a bowl. Mix in the lime juice and set aside. Heavily spray a nonstick skillet with cooking spray. Over med-high heat, add the potato, stirring to coat it with the spray. Cook until potato is well browned in spots, about 2 minutes, stirring several times. Pour in the broth. Cook, stirring often, until potatoes are almost soft and almost all the liquid has been absorbed. Season to taste with pepper. Cover a tortilla with some of the potato. Sprinkle cheese over that. Place in quesadilla maker and bake according to directions. Or can put in a skillet sprayed with nonstick spray.

BREAKFAST PIZZA

1 tube crescent rolls
1/2 lb. bacon, cut up, browned & drained
1/2 lb. sausage, crumbled, browned & drained
12 oz. frozen hash browns
1/2 C. chopped peppers
1/2 C. chopped onion
1/2 C. chopped tomatoes
2 C. cheddar cheese, shredded
5 eggs
1/2 C. milk
1 tsp. salt
pepper

Spray a 9X13 pan with cooking spray. Unroll crescent dough and place on bottom of pan. Press perforations together to form a rectangle. Top with bacon, sausage and hash browns. Sprinkle on any of the vegetables you want. Top with cheese. Beat the eggs with the milk. Add salt and pepper. Pour over top of ingredients in pan. Bake at 350 for 20-30 minutes.

RUSTIC PIZZA

1 pie crust
2-5 slices Genoa salami
1/4 lb. ham, cut into chunks
1 small pepperoni, sliced or in chunks
1/4 lb. cooked salami, sliced or chunked
5 eggs, beaten
2 lbs. cottage cheese or ricotta
8 oz. pkg. mozzarella, shredded or in chunks
1/4 C. grated Romano cheese

Place the pie crust in a greased spring form pan. Push with fingers to cover the bottom completely. Mix all ingredients and pour into pan. Bake at 350 for 1 hour or until the top is brown. Allow to cool in the oven with the door open for 1 hour. (I actually cooked it a little longer, until a knife inserted came out clean, and then served it). I also think putting it in a 9X13 works better.

SAUSAGE APPLE BRAID

1/2 pack of frozen puff pastry or pkg. of croissant rolls
10 oz. hot pork sausage
1 egg, beaten
1 small onion, finely chopped
2 small apples, finely chopped
3/4 C. dried herb stuffing mix
1 beaten egg or glaze
1 Tbs. sesame seeds

Roll the pastry out to 18" X 14". Place on greased cookie sheet.
In a large bowl mix together the sausage, egg, onion, apple and stuffing.
Spoon onto pastry leaving 4" on each side and 2" on each end. Brush
edges with egg. Make 3" cuts down each side of the pastry. Braid. Brush
with egg and sprinkle with sesame seeds. Bake at 400 for 30 minutes
or until golden brown.

ORANGE SCONES

2 C. flour
2 tsp. baking powder
1/2 tsp. salt
3/4 C. sour cream
6 Tbs. can frozen orange juice
1/4 C. sugar
1 tsp. baking soda
1/2 C. butter
1 egg

Combine flour, sugar, baking powder, soda and salt. Cut in butter with
pastry blender until mixture resembles coarse cornmeal. In a small bowl,
beat sour cream, egg and 4 Tbs. orange juice. Add to the flour mixture.
Stir until a soft dough forms. Turn onto a lightly floured surface and
knead several times. Divide in half. Pat dough into 6 inch circles. Cut
into 6 wedges. Place on greased baking sheet. Brush with remaining
orange juice. Bake at 425 for 11-12 minutes.

CORUM'S ORANGE SCONES
WITH ORANGE BUTTER

2 C. flour
5 Tbs. sugar
2-1/2 tsp. baking powder
2 tsp. grated orange peel
1/3 C. margarine
1/2 C. mandarin oranges in light syrup, drained
1/4 C. milk
1 egg, slightly beaten
1 Tbs. sugar

Combine flour, 5 Tbs. sugar, baking powder and orange peel. Cut in margarine until mixture resembles coarse crumbs. Add orange segments, milk and egg. Stir just until mixture leaves the sides of the bowl and soft dough forms. Turn dough onto floured surface. Knead lightly 10 times. On greased cookie sheet, roll or pat into 6" circle. Sprinkle with 1 Tbs. sugar. Cut into 8 wedges, separating slightly. Bake at 400 for 15-20 minutes, or until golden brown.

ORANGE BUTTER:

1/2 C. butter, softened
2 Tbs. orange marmalade

Beat butter in a small bowl until light and fluffy. Stir in marmalade. Serve with warm scones.

BREAKFAST FRUIT SALAD

2 C. cubed cantaloupe
2 large red apples, chopped
1 C. grapes
1 firm bananas, sliced
1/2 C. yogurt
1 Tbs. orange juice concentrate

Combine fruit. Combine yogurt and orange juice, drizzle over the fruit.

BREAKFAST FRUIT PARFAIT

1 C. plain yogurt
1 C. granola
2 Tbs. honey
2 C. strawberries, sliced or chopped
2 kiwis, sliced
whipped cream

Place in layers in given order in parfait glasses.

New found recipes

New found recipes

New found recipes

New found recipes

New found recipes

New found recipes

New found recipes

CAKES

RED VELVET CAKE

1/2 C. shortening
1-1/2 C. sugar
2 eggs
1 oz. red food coloring
2 Tbs. cocoa
2-1/4 C. flour
1 tsp. salt
1 C. milk
1 tsp. vanilla
1 Tbs. vinegar
1 tsp. baking soda

Cream shortening, sugar and eggs. Make a paste with food coloring and cocoa. Add to creamed mixture. Sift flour and salt together. Mix with milk and vanilla. Add to creamed mixture, a little at a time. Stir in vinegar and soda by hand. Pour into 2 round pans or a 9X13 pan greased and floured. Bake at 350 for 20-30 minutes. Cool completely.

CREAM FROSTING:

1 C. milk
pinch of salt
3 Tbs. flour
1 C. margarine
1 C. sugar
1 tsp. vanilla

Add milk and salt to flour in saucepan. Cook, stirring constantly until thick. Cool. Cream margarine and sugar with mixer for 7 minutes. Add flour paste a little at a time, beating for 5 minutes or until fluffy. Stir in vanilla. Spread on cake. Keep refrigerated.

POPPY SEED CAKE

3 C. flour
1-1/2 tsp. baking powder
1-1/2 tsp. salt
3 eggs
1-1/2 C. milk
1 C. oil
2-1/4 C. sugar
1-1/2 Tbs. poppy seed
1-1/2 tsp. each, vanilla, almond, butter and orange flavorings

Mix all ingredients together with a mixer for 2 minutes. Pour into a greased pan. Can use a 9X13 pan, 2 loaf pans or a bundt pan. Bake at 350 for 1 hour. Make a glaze with 1 C. powdered sugar and 1/2 tsp. each of vanilla, almond, butter and orange flavorings. Add enough water to make it pouring consistency. Drizzle over warm cake.

COCONUT POPPY SEED CAKE

My poppyseed cake recipe
2 pkg. instant coconut pudding mix
3-1/2 C. milk
whipped topping
1/3 C. coconut

Bake the cake and cool.
Beat the pudding mix and milk for 2 minutes, or until thick. Spread over cake. Spread whipped topping on top of this. Sprinkle with coconut, if desired.

PEANUT BUTTER SHEET CAKE

2 C. flour
2 C. sugar
1 tsp. baking soda
1/2 tsp. salt
1/2 C. oil
1-1/2 sticks margarine
1/2 C. peanut butter
1 C. water
1/2 C. milk
2 eggs
1 tsp. vanilla

Blend together dry ingredients. Bring to boil; oil, margarine, peanut butter and water. Pour over dry ingredients. Add milk, eggs and vanilla. Pour into a greased cookie sheet. Bake at 350 for 15-20 minutes.

ICING:

1/2 C. peanut butter
1/3 C. milk
1 stick margarine
1 tsp. vanilla
3-1/2 C. powdered sugar

Bring to boil, peanut butter, milk, margarine and vanilla. Add powdered sugar. Beat with mixer. Spread on cooled cake.

PEANUT BUTTER CAKE

2 C. sugar
1 stick margarine
1 C. peanut butter
1/4 tsp. vanilla
2 C. milk
2 tsp. baking soda
3 C. flour
1/4 tsp. salt

Blend sugar, margarine, peanut butter and vanilla. Mix the milk and baking soda together. Add to the first ingredients. Add flour and salt. Mix well. Pour into a 9X13 pan. Bake at 375 for 40 minutes. Or place into muffin tins and bake at 400 for 15-20 minutes.

FROSTING:

3 Tbs. peanut butter
1-1/2 C. powdered sugar
4 Tbs. hot milk

Cream peanut butter. Add sugar, gradually. Add milk and beat until smooth.

TRACY'S COCONUT CAKE

1 white cake mix
1 can coconut cream
1 can sweetened condensed milk
whipped topping
coconut

Prepare cake at directed on box. Bake in a 9X13 pan, also as directed on box. Poke holes in cooled cake. For topping: Mix together coconut cream and milk. Spread on cake. Spread whipped topping over that. Sprinkle with coconut.

COCONUT CREAM CAKE

1/2 C. shortening
1 stick margarine
2 C. sugar
5 eggs, separated
1 tsp. baking soda
2 C. flour
1 C. buttermilk
1-2/3 C. coconut
1 tsp. vanilla

Blend shortening and margarine. Gradually add the sugar. Add the egg yolks one at a time, beating after each egg. Sift flour and soda. Add alternately with buttermilk, beginning and ending with the flour mixture. Add coconut and vanilla. Beat the egg whites until stiff peaks form. Fold into batter. Pour into 3 greased round pans. Bake at 350 for 25-30 minutes.

FROSTING:

1/2 C. margarine
1-8 oz. pkg. cream cheese
1 lb powdered sugar
1 tsp. vanilla
1/2 tsp. salt
1/2 C. nuts, chopped

Mix well and spread on cakes.

CHOCOLATE CAKE

2 C. flour
2 C. sugar
1/4 tsp. salt
1/2 C. cocoa
2 tsp. baking soda
1 C. oil
1 C. milk
1 C. boiling water

Mix together flour, sugar, salt, cocoa and baking soda. Add the oil and milk. Mix well and add the boiling water. Beat very slowly. Pour into a 9X13 greased pan. Bake at 350 for 30 minutes. Batter will be very thin. Makes a very moist cake. Great with homemade ice cream. Can serve with whipped topping.

CREAMY CHOCOLATE CAKES

4 sq. semi-sweet baking chocolate
1/2 C. butter
1 C. powdered sugar
2 eggs
2 egg yolks
6 Tbs. flour
1/2 C. whipped topping

Microwave chocolate and butter in microwave for 1 minute or until butter is melted. Stir with a whisk until chocolate is completely melted. Stir in sugar until well blended. Blend in eggs and egg yolks with whisk. Stir in flour. Divide evenly between 4 buttered custard cups or soufflé dishes. Place on baking sheet. Bake at 425 for 13-14 minutes. Let stand 1 minute, Carefully run knife around cakes to loosen. Invert onto dessert dishes. Serve immediately, topping with whipped topping or ice cream.

MISSISSIPPI MUD CAKE

4 eggs
2 C. sugar
2 sticks margarine, melted
1-1/2 C. flour
1/3 C. cocoa
1 tsp. vanilla
1 C. nuts, chopped
1 jar marshmallow cream

Combine eggs and sugar. Beat until thick. Combine margarine, flour, cocoa, vanilla and nuts. Mix well and add to eggs and sugar. Pour into greased and floured cookie sheet or jelly roll pan. Bake 30 minutes at 350. When done, immediately spread marshmallow cream over top. Set in refrigerator while preparing frosting.

FROSTING:

1 stick margarine, melted
6 Tbs. milk
1 box powdered sugar
1/3 C. cocoa
1 tsp. vanilla
1 C. nuts, chopped

Mix all but the nuts and beat well. Spread on cake. Then swirl with marshmallow cream. Sprinkle with nuts.

TUNNEL OF FUDGE CAKE

1-3/4 C. sugar
1-3/4 C. margarine, softened
6 eggs
2 C. powdered sugar
2-1/4 C. flour
3/4 C. cocoa
2 C. chopped walnuts
Glaze:
3/4 C. powdered sugar
1/4 C. cocoa
4-6 tsp. milk

Combine sugar and margarine. Beat until light and fluffy. Add eggs, one at a time, beating well after each addition. Gradually add 2 C. powdered sugar. Blend well. By hand stir in flour and remaining cake ingredients until well blended. Spoon batter into a greased and floured bundt pan. Spread evenly. Bake at 350 for 45-50 minutes. Cool upright in pan on wire rack for 1-1/2 hours. Invert onto serving plate. cool at least 2 hours. For glaze, combine all the ingredients, adding enough milk for desired drizzling consistency. Spoon over cake, allowing some to run down sides.

TRIPLE BLISS BUNDT CAKE

1 pkg. chocolate cake mix
1 C. sour cream
1 pkg. instant chocolate pudding
4 eggs
1/2 C. oil
1/2 C. water
1 container dark chocolate frosting
whipped topping

Beat together all but the whipped topping and frosting. Pour into a greased bundt pan. Bake at 350 for 50 minutes to 1 hour or until toothpick comes out clean after inserting in center. Cool. Turn onto serving plate. Warm the frosting in microwave for a few seconds. Stir and return to microwave until able to pour and spread over cake. Drop small spoonfuls of whipped topping around cake top. Create a star shape by drawing a toothpick through middle several times. Serve with whipped topping. Keep refrigerated.

RASPBERRY CHOCOLATE CUPCAKES

4 sq. unsweetened baking chocolate
1/4 C. sugar
1/2 C. raspberry syrup
1-2/3 C. flour
1-1/2 tsp. baking soda
1/2 tsp. salt
1/2 C. margarine
1-1/2 C. sugar
3 eggs
1/3 C. milk

Microwave chocolate, raspberry syrup and 1/4 cup sugar for 1 minute. Stir and microwave another minute and stir until smooth. Let cool to lukewarm. Mix together flour, baking soda and salt. Set aside. With mixer, beat margarine and 1-1/2 cup sugar until light and fluffy. Add eggs, one at a time, beating after each addition. Add about 1/3 the flour mixture and 1/3 of the milk. Mix and add another third of each. Mix and add the rest. Mix thoroughly. Add the cooled chocolate. Let batter rest 5 minutes. Stir again and fill cupcake papers 3/4 full. Or you can put into a greased 9" pan. Bake cupcakes at 350 for 20-25 minutes. Pan will need an additional 5 minutes.

FROSTING:

2 C. chocolate chips
1-14 oz. can sweetened condensed milk

Put chocolate chips in a double boiler. Stir until melted. Stir in condensed milk and cook about 2 minutes, stirring constantly until frosting is shiny and of spreading consistency. Spread on cupcakes.

CHOCOLATE ZUCCHINI CAKE

1/2 C. margarine
1/2 C. oil
1-3/4 C. sugar
2 eggs
1 tsp. vanilla
1/2 C. milk
2 C. shredded zucchini
2-1/2 C. flour
4 Tbs. cocoa
1/2 tsp. baking powder
1 tsp. baking soda
1/2 tsp. cinnamon
1/2 tsp. cloves (optional)
1/2 C. chocolate chips

Cream margarine, oil and sugar. Add eggs, vanilla and milk. Beat well with mixer. Mix dry ingredients and add to the creamed mixture. Beat well. Stir in zucchini. Pour into a greased 9X13 pan. Sprinkle with chocolate chips. Bake at 350 for 40-45 minutes.

ZUCCHINI CAKE

1-1/2 C. oil
3 C. sugar
4 eggs
3 C. zucchini, grated
1/2 C. nuts, chopped
3 C. flour
1-1/2 tsp. cinnamon
2 tsp. baking powder
1 tsp. baking soda
1/2 tsp. salt

Add sugar, one cup at a time while beating, to the oil. Then add the eggs, one at a time, while beating. Add zucchini. Mix well. Add the dry ingredients and nuts. Mix. Pour into a 9X13 greased pan. Bake at 350 for 45 minutes. Frost with cream cheese frosting if desired.

CHOCOLATE SHEET CAKE

1 stick margarine
4 Tbs. cocoa
1 C. water
1/2 C. shortening
2 C. sugar
2 C. flour
1 tsp. vanilla
1/2 C. milk
1/2 tsp. salt
1 tsp. baking soda
2 eggs

Combine margarine, cocoa, water and shortening. Bring to a boil. Pour over sugar and flour. Mix well. Add the rest of the ingredients and mix well. Pour into a greased cookie sheet. Bake at 400 for 20 minutes.

ICING:

4 Tbs. cocoa
1 stick margarine
5 Tbs. milk
1/2 C. nuts, chopped
3-1/2 C. powdered sugar

Bring the cocoa, margarine and milk to a boil. Add nuts and powdered sugar. Mix well and spread on cake.

HOT FUDGE CAKE

1 C. flour
3/4 C. sugar
6 Tbs. cocoa, divided
2 tsp. baking powder
1/4 tsp. salt
1/2 C. milk
2 Tbs. oil
1 tsp. vanilla
1 C. brown sugar
1-3/4 C. hot water

Combine flour, sugar, 2 Tbs. cocoa, baking powder and salt. Stir in milk, oil and vanilla. Spread in an ungreased 9" square pan. Combine brown sugar and remaining cocoa. Sprinkle over cake batter. Pour hot water over all. Do not stir. Bake at 350 for 35-40 minutes. Serve warm. Top with whipped topping or ice cream.

GERMAN CHOCOLATE CAKE

1 pkg. German sweet chocolate
2-1/4 C. flour
1-1/2 C. sugar
1 tsp. baking soda
1/2 tsp. baking powder
1/2 tsp. salt
2/3 C. margarine, softened
1 C. milk
1 tsp. vanilla
2 eggs

Melt chocolate. Mix together the dry ingredients. Add the rest of the ingredients and the chocolate. Mix together well. Pour into 2 round greased pans. Bake at 350 for 30 minutes.

FILLING AND FROSTING:

3/4 C. evaporated milk
1/2 C brown sugar
1/2 C sugar
1/2 C. margarine
1 tsp. vanilla
3 egg yolks, slightly beaten
1-1/3 C. coconut
1 C. chopped pecans

Combine milk, sugars, margarine and vanilla. Bring to a full boil, stirring constantly. Remove from heat. Quickly stir a small amount into the egg yolks. Then stir into the hot mixture. Return to a boil, stirring constantly. Remove from heat. Add coconut and pecans. Cool to spreading consistency, beating occasionally. Spread on cake.

FLOURLESS CHOCOLATE CAKE

7 oz. (1-3/4 stick) butter
7 oz. semi-sweet chocolate
5 eggs, separated
2 Tbs. cocoa
7 Tbs. sugar
1 Tbs. vanilla
white chocolate cream

Sift cocoa and sugar together and sift into egg mixture. Stir until smooth. Add the vanilla. Beat the egg whites to soft peaks. Fold half the egg whites into the chocolate mixture, then pour the chocolate mixture into the remaining egg whites and fold in. Pour batter into a greased 10" spring form pan. Bake at 350 for 25 minutes or until cake is puffed and center is no longer moist. Remove cake from oven and press cake down to deflate it. Cool, then remove from pan.

SERVE WITH WHITE CHOCOLATE CREAM:

6 oz. white chocolate, chopped
1-3/4 C. whipping cream

Over low heat, melt the chocolate with 3/4 C. of cream, stirring constantly. When the mixture is smooth, remove from heat. Pour into a bowl and allow the mixture to come to room temperature. Whip the remaining cream and whisk constantly, making it smooth, stir into the chocolate mixture. Chill before serving.

RASPBERRY FUDGE CAKE

unsweetened cocoa
1 C. flour
3/4 tsp. baking powder
1/4 tsp. salt
3 oz. semi-sweet chocolate chips
2 oz. unsweetened chocolate, cut into pieces
3/4 C. margarine
3/4 C. sugar
3/4 C. seedless raspberry jam
1 Tbs. maraschino cherry liquid
3 eggs

Grease a 9" spring form, pan. Dust with cocoa. Combine flour baking powder and salt. In a saucepan, melt together the chocolates and margarine. Stirring until smooth. Remove from hear. Whisk sugar, jam, cherry liquid and eggs until well blended. Stir in melted chocolate mixture and flour mixture. Mix well. Pour into pan. Bake at 350 for 40-45 minutes.

TOPPING:

1/4 C. seedless raspberry jam
Spread over cake.

Melt the following ingredients together and drizzle over cake:
1 Tbs. margarine and 1 tsp. light corn syrup.

CHOCOLATE MACAROON CAKE

2 C. flour
1-3/4 C. sugar
1/3 C. cocoa
1 tsp. salt
1 tsp. baking soda
2 tsp. vanilla
3/4 C. cold water
1/2 C. shortening
1/2 C. sour cream
4 eggs, reserve 1 egg white for filling

COCONUT-MACAROON FILLING:

reserved egg white
1/4 C. sugar
1 C. grated coconut
1 Tbs. flour
1 tsp. vanilla

VANILLA GLAZE:

2 C. powdered sugar
1 Tbs. margarine, softened
1 tsp. vanilla
2-3 Tbs. milk

CHOCOLATE GLAZE:

2 C. powdered sugar
2 Tbs. cocoa
1 Tbs. margarine, softened
1/2 tsp. vanilla
2-4 Tbs. milk

CAKE:

Combine all the ingredients and blend at low speed until moistened. Beat 3 minutes at med. speed. Pour batter into a greased and floured bundt pan. Drop teaspoonfuls of the coconut filling over the chocolate batter. Bake at 350 for 55-60 minutes. Cool 10-15 minutes in pan. Turn out onto a serving plate to cool completely. Top with either glaze or some of both.

FILLING:

Beat egg white at high speed until soft peaks form. Gradually add sugar. Beat until soft peaks form. By hand, stir in coconut, flour and vanilla. Blend well.

GLAZE:

Combine sugar and margarine.(And cocoa for chocolate). Add vanilla. Add milk gradually to achieve desired consistency and stir until smooth.

WHITE CHOCOLATE FUDGE CAKE

1 pkg. white cake mix
1-1/4 C. water
3 eggs
1/3 C. oil
1 tsp. vanilla
3 sq. (1 oz. ea.) white baking chocolate, melted

FILLING:

3/4 C. semisweet chocolate chips
2 Tbs. butter (no substitutes)

FROSTING:

1 can vanilla frosting
3 sq. white baking chocolate, melted
1 tsp. vanilla
1 carton whipped topping

Combine cake mix , water, egg whites, oil and vanilla. Beat 2 minutes. Stir in white chocolate. Pour into a greased 9X13 pan. Bake at 350 for 25-30 minutes. Cool 5 minutes. Meanwhile, melt chocolate chips and butter in microwave. Stir until smooth. Spread over cake. Cool completely. Beat frosting, stir in white chocolate and vanilla. Fold in whipped topping. Frost cake. Store in refrigerator.

MENDI'S OCTOBERFEST WINE CAKE

1 pkg. yellow cake mix
1 box instant vanilla pudding
4 eggs
½ C. water
½ C. oil
½ C. white wine
½ C. nuts

Mix all the ingredients well. Pour into a greased and floured bundt pan. Sprinkle nuts in bottom of pan. Pour batter over nuts. Bake at 350 for 45 minutes.

GLAZE:

1 stick margarine
¼ C. water
¼ C. wine
1 C. sugar

Bring all the ingredients to a boil for 3 minutes. Pour over hot cake while still in the pan. Cool and remove from pan.

WHITE CAKE

3/4 C. shortening
1-1/2 C. sugar
1-1/2 tsp. vanilla
2-1/4 C. flour
3 tsp. baking powder
1 tsp. salt
1 C. milk
5 stiffly beaten egg whites

Cream together the shortening and sugar. Add vanilla. Sift together the dry ingredients and add to the creamed mixture alternately with the milk, beating after each addition. Gently fold in the egg whites. Bake at 375 for 18-20 minutes.

GOOEY BUTTER CAKE

1 yellow cake mix
2 eggs
1 stick margarine
2 eggs
1 tsp. vanilla
1-8 oz. pkg. cream cheese
1 lb. powdered sugar

Mix together the cake mix, 2 eggs and margarine. Pat into a 9X13 pan. Mix the rest of the ingredients and spread over the other mixture. Bake at 375 for 40 minutes.

NOVA'S ANGEL FOOD CAKE

Angel food cake mix
Instant gelatin (any flavor)
3 peaches (or any fruit)
1 C. water

Mix the cake mix and gelatin together. In a blender, puree the fruit. Add to cake. Add the water and mix well. Bake as directed on cake mix box.

CHAMPAGNE CAKE

FROSTING:

16 oz. white chocolate, divided
3/4 C. whipping cream
10 Tbs. unsalted butter, cut up
2 tsp. light corn syrup

CAKE:

1/4 C. unsalted butter
6 eggs
1 C. sugar
1/8 tsp. salt
2 tsp. vanilla
1 C. flour

SYRUP, FILLING AND SAUCE:

2-1/2 C. sweet champagne
1/4 C. sugar
1 (12 oz.) pkg. frozen raspberries
1/2 C. seedless raspberry jam, divided

Finely chop 12 oz. of the white chocolate and place in a large bowl. Reserve remaining for garnish. Place remaining frosting ingredients in medium saucepan. Cook over med. heat 2-3 minutes or until butter is melted and cream is hot. (Do not let cream boil.) Pour over chocolate. Let stand 3-4 minutes or until chocolate is soft and melted. Gently whisk until smooth. Pour into a 9X13 pan. Refrigerate 2-4 hours.

FOR CAKE: Melt 1/4 C. butter in pan or microwave. Skim foam from top. In a large bowl, whisk together eggs, 1 C. sugar and salt until blended. Set bowl over saucepan with barely simmering water. Cook 2-3 minutes or until sugar dissolves and mixture is warm to touch, whisking constantly. Remove from heat. Beat with mixture for 5 minutes or until pale and thick. Beat in vanilla. Sift half the flour over egg mixture. Gently fold until combined. Sift and fold in remaining flour. Stir about 1 cup of the cake batter into melted butter. Fold mixture back into batter. Grease and flour 2 round cake pans. Divide the batter evenly between the two. Bake at 350 for 18-20 minutes. Cool. Remove from pans.

FOR SYRUP : Combine 1/2 C. champagne and 1/4 C. sugar in a pan. Bring to a boil, boiling constantly for 2 minutes or reduced to 1/2 C. Place in a small bowl. Cool.

FOR SAUCE : Place remaining 2 C. champagne in a pan. Bring to a boil. Boil until reduced to 1-1/4 C. About 10 minutes. Stir in raspberries and 1/4 C. jam. Simmer 1 minute. Cool. Place in blender. Process. Strain. Cover and refrigerate.

ASSEMBLING THE CAKE: Place one layer of cake on a plate. Brush with half the syrup. Spread remaining jam on top. Spread about 1/2 C. frosting over this. Put 2nd layer cake on top. brush with remaining syrup. Frost top and sides of cake. make curls with leftover chocolate. Press onto cake. Refrigerate. Serve with raspberry sauce

DREAM CAKE

4-1/2 C. flour
1-1/2 C. sugar
1-1/2 C. butter
2 eggs, beaten
1-1/2 C. sour cream
1/2 tsp. salt
1 tsp. baking powder
1 tsp. baking soda
2 tsp. almond flavoring
1-lb cream cheese, softened
1/4 tsp. vanilla
2 eggs, beaten
1/2 c. sugar
1/2 C. raspberry preserves
2/3 C. almonds

Mix the flour and sugar. Cut in the butter to make a crumb mixture. Reserve 2 C. crumb mixture. To the rest add two eggs, sour cream, salt, baking powder, soda and almond flavoring. Mix well and spread over bottom and up sides of 2 round 10 inch pans that have been greased. Combine the cream cheese, vanilla, 2 eggs and sugar. Spread over the batter in pan. On top of the cream cheese mixture on each cake spread the raspberry preserves. Whirl the almonds in a food processor until chunky. Combine with the reserved crumbs and sprinkle over preserves. Bake at 350 for 45-55 minutes. Cool 30 minutes. Keep refrigerated.

PUDDING CAKE

1 pkg. cake mix, any flavor
2 pkg. instant pudding, any flavor
1 C. powdered sugar
4 C. milk

Prepare cake as directed on box. Bake in a 9X13 pan. Remove from oven and poke holes at once down through the cake with the handle of a wooden spoon. Holes should be 1 inch apart. Only after poking holes, combine the pudding mix with sugar. Gradually add milk. Beat at low speed for not more than 1 minute. Quickly pour about 1/2 of the pudding evenly over the warm cake. Allow remaining pudding to thicken slightly. Then spoon over the top, swirling it to "frost" the cake. Chill at least 1 hour.

VANILLA WAFER CAKE

2 sticks margarine
2 C. sugar
6 eggs
1-12 oz. pkg. vanilla wafers, crushed
1/2 C. milk
1 C. coconut
1 C. nuts

FROSTING:

1 C. sugar
1/2 C. margarine
2 Tbs. (heaping) flour
1 C. evaporated milk
1 tsp. vanilla
dash of salt

For cake:
Cream margarine and sugar. Add eggs, one at a time. Beat well. Add crushed wafers and milk alternately. Add the coconut and nuts. Pour into a greased 9X13 pan. Bake at 350 for 35-40 minutes.

For frosting:
Mix flour and sugar in saucepan. Add all but the vanilla and mix well. Cook until thick, stirring constantly. Remove from heat and stir in vanilla. Spread on cooled cake.

GELATIN CAKE

1 white cake mix
1 pkg. gelatin, any flavor
1 C. boiling water
1 C. cold water

Prepare cake as directed on box. Bake in a 9X13 pan as directed on box. Mix gelatin with the boiling water until gelatin is dissolved. Add the cold water. Mix well. Poke holes with a fork through the cake a couple inches apart. Pour gelatin onto cake, letting it absorb into the cake. Refrigerate until set. Serve with whipped topping.

PISTACHIO CAKE

1 pkg. white cake mix
3/4 C. oil
3 eggs
1 C. lemon lime soda pop
1 pkg. Pistachio instant pudding
1 C. pecans, chopped
1/2 C. coconut

ICING:

2 envelopes whipped topping mix
1-1/2 C. milk
1 pkg. pistachio instant pudding
1/2 C. coconut
3/4 C. pecans, chopped

For cake, combine all the ingredients and mix well. Pour into a greased 9X13 pan. Bake at 350 for 45 minutes.

For Icing: Combine topping mix, milk and pudding. Beat until thick. Spread on cake. Sprinkle with coconut and nuts. Keep refrigerated and covered.

BANANA CAKE

1/2 C, shortening
1-1/2 C. sugar
2 eggs
2 C. flour
1/4 tsp. baking powder
3/4 tsp. baking soda
1 tsp. salt
1/4 C. buttermilk
1 C. mashed bananas

Cream shortening and sugar until fluffy. Add eggs, beating until smooth. Sift flour, baking powder, soda and salt together. Stir alternately with milk and bananas. Pour into a greased 9X13 pan. Bake at 350 for 35-45 minutes. Frost with a cream cheese frosting.

APPLE CAKE

1 white or yellow cake mix
2/3 C. oil
3 eggs
1-2 tsp. cinnamon
1 can apple pie filling

TOPPING:

3 Tbs. flour
3 Tbs. brown sugar
3 Tbs. margarine
1/2 C. nuts
dash of cinnamon

Mix all together and stir in pie filling. Pour into a 9X13 pan. Mix the topping ingredients (flour, brown sugar and margarine.) until crumbly. Add the nuts and cinnamon. Sprinkle over top of cake. Bake at 350 for 45 minutes.

GERMAN APPLE CAKE

2 C. sugar
2 C. flour
2 tsp. cinnamon
1 tsp. baking soda
1/2 tsp. salt
4 C. apples, peeled and sliced
1/2 C. nuts
2 eggs
1 C. oil
1 tsp. vanilla

FROSTING:

8 oz. cream cheese
3 Tbs. margarine, melted
1 tsp. vanilla
1-1/2 C. powdered sugar

Mix dry ingredients together. Add the apples and nuts. Mix until well coated. Mix eggs, oil and vanilla. Add to the apple mixture. Pour into a 9X13 pan. Bake at 350 for 1 hour. For frosting: Mix all the ingredients well and spread on cooled cake.

CARAMEL APPLE CAKE

1-1/2 C. vegetable oil
1-1/2 C. sugar
1/2 C. brown sugar
3 eggs
3 C. flour
2 tsp. cinnamon
1/2 tsp. nutmeg
1 tsp. baking soda
1/2 tsp. salt
3-1/2 C. peeled diced apples
1 C. pecans or walnuts
2 tsp. vanilla

CARAMEL ICING:

1/2 C. butter
1 C. brown sugar
1/4 C. milk
1 tsp. vanilla
1 C. powdered sugar

Combine oil and sugars. Add eggs, one at a time, beating well after each addition. Combine dry ingredients. Add to batter and stir well. Fold in apples, nuts and vanilla. Pour into a greased 10" tube pan. Bake at 325 for 1-1/2 hours. Cool 10 minutes. Remove from pan. Cool completely. (Or can bake in a 9X13 pan, about a hour cooking time).

For Icing: In double boiler, heat butter, brown sugar, milk and vanilla until sugar is dissolved. Cool to room temperature. Beat in the powdered sugar until smooth. Drizzle over cake. Sprinkle with nuts if desired.

FASTEST CAKE IN THE WEST

2 C. flour
1-1/2 C. sugar
1/2 tsp. salt
1-1/2 tsp. baking soda
1 tsp. cinnamon
1 C. nuts
1 can cherry pie filling
2 eggs, beaten

Mix this in the pan you are going to bake it in. Use a 9X13 pan. Do not grease. Mix dry ingredients together. Add the remaining ingredients. Mix together with a fork until well mixed. Bake at 350 for 30 minutes. Serve with whipped topping or ice cream. Or you can use a cream cheese frosting.

OATMEAL CAKE

1-1/2 C. boiling water
1 C. quick cooking oatmeal
1/2 C. margarine
1 C. sugar
1 C. brown sugar
2 eggs
1-1/2 C. flour
1 tsp. cinnamon
1 tsp. baking soda
1/2 tsp. salt
1 tsp. nutmeg

TOPPING:

1/2 C. evaporated milk
1/2 C. sugar
1 C. nuts
1/4 tsp. vanilla
1/4 C. brown sugar
1 C. coconut
6 Tbs. margarine

For cake: Pour hot water over oatmeal. Let soak 20 minutes. Cream margarine and sugars. Beat in eggs. Sift dry ingredients and mix well with creamed mixture. Pour into a greased 9X13 pan. Bake at 350 for 30-35 minutes. Cool.

For topping:
In a pan, mix all the ingredients. Heat until bubbly. Pour over cooled cake. May put under broiler until lightly browned if desired. Watch carefully!!!!!

STRAWBERRY CAKE

1 pkg. white cake mix
1 pkg. strawberry gelatin
4 eggs
1/2 C. drained strawberries
1/2 C. strawberry juice
3 Tbs. flour
1 C. oil

ICING:

3-1/2 C. powdered sugar
3/4 stick margarine
1 C. drained strawberries

Mix all the cake ingredients together. Pour into a greased 9X13 pan. Bake at 350 for 1 hour.

For icing:
Mix all the ingredients together until creamy. Spread on cooled cake.

MOM'S FRUIT COCKTAIL CAKE

2 C. flour
1 tsp. baking soda
1-1/2 C. sugar
2 eggs
1/2 tsp. salt
1 can fruit cocktail, do not drain
3/4 C. brown sugar
1/2 C. nuts

ICING:

3/4 C. sugar
1 tsp. vanilla
3/4 C. evaporated milk
1/4 C. coconut
1 stick margarine

For cake: Mix all the ingredients together except the brown sugar and nuts. Pour into a 9X13 pan. Mix the brown sugar and nuts together and sprinkle over cake. Bake at 350 for 45 minutes.

For icing: Put all the ingredients in a pan and bring to a boil. Boil 5 minutes. Pour over cake. Keep refrigerated.

CARROT CAKE

2 C. flour
2 C. sugar
1/2 tsp. salt
1 tsp. baking powder
2 tsp. cinnamon
2 tsp. baking soda
4 eggs
1 tsp. vanilla
1-1/2 C. oil
3 C. grated carrots

Mix all the dry ingredients. Add the rest of the ingredients and mix well. Pour into a greased and floured 9X13 pan. Bake at 350 for 1 hour.

ICING:

1 stick margarine
1 tsp. vanilla
1 (8 oz.) pkg. cream cheese
2 C. powdered sugar
1 C. chopped walnuts

Cream margarine and cream cheese until smooth. Add the rest of the ingredients and mix well. Put on cooled cake.

PUMPKIN CAKE

1 large can pumpkin
4 eggs
1 can evaporated milk
1-1/2 C. sugar
2 tsp. cinnamon
1/2 tsp. nutmeg
1 yellow cake mix
1 C. margarine
1 C. nuts

Mix the first 6 ingredients. Pour into an ungreased 9X13 pan. Sprinkle cake mix over the top. Melt margarine and drizzle over top. Sprinkle with nuts. Bake at 350 for 40 minutes. Serve with whipped topping.

PUMPKIN SHEET CAKE

1 can pumpkin (16 oz)
2 C. sugar
1 C. oil
4 eggs, lightly beaten
2 C. flour
2 tsp. baking soda
1 tsp. cinnamon
1/2 tsp. salt

Beat pumpkin, sugar and oil. Add eggs. Mix well. Combine flour, soda, cinnamon and salt. Add to mixture. Beat until well blended. Pour into a greased jelly roll pan or cookie sheet. Bake at 350 for 25-30 minutes. Cool.

CREAM CHEESE FROSTING:

1-3 oz. pkg. cream cheese
5 Tbs. margarine
1 tsp. vanilla
1-3/4 C. powdered sugar
3-4 tsp. milk

Beat cream cheese, margarine and vanilla until smooth. Gradually add powdered sugar. Mix well. Add milk until frosting reaches spreading consistency. Frost cake.

PEACH POUND CAKE

1 C. margarine
3 C. sugar
6 eggs
1 tsp. vanilla
1/2 tsp. almond flavoring
3 C. flour
1/4 tsp. baking soda
1/2 tsp. salt
1/2 C. sour cream
2 C. peaches

Cream margarine and sugar. Add eggs, one at a time. Stir in vanilla and almond flavoring. Combine the dry ingredients. Add to creamed mixture. Fold in sour cream and peaches. Pour into a greased and floured bundt pan or a tube pan. Bake at 350 for 75-85 minutes.

FESTIVE CAKE

3 C. flour
2 C. sugar
1-1/2 tsp. baking soda
1 tsp. salt
1 tsp. cinnamon
1 C. nuts
3 eggs, beaten
1-1/2 C. oil
1 tsp. vanilla
2 C. bananas, chopped
1 C. drained crushed pineapple

Mix the first 6 ingredients together and set aside. Mix the rest of the ingredients together and add to the first set of ingredients. Pour into a tube pan or bundt pan. Bake at 325 for 1 hour 20 minutes.

PEAR CAKE

1 can pears
1 pkg. cake mix
2 egg whites
1 egg
powdered sugar

Drain pears, reserving syrup. Chop pears and place them and the syrup in mixing bowl. Add cake mix, egg whites and egg. Beat on high for 4 minutes. Grease and flour a bundt pan. Pour batter in. Bake at 350 for 50-55 minutes. Cool. Remove from pan. Dust with powdered sugar.

PLUM CAKE

1 C. butter
3/4 C. sugar
3/4 C. brown sugar
2 eggs
1 tsp. vanilla
2-1/2 C. flour
2 tsp. baking powder
1 tsp. baking soda
1/2 tsp. salt
2 tsp. cinnamon
1-16 oz. can purple plums, packed in syrup.
powdered sugar

Beat the butter until creamy and light. Gradually add the sugars, beating until creamy and smooth. Beat in the eggs, then the vanilla. Drain the syrup from plums and reserve the syrup. Chop the plums. Sift the dry ingredients and and stir into the butter mixture, alternating with 1/2 C. reserved syrup, beginning and ending with dry ingredients. Stir in the plums. Pour batter into a buttered 9X13 pan. Bake at 400 for 25-30 minutes. Turn cake out onto a rack and allow to cool. Dust with powdered sugar.

CINNAMON FLOP CAKE

2 C. flour
1 C. sugar
pinch of salt
2 tsp. baking powder
1 heaping Tbs. shortening
1 egg
1 C. milk
1/3 stick margarine, melted
brown sugar
cinnamon

Mix flour, sugar, salt and baking powder in a bowl. Cut in shortening. Blend egg and milk together. Add to dry ingredients. Mix well. Spread in a square pan. Pour margarine over top. Sprinkle with brown sugar and cinnamon. Take a knife and swirl through the mixture to give it a marbled look. Bake 375 for 30 minutes.

RHUBARB PUDDING CAKE

4 C. diced rhubarb
1 C. sugar
3/4 C. water
1/4 C. shortening
1/2 C. sugar
1 C. flour
1/4 tsp. salt
1 egg
1/2 tsp. vanilla
2 tsp. baking powder
1/2 C. milk

Cook rhubarb, 1 C. sugar and water until rhubarb is tender. Keep hot. Cream shortening and 1/2 C. sugar. Beat in eggs and vanilla. Sift together flour, baking powder and salt. Add alternately with milk to creamed mixture. Pour into a greased 9" square pan. Spoon hot rhubarb over batter. Bake at 350 for 40 minutes.

RHUBARB UPSIDE DOWN CAKE

TOPPING:

3C. rhubarb, cut into 1/2 slices
1 C. sugar
2 Tbs. flour
1/4 tsp. nutmeg
1/4 C. margarine, melted

BATTER:

1-1/2 C. flour
3/4 C. sugar
2 tsp. baking powder
1/4 tsp. salt
1/2 tsp. nutmeg
1/4 C. margarine, melted
2/3 C. milk
1 egg
whipped topping

Sprinkle rhubarb in a greased 10" heavy skillet. Combine sugar, flour and nutmeg. Sprinkle over rhubarb. Drizzle with margarine. For batter, combine flour, sugar, baking powder, salt and nutmeg in a bowl. Add margarine, milk and egg. Beat until smooth. Spread over rhubarb. Bake at 350 for 35 minutes. Loosen edges immediately and invert onto a serving plate. Serve warm with whipped topping.

RHUBARB CAKE

1 C. rhubarb, cut fine
1/2 C. sugar
2 C. flour
1-1/2 C. sugar
1/2 C. oil
1 egg
1 C. milk
1 tsp. baking soda
1 tsp. cinnamon
1 tsp. vanilla

Combine rhubarb and the 1/2 C. sugar. Mix the rest of the ingredients together. Add the rhubarb and sugar mixture. Stir until well blended. Pour into a 9X13 greased pan. Bake at 350 for 1 hour.

TOPPING:

1 C. coconut
1 C. brown sugar
1/4 C. milk
1 Tbs. margarine
1/2 C. nuts

Combine all the ingredients and cook 3 minutes. Pour on cake and spread while cake is hot.

BUTTER CREAM FROSTING

3 C. powdered sugar
1 stick margarine, softened
1 tsp. vanilla

Cream together with mixer until smooth. Spread on any cake.

ORANGE FROSTING

2 Tbs. butter, softened
2 Tbs. orange juice
1 to 1-1/2 C. powdered sugar

Beat the butter and orange juice together. Add the powdered sugar until the desired consistency is reached. Spread on cake or cookies.

CREAM FROSTING

1 C. milk
pinch of salt
3 Tbs. flour
1 C. margarine
1 C. sugar
1 tsp. vanilla

Add milk and salt to flour in a saucepan. Cook, stirring constantly until thick. Cool. Cream margarine and sugar with mixer for 7 minutes. Add flour paste a little at a time, beating for 5 minutes or until fluffy. Stir in vanilla. Spread on cake. Keep refrigerated.

CREAMY FROSTING

1 C. sugar
1/2 C. margarine
2 heaping Tbs. flour
1 C. evaporated milk
1 tsp. vanilla
dash of salt

Mix flour and sugar in saucepan. Add all but the vanilla and mix well. Cook until thick. Remove from heat and stir in vanilla. Spread on cooled cake.

CREAM CHEESE FROSTING

8 oz. pkg. cream cheese
3 Tbs. margarine, melted
1 tsp. vanilla
1-1/2 C. powdered sugar

Mix well with mixer and spread on cooled cake.

CHOCOLATE FROSTING

1 stick margarine
6 Tbs. milk
1 lb. powdered sugar
1/3 C. cocoa
1 tsp. vanilla

Mix all the ingredients together and beat well with mixer. Spread on cake.

WHIPPED CREAM FROSTING

2-12 oz. cartons heavy whipping cream
3/4 C. powdered sugar

Using electric mixer, whip cream until stiff. Add powdered sugar 1/4 C. at a time, mixing between each addition. Mix until stiff and cream forms peaks. Frost cake. Refrigerate before serving or serve immediately. Cake must be stored in refrigerator. Note: The more powdered sugar, the stiffer the frosting.

New found recipes

New found recipes

New found recipes

New found recipes

New found recipes

New found recipes

New found recipes

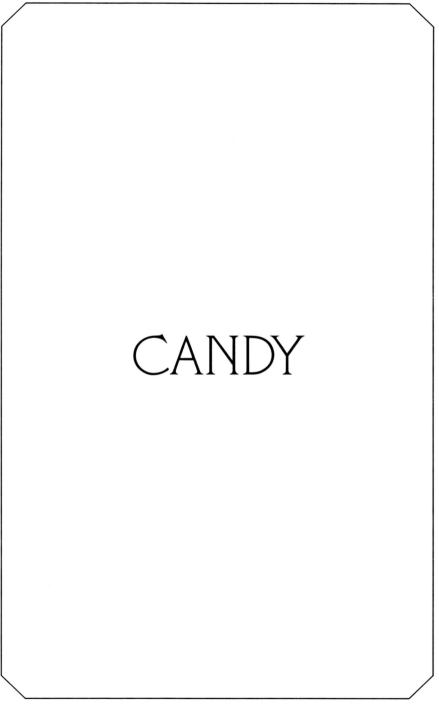

CANDY

CREAM CHEESE MINTS

8 oz. cream cheese, softened
2 lbs. powdered sugar
2 tsp. peppermint flavoring

Mix cream cheese, sugar and flavoring with mixer. Mix until mixture resembles clay. Color if desired by kneading in color. Make small balls, dip in sugar and press into rubber mint mold. Immediately drop onto waxed paper. Or you can use a decorator bag and large tip and squeeze mints onto waxed paper. Air dry completely before removing from waxed paper.

PEANUT CLUSTERS

1 (12 oz.) pkg. chocolate chips
1 can sweetened condensed milk
3 C. salted peanuts
2 tsp. vanilla

Melt chocolate chips in microwave. Add milk, peanuts and vanilla. Stir together. Drop by teaspoon on waxed paper.

MICROWAVE PEANUT BRITTLE

1-1/2 C. sugar
1/2 C. corn syrup
1/2 C. water
2 C. raw peanuts
dash salt
1 tsp. margarine
1 tsp. baking soda
1 tsp. vanilla

Place sugar, syrup, water, salt and peanuts in a 2 qt. bowl. Cook on high 5 minutes. Stir. Cook 13-15 minutes on high or until syrup separates into threads. (Hard crack stage, 300 degrees). Stir in margarine, soda and vanilla until light and bubbly. Pour into buttered cookie sheet. Spread thin. Cool. Break into pieces.

CARAMEL DELIGHTS

1-12 oz. pkg. chocolate chips
2 Tbs. shortening
30 caramels
3 Tbs. margarine
2 Tbs. water
1 C. chopped pecans

Melt chocolate chips and shortening in microwave. Stir until smooth. Pour 1/2 of it into an 8" foil lined square pan. Spread evenly. Refrigerate until firm. About 15 minutes. Combine caramels, water and margarine. Melt in the microwave. Stir until smooth. Stir in nuts. Pour over chocolate in pan. Spread evenly. Refrigerate about 15 minutes. Top with remaining chocolate. Spread evenly. Return to refrigerator and chill until firm. About 1 hour. Cut into squares.

CHOCOLATE COCONUT BALLS

2 lbs. powdered sugar
1 stick margarine
1-7 oz. pkg. flaked coconut
1 can sweetened condensed milk
12 oz. pkg. chocolate chips
1/2 lb. paraffin wax

Mix the first 4 ingredients together. Form into balls. Let stand for at least 2 hours in refrigerator. Melt chocolate chips and wax together. Twirl balls in the chocolate and wax mixture. Sit on waxed paper.

CHOCOLATE TRUFFLES

1/4 C. heavy cream
2 Tbs. Grand Marnier
6 oz. semi-sweet chocolate
4 Tbs. butter, softened
1 large chocolate candy bar
6 oz. chocolate chips
3/4 bar paraffin wax

In a heavy saucepan, reduce cream over a medium heat by 1 Tbs. Add Grand Marnier and chocolate. Stir until melted. Remove from heat and stir in butter. Place in a shallow glass dish and refrigerate 2-3 hours. Scoop out balls. Melt the chocolate bar, chocolate chips and wax over boiling water. Dip balls in chocolate until coated. Set on waxed paper. Refrigerate until firm.

EASY CHOCOLATE TRUFFLES

6 Tbs. butter
12 oz. semi-sweet chocolate chips
1/2 C. powdered sugar, firmly packed
6 egg yolks
1 Tbs. rum, brandy or vanilla flavorings

In double boiler, melt the butter, chocolate chips and powdered sugar. Remove from heat. Beat egg yolks and a little at a time to melted chocolate, stirring until smooth and glossy. Stir in rum brandy or vanilla. Place in refrigerator for 3 hours.

Form into small balls and roll in and of the following:

Finely chopped nuts
Powdered sugar
Chocolate sprinkles
Shaved chocolate
Cocoa powder
Finely chopped coconut

Place on bon bon paper and store in refrigerator.

TRUFFLES

1/4 C. heavy cream
6 oz. semi-sweet chocolate
4 Tbs. butter, softened
4 oz. chocolate
2 Tbs. butter
1 inch paraffin
1/4 tsp. vanilla

In a heavy saucepan, reduce cream over a medium heat with semi-sweet chocolate. Stir until melted. Remove pan from heat. Stir in 4 tbs. butter. Place in a shallow glass bowl and refrigerate 2-4 hours. Scoop out and roll into balls. Melt 4 oz. chocolate, 2 Tbs. butter and paraffin wax. Stir in vanilla. Dip chocolate in this and place on waxed paper and refrigerate until firm.

FUDGE

4-1/4 C. sugar
1/2 C. margarine
1 can evaporated milk
2 (12 oz.) pkg. chocolate chips
2 C. nuts, chopped
2 pints marshmallow cream
2 large chocolate candy bars (4-1/2 oz. ea.)

Boil together sugar, margarine and milk for 8 minutes, stirring constantly. Place candy and chocolate chips in a large bowl. Pour the sugar and milk mixture over the top. Beat well and add the marshmallow cream and nuts. Stir until cool. Spread into a 9X13 pan.

DARK CHOCOLATE FUDGE

3 C. semi-sweet chocolate chips
1 can sweetened condensed milk
dash of salt
1 C. walnuts, chopped
1-1/2 tsp. vanilla

Melt chocolate chips with the milk and salt. Remove from heat and stir in nuts and vanilla. Spread evenly in a wax-lined square pan. Chill until firm.

FUDGE CRISPIES

1-12 oz. pkg. chocolate chips
1/2 C. margarine
1/2 C. corn syrup
2 tsp. vanilla
1 C. powdered sugar
4 C. crispy rice cereal

Combine chocolate chips, margarine and corn syrup. Melt in microwave. Stir until smooth. Stir in vanilla and sugar. Add cereal. Spread into a buttered 9X13 pan. Chill until firm.

EASY TURTLE CANDY

57 caramels (1 lb.)
8 Tbs. water
1 tsp. vanilla
1 pkg. semi-sweet chocolate chips (12 oz.)
1-1/2 C. pecan halves

Melt caramels with water and vanilla in a double boiler. Cool slightly. Separately, melt chocolate and set aside in a warm place. Place pecans on greased baking sheet. Spoon about 1 teaspoonful of caramel mixture in center of each nut, half covering each one. Let stand 10 minutes, spread some melted chocolate over each candy. Let stand until set.

TOFFEE BARS

2 lbs. butter
4 C. brown sugar
2 lbs. chocolate

Melt and cook to 300 degrees, the butter and brown sugar. Pour into 2 cookie sheets. Put 1 lb of chocolate on each one. Smooth around as it melts.

PEANUT BUTTER CHOCOLATE BALLS

4 C. crispy rice cereal
1 lb. powdered sugar
1 stick margarine
1 C. plus 3 Tbs. peanut butter
1 large chocolate candy bar
6 oz. chocolate chips
3/4 bar paraffin wax

Combine margarine and peanut butter. Add powdered sugar. Mix and add cereal. Shape into a ball. Melt the chocolate, chips, and wax over boiling water in a double boiler. Leave over the hot water and dip balls until coated. Place on waxed paper and let set.

PEANUT BUTTER SNOWBALLS

1 C. powdered sugar
1/2 C. creamy peanut butter
3 Tbs. margarine
1 lb. almond bark

Combine sugar, peanut butter and margarine. Mix well. Shape into 1" balls and place on waxed paper lined cookie sheet. Chill for 30 minutes. Meanwhile, melt almond bark in microwave. Dip balls and place on waxed paper to harden.

CHRISTMAS BARK CANDY

1 pkg. vanilla chips or milk chocolate chips
2 tsp. vegetable oil
1-1/4 to 1-1/2 C. miniature candy coated chocolate pieces
  or pretzel pieces or peppermints, crushed

In microwave, melt chips in oil. Cool 5 minutes. Stir in candies or pretzels. Spread on waxed paper. Chill 10 minutes. Break into pieces.

CINNAMON ROCK CANDY

1 C. water
3-3/4 C. sugar
1-1/4 C. light corn syrup
1 tsp. red good coloring
1 tsp. cinnamon oil

Line a 9X13 pan with foil. Butter the foil. Combine water, sugar, syrup and food coloring. Bring to a boil, stirring occasionally. Cover and cook for 3 minutes to dissolve sugar. Uncover and cook without stirring until candy thermometer reads 300 (hard crack stage). About 25 minutes. Remove from heat and stir in cinnamon oil. Immediately pour into prepared pan. Cool completely. Break into pieces.

DIVINITY

3 C. sugar
3/4 C. corn syrup
3/4 C. water
3 egg whites
1/4 tsp. salt
1 tsp. vanilla
3/4 C. pecans or walnuts, chopped

Combine sugar, corn syrup and water. Cook until it reaches 262 degrees. Or, you can microwave this for 8-12 minutes. While the syrup is cooking, add the salt to the egg whites and beat until they cling to the sides of the bowl. Slowly, pour the hot syrup over the egg whites, beating constantly. Beat this for 12-15 minutes or until candy will not flow from spoon in a continuous ribbon, but rather in broken pieces. Mixture will become dull looking. Pour in the nuts and vanilla. Drop by spoonfuls onto waxed paper.

LEMON FUDGE

1 stick margarine
1/2 C. milk
2 pkg. lemon pudding, cook and serve kind
3-1/4 C. powdered sugar

In saucepan, melt margarine. Add milk and pudding. Stir constantly and boil 1 minute. Remove from heat and add powdered sugar. Stir until lumps are gone. Pour into a buttered pie plate. Cool and cut into squares.

NO COOK CANDY

8 oz. pkg. cream cheese
5 C. sifted powdered sugar
1 C. chopped English walnuts
1 tsp. vanilla
flaked coconut

Mix in bowl and refrigerate. When firm, shape into balls and roll in flaked coconut.

CHOW MEIN NOODLE CLUSTERS

1 pkg. (12 oz.) semi-sweet chocolate chips
1 can sweetened condensed milk
2 C. chow Mein noodles

Melt chocolate chips in microwave. Stir in milk until smooth. Add chow mien noodles. Drop by teaspoon onto waxed paper. Chill.

CHOCOLATE CHERRY BALLS

2 boxes cherry frosting mix
1- 2lb bag of powdered sugar
1 stick margarine
1 can sweetened condensed milk
1 tsp. vanilla
1 large jar maraschino cherries, drained and chopped
3 oz. paraffin
2-12 oz. pkg. milk chocolate chips
1 lb. Spanish peanuts

Mix frosting mix, 1 lb. powdered sugar, margarine, milk, vanilla and cherries in a very large bowl with hands, mixture should be like a thin dough, add more powdered sugar until it is. Roll into individual small balls. (1-1/2 to 2 inch in size.) Freeze. Melt paraffin, chocolate chips and peanuts. Dip frozen cherry balls into chocolate mixture. Let set.

BUTTERSCOTCH HAYSTACKS

1-2/3 C. butterscotch morsels
3/4 C. creamy peanut butter
1 can (8.5 oz) chow Mein noodles
3-1/2 C. miniature marshmallows

Line baking sheet with waxed paper. Microwave morsels for 1 minute. Stir. Microwave 10-20 seconds stirring until smooth. Stir in peanut butter until well blended. Add noodles and marshmallows. Toss until coated. Drop by tablespoon onto waxed paper. Refrigerate until ready to serve.

PEANUT BUTTER CANDY

1/2 C. peanut butter
1/4 C. crushed graham crackers
1/2 C. powdered sugar
1 Tbs. margarine
1 bag chocolate chips
1 tsp. oil

Mix first 4 ingredients and put into the refrigerator until firm. Mix and melt the last two ingredients. Make balls of the peanut butter mixture. Dip the balls into the chocolate mixture. Put on waxed paper and refrigerate until set.

DELMA'S ALMOND BARK CANDY

20 oz. white almond bark
1 C. peanut butter
2-1/2 C. miniature marshmallows
2-1/2 C. dry roasted peanuts

Melt almond bark in microwave, about 2 minutes. Add the peanut butter and mix well. Add the remaining ingredients and drop by teaspoon onto waxed paper. Let cool until firm.

The original recipe calls for:

1 C. miniature marshmallows
1 C. dry roasted peanuts
3 C. crispy rice cereal

And you can add anything you want with these....dried cranberries, almonds, pecans, candies....just whatever you have on hand.

New found recipes

New found recipes

New found recipes

New found recipes

New found recipes

New found recipes

173

New found recipes

COOKIES, BROWNIES & BARS

OATMEAL COOKIES

1 C. shortening
1 C. sugar
1 C. brown sugar
2 eggs
1 tsp. vanilla
1-1/2 C. flour
1 tsp. salt
1 tsp. baking soda
3 C. oatmeal

Cream shortening and sugars. Mix in eggs and vanilla. Sift flour, salt and baking soda and fold in. Add oatmeal and mix. Roll into balls and bake at 10-12 minutes at 350.

PEANUT BUTTER COOKIES

1/4 C. shortening
1/4 C. margarine, softened
1/2 C. peanut butter
1/2 C. sugar
1/2 C. brown sugar
1 egg
1-1/4 C. flour
3/4 tsp. baking soda
1/2 tsp. baking powder
1/4 tsp. salt

Mix well the shortening, margarine, peanut butter, sugars and egg. Blend in the rest of the ingredients. Cover and chill for an hour. Shape into 1 inch balls and place 3 inches apart on greased cookie sheet. With fork dipped in sugar, flatten in crisscross pattern. Bake at 375 for 10-12 minutes.

You can make peanut butter and jelly cookies by using this recipe and shaping the dough into balls and making an indention in the center and spoon some jelly or jam in it. Bake the same.

SNICKERDOOLES

1/2 C. margarine
1/2 C. shortening
1-1/2 C. sugar
2 eggs
2-3/4 C. flour
2 tsp. cream of tartar
1 tsp. baking soda
1/4 tsp. salt
2 Tbs. sugar
2 tsp. cinnamon

Mix thoroughly margarine, shortening, sugar and eggs. Blend in flour, cream of tartar, soda and salt. Shape into balls. Mix the sugar and cinnamon and roll the balls into this. Place 2 inches apart on ungreased cookie sheet. Bake at 400 for 8-10 minutes.

TRACY'S CHOCOLATE CHIP COOKIES

1 C. softened margarine
3/4 C. brown sugar
1 small box vanilla instant pudding
2 eggs
1 C. chocolate chips
1/4 C. sugar
1 tsp. vanilla
2-1/4 C. flour
1 tsp. baking soda

Mix together all the ingredients except chocolate chips with a mixer. Add chocolate chips, drop onto cookie sheets. Bake at 375 for 8-10 minutes.

CHOCOLATE CHIP COOKIES

2 C. margarine
2 C. brown sugar
1 C. sugar
4 eggs
2 tsp. vanilla
5 C. flour
2 tsp. baking soda
1-1/2 tsp. salt
1-24 oz. pkg. chocolate chips
2 C. chopped pecans

Blend together margarine and sugars until smooth. Add eggs and vanilla. Beat well. Mix together flour, soda and salt. Add to the creamed mixture and mix well. Fold in chocolate chips and nuts. Drop by teaspoon onto cookie sheet 2" apart. Bake at 350 for 10 minutes.

BEST CHOCOLATE CHIP COOKIES

1-1/2 C. flour
1 tsp. baking soda
1 tsp. cinnamon
1 C. margarine
1/2 C. brown sugar
1 C. sugar
1 egg
1 tsp. vanilla
1-1/2 C. old fashion oats
1 C. chocolate chips

Mix together flour, baking soda and cinnamon. Beat together margarine and sugars until light and fluffy. Beat in egg and vanilla. Beat in flour mixture until blended. Fold in oats and chips. Cover and chill for 1 hour. Drop by teaspoon on greased cookie sheet. Bake at 350 for 10-12 minutes.

CHIPS GALORE COOKIES

1 C. margarine
3/4 C. sugar
3/4 C. brown sugar
2 eggs
1 Tbs. almond flavoring
2-1/4 C. flour
1 tsp. baking soda
1/2 tsp. salt
1-1/2 C. each:
semi-sweet chocolate chips
milk chocolate chips
vanilla chips
1-1/2 C. chopped pecans
1-1/2 C. chopped walnuts

Cream margarine and sugars. Add eggs, one at a time, beating well after each addition. Beat in almond flavoring. Combine flour, baking soda and salt. Gradually add to creamed mixture. Combine chips and nuts. Stir into dough. Cover and chill 1 hour. Drop by teaspoon onto a greased baking sheet. Bake at 325 for 18-20 minutes.

OATMEAL CHOCOLATE CHIP COOKIES

1/2 C. quick oats
2-1/4 C. flour
1-1/2 tsp. baking soda
1/2 tsp. salt
1/4 tsp. cinnamon
1 C. margarine
3/4 C. brown sugar
3/4 C. sugar
2 tsp. vanilla
1 tsp. lemon juice
2 eggs
2 C. chocolate chips
1-1/2 C. walnuts

Combine oats, flour, baking soda, salt and cinnamon. In another bowl, cream the margarine, sugars, vanilla and lemon juice. Add the eggs and beat until fluffy. Stir in the flour mixture. Blend well. Add the chocolate chips and nuts. Using 1/4 C. of the dough for each cookie scoop round balls with an ice cream scoop and place on greased cookie sheet. Bake at 350 for 16-18 minutes.

CHOCOLATE NO BAKE COOKIES

2 C. sugar
1/2 C. milk
1 stick margarine
5 Tbs. cocoa
3 C. oatmeal
2 tsp. vanilla
1/2 C. peanut butter

Mix sugar, milk, margarine and cocoa in a saucepan. Bring to a boil. Boil 2 minutes. Remove from heat and add peanut butter. Stir, then add the vanilla and oatmeal. Drop by teaspoonful onto waxed paper.

CHOCOLATE KISS COOKIES

1-3/4 C. flour
1 tsp. baking soda
1/2 tsp. salt
1/2 C. margarine
1/2 C. peanut butter
1/2 C. sugar
1/2 C. brown sugar
1 egg
1 tsp. vanilla
1 pkg. kiss chocolate candies

Sift flour, salt and baking soda together. In another bowl, cream margarine, peanut butter and sugars. Add egg and vanilla. Gradually blend in the dry ingredients. Shape into balls and place onto an ungreased cookie sheet. Bake at 375 for 8 minutes. Place a kiss in the center and press firmly. Return to the oven for 2 minutes. 1

CANDY BAR COOKIES

1 C. peanut butter
1/2 C. margarine
1/2 C. shortening
1-1/2 C. sugar
1-1/2 C. brown sugar
1-1/2 tsp. baking soda
2 eggs
1 tsp. vanilla
2-1/4 C. flour
40 miniature candy bars, with or without nuts

Beat peanut butter, margarine and shortening. Add the sugars and baking soda. Beat until combined. Beat in eggs and vanilla. Beat in flour. Form about 2 tablespoons of the dough around each candy bar. Make sure candy is completely covered. Place on cookie sheet 2-1/2 inches apart. Make at 325 for 15-20 minutes.

SUGAR COOKIES

1 C. margarine
2 C. sugar
2 eggs
1 C. milk
2 tsp. vanilla
1 tsp. baking soda
1 tsp. baking powder
1/2 tsp. salt
enough flour to make a soft dough

ICING:

1/3 C. margarine
3-1/2 C. powdered sugar
5 Tbs. milk
1/8 tsp. salt
1 tsp. vanilla

Mix the margarine, sugar, eggs, milk and vanilla together until smooth. Add a couple of cups of flour and the soda, baking powder and salt. Mix well. Then continue to add flour until you the soft dough. Chill overnight. Roll out and cut into desired shapes. Bake at 375 for 10 minutes.

For icing: Mix all the ingredients together and add any color of food coloring desired. Spread on cooled cookies.

CHOCOLATE COOKIES

2 C. oatmeal
2 C. semisweet chocolate chips
1 C. butter
1 C. brown sugar
1/2 C. sugar
1-1/2 C. flour
1/2 tsp. baking soda
1/2 tsp. salt
1/4 C. unsweetened cocoa
2 eggs slightly beaten
1 Tbs. milk
1-1/2 tsp. vanilla
9 oz. white chocolate
1-1/2 Tbs. shortening

Beat together the butter and sugars until creamy. Sift together the flour, baking soda, salt and cocoa. Add to the butter mixture, mix thoroughly. Stir in the milk and vanilla into the eggs. Add to the batter and mix well. add the oatmeal and chocolate chips. Drop by teaspoon onto buttered cookie sheets. Bake at 350 for 9-12 minutes. Cool 1 minute.

Melt the white chocolate with the shortening. Dip the bottom third of the cookie into the warm white chocolate. Place on wax paper and cool.

MONSTER COOKIES

1 dozen eggs
2 lbs. brown sugar
2 C. sugar
1 lb. margarine
8 tsp. baking soda
3 lb. chunky peanut butter
18 C. oatmeal
1 lb. candy coated chocolate candies (they melt in your mouth)
1 lb. chocolate chips
1 lb. butterscotch chips

Mix all the ingredients except the oatmeal, candies and chips together with mixer in a very large bowl. Stir in the rest of the ingredients by hand. Drop by spoonful onto an ungreased cookie sheet. Bake at 350 for 12 minutes. Do not over bake. Cookies will not appear done. Let them set a few minutes then remove them onto waxed paper. Make 12 dozen. These freeze well.

DISHPAN COOKIES

2 C. brown sugar
2 C. sugar
2 C. oil
4 eggs
2 tsp. baking soda
1/2 tsp. baking powder
1 tsp. salt
4 C. flour
1-1/2 C. quick cook oatmeal
2 C. coconut
4 C. cornflakes
6 oz. chocolate chips
1/2 C. nuts, chopped

Cream together the sugars, oil and eggs. Stir in the soda, baking powder, salt and flour. Add the rest of the ingredients. Mix well. Drop by teaspoon on an ungreased cookie sheet. Bake at 325 for 10 minutes.

COWBOY COOKIES

1/2 C. margarine, softened
1 egg
1 tsp. vanilla
1-1/3 C. flour
1-1/3 C. quick cooking oatmeal
1 C. semi-sweet chocolate chips
1/2 C. brown sugar
1/2 C. sugar
1/2 C. chopped pecans
1 tsp. baking soda
1 tsp. baking powder
1/4 tsp. salt

Place the margarine, egg and vanilla in a bowl and cream together. Add the rest of the ingredients to the butter mixture and mix well. Drop by teaspoon onto an ungreased cookie sheet. Bake at 350 for 11-13 minutes. Allow to cool on the baking sheet for 5 minutes before removing.

CREAM WAFERS

1 C. butter
1/3 C. whipping cream
2 C. flour
sugar

CREAM FILLING:

1/4 C. soft butter
3/4 C. powdered sugar
1 tsp. vanilla

Mix butter, cream and flour thoroughly. Cover and chill. Roll about 1/3 of dough at a time 1/8 inch thick on a floured surface. (Keep remaining in refrigerator). Cut into 1-1/2 inch circles. Transfer rounds with spatula to piece of wax paper that is heavily covered with sugar. Turn each round so that both sides are coated with sugar. Place on ungreased cookie sheet. Prick round with fork about 4 times. Bake at 375 for 7-9 minutes. Put cookies together in pairs with cream filling.

Cream filling:
Cream all the ingredients until smooth and fluffy. Tint with a few drops of food coloring. Add a few drops of water if necessary for proper spreading consistency.

GELATIN COOKIES

4 C. flour
1 tsp. baking powder
1-1/2 C. margarine
1 C. sugar
1 pkg. gelatin
1 egg
1 tsp. vanilla

Sift flour and baking powder together. Cream margarine, sugar and gelatin. Add egg. Beat well. Gradually add flour mixture. Mix well. Put dough through cookie press onto ungreased cookie sheet. Or shape into balls. Bake at 350 for 15 minutes.

CHOCOLATE CRINKLES

1/2 C. shortening
1-2/3 C. sugar
2 tsp. vanilla
2 eggs
2-1 oz. sq. unsweetened chocolate, melted
2 C. flour
1/2 tsp. salt
2 tsp. baking powder
1/3 C. milk
1/2 C. chopped
walnuts
powdered sugar

Cream together the shortening, sugar and vanilla. Beat in eggs, then the melted chocolate. Sift together the flour, salt and baking powder. Add alternately with milk. Add walnuts. Chill 3 hours. Form into 1 inch balls, roll into powdered sugar. Place on a greased cookie sheet. Bake at 350 for 15 minutes.

GERMAN CHOCOLATE COOKIES

1 pkg. German chocolate cake mix
2 eggs
1/2 C. margarine, melted
1/2 C. oatmeal
1 C. chocolate chips

Combine cake mix, eggs, margarine and oats. Mix well. Stir in chocolate chips. Drop by teaspoon on ungreased cookie sheet. Bake at 350 for 9-11 minutes.

MACADAMIA NUT COOKIES

1 C. margarine
3/4 brown sugar
1/4 C. sugar
2 eggs
1 tsp. vanilla
2-1/2 C. flour
1 pkg. instant vanilla pudding
1 tsp. baking powder
1/4 tsp. salt
1 pkg. vanilla chips (10-12 oz)
2 jars macadamia nuts, chopped (3-1/2 oz. each)
1/2 C. finely chopped peanut brittle

Cream margarine and sugars until smooth. Add eggs, one at a time, beating well after each addition. Beat in vanilla. Combine flour, pudding mix, baking soda and salt. Gradually add to creamed mixture and mix well. Stir in chips, nuts and brittle. Drop by teaspoon onto greased cookie sheet. Bake at 375 for 10-12 minutes.

VANILLA WAFER COOKIES

1/2 C. butter
1 C. sugar
1 egg
1 tsp. vanilla
1-1/3 C. flour
3/4 tsp. baking powder
1/4 tsp. salt

Cream butter and sugar. Beat in egg and vanilla. Combine dry ingredients and add to creamed mixture. Drop by teaspoon onto ungreased cookie sheet. Bake at 350 for 12-15 minutes.

MACAROONS

4 eggs
1-1/2 C. sugar
2/3 C. flour
1/2 tsp. baking powder
2 Tbs. margarine, melted and cooled
1 tsp. vanilla
5 C. flaked coconut
1/4 tsp. salt

Beat eggs until foamy. Gradually add sugar, beating constantly until thick and pale yellow. Stir together dry ingredients. Fold into egg mixture. Stir in margarine, vanilla and coconut. Drop by teaspoon onto a greased and floured cookie sheet. Bake at 325 for 10-13 minutes.

COCONUT MACAROONS

1/3 C. flour
2-1/2 C. flaked coconut
1/8 tsp. salt
2/3 C. sweetened condensed milk
1 tsp. vanilla

Combine flour, coconut, and salt. Add milk and vanilla. Mix well. Drop by teaspoon onto a greased baking sheet. Bake at 350 for 15-20 minutes.

STRAWBERRY COOKIES

1 c. butter, softened
1- 3 oz. pkg. cream cheese, softened
1/2 C. sugar
1 tsp. vanilla
2 C. flour
36 small ripe strawberries, hulled and halved

Beat butter with cream cheese until well blended. Beat in the sugar and vanilla. Stir in flour until well blended. Shape 1/2 tablespoon into balls and place on a cookie sheet. Make a small indentation in the top of each cookie with your thumb. Carefully place a strawberry half, cut side down in each indentation. Bake at 350 for 12-18 minutes.

FRENCH COOKIES

1-1/4 lbs. margarine
2 C. sugar
2-1/2 C. brown sugar
8 eggs
1/2 tsp. vanilla
1 tsp. rum flavoring
10 C. flour

Mix all and let stand overnight in the refrigerator. Roll into balls the size of walnuts. Bake in French cookie iron.

CHOCOLATE PIZELLES

6 eggs
2 C. sugar
1/4 tsp. vanilla
2 sticks margarine, melted
1/2 C. cocoa
3-1/2 C. flour
4-1/2 tsp. baking powder

Beat eggs, adding sugar gradually. Beat until smooth. Add cooled margarine and vanilla. Blend the cocoa, flour and baking powder into the mixture. Beat until smooth. Drop by teaspoon in center of pizzelle maker. Bake 30-45 seconds.

PIZELLES

3-1/2 C. eggs
3 C. sugar
2-1/4 C. melted shortening
1 C. artificial vanilla (or 8 Tbs. real vanilla)
1 tsp. anise oil
2 tsp. lemon extract
3 tsp. orange extract
Approximately 7 C. flour

Melt the shortening and cool it. Whip the eggs until frothy. Add the sugar and whip until creamy. Add the flavorings and mix after each addition. Mix in the shortening. Transfer the mixture to a very large bowl. Add about 1/2 the flour and mix well. Continue mixing the flour a cup or two at a time until all is mixed well. The dough should be heavy, not runny and sort of "glumps" off the spoon. Drop the dough by teaspoon into center of the pizzelle iron, close tightly and cook for approximately 30-45 seconds or until the golden color you like.

PIZELLES 2

6 eggs
1-1/2 C. sugar
2 Tbs. anise or almond flavoring
1/4 tsp. vanilla
2 sticks margarine, melted
3-1/2 C. flour
4 tsp. baking powder

Beat the eggs. Gradually add the sugar. Beat until smooth. Add cooled margarine and flavorings. Blend the flour and baking powder into mixture until smooth. Drop by teaspoon onto center of pizzelle maker. Bake until golden. About 30-45 seconds.

FUDGE BROWNIES

1-1/2 C. margarine
3/4 C. cocoa
2 C. sugar
4 eggs
2 tsp. vanilla
1-1/2 C. flour

In a saucepan, melt margarine and cocoa together. Remove from heat and stir in sugar. Blend in eggs, one at a time. Add vanilla. Stir in flour. Spread in a greased 9X13 pan. Bake at 350 for 30 minutes.

YUMMY BROWNIES

1 C. butter
3-1/2 oz. unsweetened chocolate
3 Tbs. dark unsweetened cocoa
1-1/2 C. flour
1/2 tsp. baking powder
1 tsp. salt
4 eggs
2 C. sugar
1 tsp. vanilla
1 C. chocolate chips

Melt butter with unsweetened chocolate in top of double boiler, stir occasionally. Set aside to cool. Sift together the cocoa, flour baking powder and salt. Beat eggs until creamy, then gradually add sugar, beating constantly. Add vanilla and cooled chocolate mixture. Stir in dry ingredients just until combined. Spread batter into a greased 9X13 pan. Sprinkle chocolate chips over top. Bake at 350 for 30-35 minutes.

CHEWY, FUDGY TRIPLE CHOCOLATE BROWNIES

5 oz. semi-sweet chocolate, chopped
2 oz. unsweetened chocolate, chopped
1 stick unsalted butter, cut in quarters
3 Tbs. cocoa
3 eggs
1-1/4 C. sugar
2 tsp. vanilla
1/2 tsp. salt
1 C. flour

In double boiler, melt chocolates and butter, stirring occasionally until mixture is smooth. Whisk in cocoa until smooth. Set aside to cool. Whisk together eggs, sugar, vanilla and salt. Whisk warm chocolate mixture into egg mixture, then stir in flour, just until combined. Pour mixture into a greased and floured square pan. Bake at 350 for 35-40 minutes. Cool.

TERESA'S BROWNIES

A brownie recipe of your choice
1 jar marshmallow cream
2 bags chocolate chips
1 C. peanut butter
3 C. crisp rice cereal

Make the brownies in a cookie sheet. Set the marshmallow cream on the stove while brownies are baking. Spread marshmallow cream on brownies that have slightly cooled. Mix together the chocolate chips, peanut butter and cereal. Spread on top of marshmallow cream. Cool completely. May stick in the fridge to cool quickly.

DOUBLE DECKER BROWNIES

3/4 C. margarine
1 C. sugar
1 C. brown sugar
3 eggs
1 tsp. vanilla
2-1/2 C. flour
2-1/2 tsp. baking powder
1/2 tsp. salt
1/3 C. cocoa
1 Tbs. margarine, melted
1 C. mini chocolate chips

Cream 3/4 C. margarine and sugars until light and fluffy. Beat in eggs and vanilla. In another bowl combine 2-1/4 C. flour, baking powder and salt. Blend into creamed mixture. Divide batter in half. Blend together cocoa and melted margarine. Stir into half of the dough. Spread cocoa dough into a greased 9X13 pan. Stir remaining 1/4 C. flour and 1/2 C chocolate chips into remaining dough. Spread over cocoa dough in pan. Sprinkle with remaining chocolate chips. Bake at 350 for 25-30 minutes.

CHOCOLATE SAUCE BROWNIES

1/2 C. margarine
1 C. sugar
4 eggs
1-1/2 C. rich chocolate sauce or 1 can chocolate syrup
1 tsp. vanilla
1 C. plus 1 Tbs. flour
1/2 tsp. baking powder
1 C. pecans

FROSTING:

1 C. sugar
6 Tbs. milk
6 Tbs. margarine
1/2 C. chocolate chips

Cream margarine and sugar. Add eggs one at a time. Beating well after each addition. Stir in chocolate sauce and vanilla. Combine flour and baking powder. Add to creamed mixture and mix well. Add nuts. Pour into a greased 9X13 pan. Bake at 350 for 20-25 minutes. Cool. For frosting: Combine sugar, milk and margarine. Bring to a boil. Boil 1 minute. Remove from heat, Add chocolate chips. Stir until melted and smooth. Spread on brownies.

MAGIC COOKIE BARS

1/2 C. margarine, melted
1-1/2 C. graham cracker crumbs
1 C. nuts
1 C. semi-sweet chocolate chips
1-1/3 C. flaked coconut
1 can sweetened condensed milk

Pour melted margarine in a 9X13 pan. Sprinkle crumbs evenly over. Sprinkle nuts over crumbs. Scatter chocolate chips. Sprinkle coconut. Pour milk evenly over top of all this. Bake at 350 for 25 minutes. Cool for 15 minutes before cutting.

MULTIPLE CHOICE BARS

1/2 C. margarine
1 can sweetened condensed milk

COLUMN A: (1-1/2 CUPS)

Graham crackers crumbs
Vanilla wafers crumbs
Chocolate wafer crumbs
Animal cracker crumbs
Sugar cookie crumbs

COLUMN B: (2 CUPS)

Chocolate chips
Butterscotch chops
Peanut butter chips
Raisins
Candy coated chocolate candies (they melt in your mouth)

COLUMN C (2 CUPS)

Flaked coconut
Crisp rice cereal
Miniature marshmallows
Frosted corn flaked cereal, crumbled

COLUMN D: (1 CUP)

Chopped walnuts
Chopped pecans
Chopped cashews

Melt margarine and pour into a 9X13 pan. Evenly drizzle one ingredient from column A. Drizzle condensed milk over the crumbs. Evenly sprinkle on an ingredient from column B. Evenly sprinkle one ingredient from column C on top of that. Evenly sprinkle one ingredient from column D over the top. Press everything down with the palms of your hands. Bake at 350 for 30 minutes. Cool.

OATMEAL BAR COOKIES

1 C. butter
1/2 C. brown sugar
1/2 C. sugar
2 eggs
2 tsp. vanilla
1 C. flour
1/2 tsp. salt
1/4 tsp. baking soda
1 C. oatmeal

Cream the butter and sugars. Beat in the eggs and vanilla. Add the flour, salt and baking soda. Stir in oats. Spread into a 9X13 greased pan. Bake at 350 for 30 minutes.

CARAMEL OATMEAL BAR COOKIES

3 C. flour
3-3/4 C quick oats
2-1/4 C. brown sugar
3/4 tsp. salt
1-1/2 tsp. baking soda
2-1/4 C. butter, melted
2 lbs. caramels
12 oz. chocolate chips
8 Tbs. half-n-half
2 C. pecans, chopped

Mix flour, oatmeal, salt, soda and sugar in a bowl. Pour melted butter over dry ingredients and mix until well blended. Cut this mixture in half. Press one half into the bottom of an ungreased sheet cake pan. Bake at 350 for 10 minutes.

BLACK AND WHITE BARS

1 pkg. white cake mix
2 eggs
1/3 C. oil
1 can sweetened condensed milk
1 C. semi-sweet chocolate chips
1/4 C. margarine

Combine cake mix, eggs, and oil. With floured hands, press 2/3 of the mixture into a greased 9X13 pan. Set remaining cake mixture aside. Combine milk, chocolate chips and margarine. Microwave on high for 45 seconds or until chips and margarine are melted. Stir until smooth. Pour over crust. Drop teaspoonfuls of remaining batter over top. Bake at 350 for 20 minutes. Cool.

CHOCOLATE PECAN BARS

1/2 C. butter
1/2 c. brown sugar
1 C. flour
1 C. pecan halves
2 eggs
1 C. brown sugar
1 tsp. vanilla
1/2 tsp. salt
1 tsp. baking powder
Additional flour
1 C. chocolate chips

In food processor, combine the first 3 ingredients with metal blade until crumbly. Or you can use a pastry cutter. Pat into a greased 9X13 pan. Bake at 375 for 10 minutes. Cool. Spread pecans on cooled crust. Beat eggs with brown sugar until thick. Add vanilla. Put salt and baking powder in bottom of a 1/4 cup measure, fill the rest of the measure with flour. Stir into egg mixture. Pour over crust. Sprinkle chocolate chips evenly over mixture. Bake at 375 for 20 minutes. Cool.

PEANUT MALLOW BARS

1 C. chopped salted peanuts
3/4 C. flour
3/4 C. quick cooking oats
2/3 C. brown sugar
1/2 tsp. salt
1/2 tsp. baking soda
1 egg, lightly beaten
1/3 C. margarine

TOPPING:

1 jar marshmallow cream (7 oz)
2/3 C. caramel ice cream topping
1-3/4 C. salted peanuts

Combine the first 6 ingredients. Stir in egg. Cut in margarine until crumbly. Pat into a greased 9X13 pan. Bake at 350 for 8-10 minutes. Spoon marshmallow cream over hot crust. Carefully spread. Drizzle with caramel topping. Sprinkle with peanuts. Bake at 350 for 15-20 minutes. Cool.

CHOCOLATE PEANUT BUTTER BARS

1 C. sugar
1 C. light corn syrup
1 C. peanut butter
6 C. crisp rice cereal
2 C. chocolate chips, melted

Combine sugar syrup and peanut butter. Cook over medium heat until sugar is dissolved. Remove from heat. Add cereal. Stir until coated. Spread into a 9X13 greased pan. Press lightly. Spread chocolate over bars.

CHOCOLATE CHIP CHEESE BARS

1 tube refrigerated, chocolate chip cookie dough or use 2 C. of you own recipe
1 pkg. (8 oz) cream cheese
1/2 C. sugar
1 egg

Cut cookie cough in half. For crust, press one half into the bottom of an 8" square pan. Beat cream cheese, sugar and egg until smooth. Spread over crust. Crumble remaining dough over top. Bake at 350 for 35-40 minutes. Keep refrigerated.

CHOCOLATE PEANUT BARS

1 pkg. white cake mix
1 C. peanut butter
1 egg
1 pkg. (8 oz.) cream cheese
1/3 C. milk
1/4 C. sugar
1 C. chocolate chips
3/4 C. salted peanuts

Beat cake mix, 2/3 cup peanut butter and egg until crumbly. Press into a greased 9X13 pan. In a bowl, combine cream cheese and remaining peanut butter. Gradually add milk and sugar. Beat well. Carefully spread over crust. Sprinkle chocolate chips and peanuts over top. Bake at 350 for 25-30 minutes. Cool.

CHERRY BARS

1 C. margarine
1-1/2 C. sugar
4 eggs
3 C. flour
1/2 tsp. salt
2-1/2 tsp. baking powder
1 can cherry pie filling or peach pie filling

Cream margarine and sugar. Add eggs and beat well. Add dry ingredients. Spread 2/3 of the mixture in a greased cookie sheet. Spoon pie filling over dough. Drop the rest of the batter over fruit with a teaspoon. Bake at 350 for 35-40 minutes.

FROSTED BANANA BARS

1/2 C. margarine
2 C. sugar
3 eggs
1 tsp. baking soda
1-1/2 C. mashed bananas
1 tsp. vanilla
2 C. flour
pinch of salt

FROSTING:

1/2 C. margarine
1-8 oz. pkg. cream cheese
4 C. powdered sugar
2 tsp. vanilla

Cream margarine and sugar. Beat in the eggs, bananas and vanilla. Combine flour, baking soda and salt. Add to creamed mixture. Mix well. Pour into a greased 9X13 pan. Bake at 350 for 25 minutes. Cool. For frosting: Cream margarine and cream cheese. Gradually add sugar and vanilla. Beat well. Spread on bars.

CONFETTI COOKIES

1 box confetti cake mix
1/2 C. margarine, melted
2 eggs
1/2 C. nuts (optional)
1 can confetti frosting

Combine cake mix, margarine and eggs. Stir by hand until moistened. Add nuts. Spread into a 9X13 pan. Bake at 375 for 13-17 minutes. Cool Frost. Sprinkle with the candies. Cut into bars.

LEMON BAR COOKIES

1 C. flour
1/4 C. powdered sugar, sifted
1/2 C. margarine
1/2 tsp. butter flavoring

FILLING:

3/4 C. sugar
1/4 C. flour
1/2 tsp. baking powder
2 eggs, beaten
2 Tbs. lemon juice
1/4 tsp. lemon flavoring
1/2 C. coconut

Combine flour and powdered sugar. Cut in the margarine until crumbly. Add flavoring. Mix. Pat into a 9" square pan. Bake at 350 for 15 minutes. Cool. For filling: Combine sugar, flour and baking powder. Add eggs. Mix well. Add remaining ingredients. Spread on top of baked crust. Bake at 350 for 25 minutes. Sprinkle with powdered sugar and coconut over top if desired.

PEANUT BUTTER BARS

2 sticks margarine
1 C. peanut butter
1 lb. powdered sugar
1 C. graham cracker crumbs
1 (12 oz.) bag chocolate chips

Melt the margarine and peanut butter. Add the rest of the ingredients. Put in a 9X13 pan. Melt the chocolate chips and pour on top. Refrigerate.

CRISPY PRETZEL BARS

1 C. sugar
1 C. light corn syrup
1/2 C. peanut butter
5 C. crisp rice cereal
2 C. pretzel sticks
1 C. plain chocolate candies (won't melt in your hands)

Combine sugar and syrup. Microwave on high for 3 minutes or until sugar is dissolved. Stir in peanut butter until well blended. Add the cereal, pretzels and candies. Stir until coated. Press into a 9X13 pan.

CRISPY RICE CEREAL BARS

6 C. crisp rice cereal
1/4 C. margarine
1 (10-1/2 oz.) bag miniature marshmallows

Melt margarine and marshmallows in a large pot over low heat. Stir until melted. Remove from heat. Add cereal. Stir until well coated. Press into a greased 9X13 pan. Cool. Cut into bars. If you wish to frost these. Melt together 6 oz. chocolate chips and 6 oz. butterscotch chips and spread over bars.

PEANUT BUTTER CRISPY RICE BARS

1 C. light corn syrup
1 C. sugar
1 C. peanut butter
6 C. crisp rice cereal

Heat syrup and sugar to boiling. Remove from heat and add peanut butter. Mix cereal in until well coated. Press into a greased 9X13 pan. Can frost with a mixture of 6 oz. chocolate chips and 6 oz. butterscotch chips, melted together.

TOFFEE PECAN BARS

2 C. flour
1/2 C. powdered sugar
1 C. margarine
1 egg
1 can sweetened condensed milk
1 tsp. vanilla
1 pkg. toffee bits (10 oz.) or almond brickle (7-1/2 oz.)
1 C. chopped pecans

Combine flour and sugar. Cut in margarine until crumbly. Press into a greased 9X13 pan. Bake at 350 for 15 minutes. Combine egg, milk and vanilla. Mix well. Fold in toffee bits and pecans. Spoon over crust. Bake for 25 minutes or until golden brown. Chill until firm before cutting.

FROSTED PEANUT BUTTER FINGERS

1 C. margarine, softened
1-1/2 C. brown sugar
2-1/2 C. creamy peanut butter, divided
1 egg
1-1/2 tsp. vanilla
2-1/2 C. quick cook oatmeal
2 C. flour
1 tsp. baking soda
1/2 tsp. salt

Cream margarine and sugars. Add 1 C. peanut butter, egg and vanilla. Mix well. Combine oats, flour, baking soda and salt. Add to creamed mixture. Spread in a greased 9X13 pan. Bake at 350 for 13-17 minutes. Cool 12 minutes. Spread on remaining peanut butter. Cool completely.

CHOCOLATE FROSTING:

6 Tbs. margarine, softened
4 C. powdered sugar
1/2 C. cocoa
1 tsp. vanilla
6-8 Tbs. milk

Combine margarine, powdered sugar, cocoa, vanilla and enough milk to achieve spreading consistency. Spoon over bars, then spread.

New found recipes

New found recipes

New found recipes

New found recipes

New found recipes

New found recipes

New found recipes

DESSERTS

FOUR LAYER DESSERT

1 C. flour
1/2 C. margarine, melted
8 oz. cream cheese
1 qt. whipped topping
2 pkg. chocolate instant pudding, or any flavor
3 C. milk
1 C. powdered sugar

Combine flour and margarine. Pat into a 9X13 pan. Bake at 350 for 15 minutes. Blend together cream cheese, powdered sugar and 1 cup whipped topping. Spread onto cooled crust. Combine pudding and milk. Beat until thick. Pour over cream cheese mixture. Top with remaining whipped topping. Chill.

CHERRY CHEESE CAKE

1 can sweetened condensed milk
8 oz. pkg. cream cheese
large container whipped topping
1/2 C. lemon juice
1 lg. or 2 regular cans cherry pie filling
1 pkg. graham crackers
1 stick margarine

Make a crust first. Crush the graham crackers. Melt the margarine and mix with the crumbs in a 9X13 pan. Pat down to form a crust. Set aside. Mix the milk and cream cheese with mixer until smooth. Fold in the whipped topping. Add the lemon juice and stir by hand. Pour into the crust. Spread filling over top. Refrigerate.

RASPBERRY SWIRL CHEESECAKE

1 pkg. graham crackers, crushed
1 stick margarine, melted
5 pkg. (8 oz each) cream cheese
1 C. sugar
3 Tbs. flour
1 Tbs. vanilla
1 C. sour cream
4 eggs
1/3 C. seedless raspberry jam

Mix the graham crackers and margarine. Press into a 9X13 pan. Bake at 325 for 10 minutes.

Beat the cream cheese, sugar, the flour and vanilla with electric mixer until well blended. Add sour cream. Mix well. Add the eggs, one at a time, mixing on low after each addition. Pour over crust. Drop small spoonfuls of jam over batter. Cut through batter several times for marble affect. Bake at 325 for 55 minutes or until center is almost set. Cool completely. Refrigerate at least 4 hours or overnight.

WHITE CHOCOLATE CHEESECAKE

2 C. vanilla wafers crumbs
3/4 stick margarine, melted
1 tsp. almond flavoring
2 C. sour cream
1/2 C. sugar
1 tsp. vanilla
cherry pie filling
1 C. sugar
3-8 oz. pkg. cream cheese
1 C. real mayonnaise
4 eggs
2 C. white chocolate chips
2 tsp. vanilla

Mix together the cookie crumbs, margarine and almond flavoring. Press into a 9X13 pan. Place in freezer for 15-30 minutes. Mix sour cream, 1/2 cup sugar and vanilla. Cover and refrigerate. With mixer, stir together 1 cup sugar, cream cheese and mayo. Whip until smooth. Add eggs, one at a time, beating after each addition. Melt the white chocolate, cool and then add gradually at low speed. Add vanilla. Mix thoroughly. Pour batter over crust. Bake at 350 for 55 minutes. Remove from oven and spread the sour cream mixture over top, starting at the center and working to within an inch of the rim. Return to oven and bake 5-10 minutes. Cool, then refrigerate. Spread pie filling on top before serving.

CHEESE CAKE

1 pkg. lemon gelatin
1 C. boiling water
3 Tbs. lemon juice
1-8 oz. pkg. cream cheese
1 C. sugar
1 tsp. vanilla
1 can evaporated milk
1 pkg. graham crackers, crushed
1 stick margarine, melted

Make a crust with the graham crackers and margarine. Pat into a 9X13 pan. Whip the evaporated milk with mixer. Set aside. Dissolve gelatin in water. Add lemon juice, cream cheese, sugar and vanilla. Mix with mixer until smooth. Add the evaporated milk. Mix well. Pour into crust. Chill.

CHOCOLATE CHIP CHEESECAKE

3 (8 oz.) pkg. cream cheese
3/4 C. sugar
3 eggs
1 tsp. vanilla
2 C. mini chocolate chips
1 graham cracker crust
2 Tbs. whipping cream

Beat cream cheese and sugar until well blended. Add eggs and vanilla. Beat well. Stir in 1-2/3 C. chocolate chips. Pour into crust. Bake at 450 for 10 minutes. Reduce to 250 and bake 30 minutes. Cool completely. Cover, refrigerate. Place remaining 1/3 chocolate chips and whipping cream in a bowl and microwave 20-30 seconds or until chips are melted and mixture is smooth. Cool slightly. Spread over cheesecake. Refrigerate 15 minutes. Cover and keep refrigerated.

PUMPKIN CHEESE CAKE

1 egg yolk
1-10" graham cracker crust
2 eggs
2 (8 oz.) pkg. cream cheese
3/4 C. sugar
1 can (16 oz) pumpkin
1-1/2 tsp. cinnamon
1/2 tsp. ginger

Brush egg yolk onto pie crust, bottom and sides. Bake at 350 for 5 minutes. Beat eggs, cream cheese and sugar until smooth. Add pumpkin, cinnamon and ginger. Pour into crust and bake at 350 for 40-45 minutes or until set. Cool. Refrigerate overnight.

CHOCOLATE COOKIE DESSERT

1-15 oz. pkg. chocolate sandwich cookies
1/2 C. margarine, melted
1 C. powdered sugar
8 oz. cream cheese
16 oz. whipped topping
2 pkg. instant chocolate pudding

Crush all the cookies except for 8 of them. Mix with margarine. Press into a 9X13 pan. Mix sugar, cream cheese and half the whipped topping. Spread on cookie crust. Make pudding according to directions. Spread on top of cream cheese mixture. Top with remaining whipped topping. Crush remaining cookies and sprinkle on top.

PISTACHIO DESSERT

1-20 oz. pkg. chocolate sandwich cookies
1/3 C. margarine, melted
12 oz. container whipped topping
2 pkg. instant Pistachio pudding
1-1/2 C. milk
1 qt. vanilla ice cream

Crush cookies and add margarine. Put half in a 9X13 pan. Combine pudding, milk and ice cream. Beat well. Pour over crumbs. Refrigerate 2 hours. Spread whipped topping over mixture and sprinkle remaining crumbs on top.

PEANUT BUTTER DESSERT

2-1/4 C. crushed peanut butter sandwich cookies
1/2 C. margarine, melted
1 C. powdered sugar
2 pkg. (3 oz. ea) cream cheese
1 carton (8 oz) whipped topping, divided
2-1/2 C. milk
2 pkg. instant chocolate pudding

Combine crushed cookies and margarine. Press into a 9X13 pan. Bake at 350 for 6-8 minutes. Cool. Beat cream cheese and powdered sugar. Fold in 1 cup whipped topping. Spread over cooled crust. In another bowl beat milk and pudding for 2 minutes or until thickened. Spread over cream cheese. Top with remaining whipped topping. Can sprinkle some cookie crumbs over top if you want. Refrigerate for at least 1 hour.

PEACHES AND CREAM DESSERT

1-1/8 C. flour
3/4 C. milk
1-1/2 tsp. baking powder
3/4 tsp. salt
1 box cook type vanilla pudding
4-1/2 tbs. margarine
2 eggs
2 (29 oz.) can sliced peaches, drained (reserve juice)
8 oz. cream cheese
1 C. sugar
1-1/4 tsp. sugar, mixed with 3/4 tsp. cinnamon

Beat first 7 ingredients for 2 minutes. Pour into a greased 9X13 pan. Top with peaches. Laying within an inch of edge. Combine Cream cheese, sugar and 4 Tbs. reserved juice. Beat for 2 minutes. Spoon over top of peaches. Sprinkle with cinnamon sugar mixture. Bake at 350 for 35 minutes.

BREAD PUDDING

2 C. bread, crumbled
4 C. scaled milk
1/4 C. margarine
3/4 C. sugar
1 tsp. vanilla
4 eggs, beaten
1/4 tsp. salt
1/2 tsp. cinnamon

Mix the milk, margarine, sugar and vanilla together until margarine is melted. Add the eggs, salt and cinnamon. Grease a large casserole dish. Put the bread in and pour the milk mixture over the top. Bake at 350 for 1 hour.

If I have leftover cinnamon rolls I will use them in place of the bread. When I do this I omit the cinnamon from the recipe.

WHITE CHOCOLATE BREAD PUDDING

6 C. whipping cream
2 C. milk
1 C. sugar
20 oz. white chocolate, broken in pieces
4 eggs
15 egg yolks
24" loaf bread, sliced 1" thick (use stale bread or dry the slices in a
275 degree oven)

WHITE CHOCOLATE SAUCE:

8 oz. white chocolate, broken in pieces
1/2 C. whipping cream

In a large saucepan, heat whipping cream, milk and sugar over medium
heat. When hot, take off the heat and add the white chocolate. Stir
until melted. Combine eggs and the yolks in a large bowl. Slowly pour
the hot cream mixture into the eggs in a steady stream, whipping the
eggs as you pour. Place the bread in a 9X13 greased pan. Pour 1/2 the
liquid over the bread. Use fingers to press the bread into the mixture
so that it absorbs the liquid and becomes soggy. Pour in the remaining
liquid. Cover the pan with foil. Bake at 350 for 1 hour. Take off the foil
and bake an additional 1/2 hour, until set and golden brown.

For sauce: Bring cream to a boil. Remove from heat and stir in the
chocolate. Stir until smooth and completely melted. Spoon over bread
pudding.

PUMPKIN DESSERT

1 can pumpkin
1 can evaporated milk
3 eggs
1 C. sugar
4 tsp. pumpkin pie spice
1 pkg. yellow cake mix
3/4 C. margarine, melted
1-1/2 C. chopped walnuts
whipped topping

Combine the first five ingredients. Put into a greased 9X13 pan. Sprinkle with dry cake mix. Drizzle with margarine. Top with walnuts. Bake at 350 for 1 hour. Serve with whipped topping. Keep refrigerated.

MOM'S CHERRY DELIGHT

1 pkg. graham crackers, crushed
1 stick margarine, melted
1 large can cherry pie filling
1 container whipped topping

Mix the graham crackers and margarine. Pat into a 9X13 pan. Top with the cherry pie filling. Spread the whipped topping over the cherries. Refrigerate.

CHOCOLATE PEANUT SUPREME

1/2 C. chunky peanut butter
1/3 C. margarine, melted
1-1/2 C. graham cracker crumbs
1/2 C. sugar
1 large pkg. instant chocolate pudding
3 C. milk
1 carton whipped topping
1 C. chopped peanuts

Combine peanut butter and margarine. Stir in graham cracker crumbs and sugar. Press into a 9X13 pan. Prepare pudding with milk according to directions on pudding box. Spoon over crust. Spread with whipped topping. Sprinkle peanuts on top.

FAIRY'S DELIGHT

1st Layer:
1 C. flour
1/2 C. margarine
1/2 C. nuts
2nd Layer:
8 oz. pkg. cream cheese
1 C. sugar
1 C. whipped topping
3rd Layer:
2 pkg. instant pistachio pudding
3 C. milk
4th Layer:
whipped topping
nuts
coconut

For 1st layer: blend ingredients together and pat into 9X13 pan. Bake at 350 for 20 minutes. Cool

For 2nd layer: blend together the cream cheese and sugar. Add the whipped topping. Spread over 1st layer.

For 3rd layer: Beat the pudding and milk together until slightly thickened and spread over 2nd layer.

For 4th layer: Top with the remaining whipped topping. May sprinkle nuts and coconut over top.

PEACH PUDDING

1/4 C. peach gelatin powder
1/2 C. hot milk
1-1/2 C. cold milk
1 pkg. (3.4 oz) instant vanilla pudding
sliced peaches
whipped topping

Dissolve gelatin in hot milk. In another bowl, beat cold milk and pudding mix on low for 2 minutes. Add gelatin mixture. Mix well. Let stand 5 minutes. Spoon into individual bowls. Garnish with peaches and whipped topping.

BERRY DELIGHT

1 graham cracker crust
1-8 oz. pkg. cream cheese
1/4 C. sugar
2 Tbs. milk
2 pints strawberries
3-1/2 C. milk
2 pkg. instant vanilla pudding
8 oz. whipped topping

Beat cream cheese, sugar and 2 Tbs. milk until smooth. Gently stir in half the whipped topping. Spread over crust. Top with strawberries. Add pudding to the 3-1/2 C. milk. Beat 2 minutes. Pour over the top of strawberries. Refrigerate 4 hours. Spread remaining whipped topping on top.

STRAWBERRY DESSERT

2 C. crushed pretzels
1/2 C. sugar
1 stick margarine
8 oz. cream cheese
8 oz. whipped topping
3/4 C. sugar
1 large pkg. strawberry gelatin
water
1 pkg. strawberries

Mix the first 3 ingredients together. Press into a 9X13 pan. Bake at 350 for 5 minutes. Mix the cream cheese with the whipped topping. Add sugar and mix well. Spread over pretzel crust. Make gelatin as directed on box. Mix strawberries with gelatin and let set up a little in the refrigerator. Spoon onto cream cheese mixture. Chill.

CHERRY ANGEL DELIGHT

1 large prepared angel food cake
1 can cherry pie filling
1 pkg. vanilla instant pudding
1-1/2 C. milk
1 C. sour cream

Cut or tear cake into 1/2 inch pieces to measure 8 cups. Place half in a square glass pan. Reserve 1/3 of the pie filling. Spread the rest over cake. Top with remaining cake cubes. Combine pudding, milk and sour cream. Spoon over cake. Cover and chill. To serve, cut into squares and top with remaining pie filling.

MANGO MOUSSE IN CRISPY CUPS

2 Tbs. butter
20 large marshmallows
3 C. crispy rice cereal
1/4 C. heavy cream
4 sq. white baking chocolate, chopped
2 pkg. (8 oz. ea.) cream cheese
3/4 C. powdered sugar
1/2 tsp. grated lime rind
1 C. diced ripe mango

Coat muffin cups with nonstick spray. Melt butter and marshmallows then add the cereal. Mix well. Press 1/4 C. mixture into bottom and sides of cups. Set aside. Combine cream and chocolate. Microwave, Stir until melted. Beat cream cheese, sugar and rind. Beat in chocolate mixture until fluffy. About 2 minutes. Refrigerate 30 minutes. Pour into crispy cups. Refrigerate.

FRUIT COBBLER

1 C. flour
2 tsp. baking powder
2/3 C. milk
3/4 C. sugar
1 tsp. vanilla
1/4 tsp. salt
2 C. cherries, peaches or blackberries

Mix all but the fruit and put into a greased square pan. Pour fruit on top of batter. Bake at 325 for 45 minutes.

CHERRY ENCHILADAS

3 C. cherry pie filling
1 pkg. large flour tortillas
1 stick margarine
1-1/2 C. sugar
1-1/4 C. water

Divide pie filling evenly between tortillas. Roll as for enchiladas. Place seam side down in a lightly greased 9X13 pan. Combine margarine, sugar and water. Heat and pour over tortillas. Place in refrigerator for 2 hours or over night. Bring to room temperature and then bake at 350 for 30 minutes.

STRAWBERRY CREPES

CREPES:

4 eggs
1-1/3 C. milk
2 Tbs. oil
1 C. flour

FILLING:

8 oz. cream cheese
1/4 C. powdered sugar
1 C. sliced strawberries

TOPPING:

1-1/2 C. sugar
1-1/2 C. strawberries, crushed

Beat eggs slightly. Add remaining ingredients. Mix just until smooth. Pour a few Tbs. into a hot skillet, tilting to spread evenly. Brown lightly on both sides. For filling: blend powdered sugar and cream cheese until smooth. Add the berries. Place about 2 Tbs. on crepe and roll up. For topping: Stir berries and sugar together in a sauce pan. Bring to a boil. Reduce heat and simmer 10 minutes. Cool. Pour over top of filled crepes. Variations: May use cherry pie filling.

APPLE TURNOVERS

3 C. flour
3 Tbs. sugar
1 tsp. salt
1/2 tsp. cinnamon
1-1/4 C. shortening
5-6 Tbs. water
1 can apple pie filling (or any kind you prefer)

Combine flour, sugar, salt and cinnamon. Cut in shortening. Sprinkle dough with water, adding 1 Tbs. at a time, stirring with a fork, until just enough has been added so the dough can be patted into a ball. Divide pastry in half. On a lightly floured surface, roll one of the halves into a 10X15 rectangle. Cut into 6 squares, 5" each. Repeat with the other half of the dough. Place 2 Tbs. of the fruit in the center of each square. Moisten edges with water. Fold over 1/2 the square to form a triangle. Seal edges by going around the edges with a fork. Prick top for steam. Bake at 425 for 12-15 minutes. Drizzle a glaze made with powdered sugar, water and vanilla while hot.

QUICK CHERRY TURNOVERS

1 tube refrigerated crescent rolls
1 C. cherry pie filling
1/2 C. powdered sugar
1-2 Tbs. milk

Unroll dough and separate into eight triangles. Make four squares by pressing the seams of two triangles together and rolling into shape. Place on ungreased baking sheet. Spoon 1/4 C. pie filling in one corner of each square. Fold to make a triangle. Bake at 375 for 10-12 minutes. Mix sugar and milk. Drizzle over turnovers.

CHOCOLATE DESSERT WRAPS

1/2 C. creamy peanut butter
4 tortillas (8")
1 C. miniature marshmallows
1/2 C. semi-sweet chocolate chips
vanilla ice cream

Spread 2 Tbs. peanut butter on each tortilla. Sprinkle 1/4 C. marshmallows and 2 Tbs. chocolate chips on half of each tortilla. Roll up, beginning with the topping side. Wrap each tortilla in heavy duty foil. Seal tightly. Grill, covered, over low heat 5-10 minutes or until heated through. Remove foil and serve with ice cream.

RASPBERRY TARTS

1 C. butter
3/4 C. sugar
2 egg yolks
1 tsp. vanilla
1 tsp. lemon juice
1-1/2 C. flour
1 tsp. cinnamon
1/4 tsp. cloves
1/4 tsp. salt
1 tsp. baking powder
1-1/4 C. blanched slivered almonds, ground
1 to 1-1/4 C. seedless red raspberry jam

Beat butter until creamy. Add the sugar and beat well. Beat egg yolks slightly with vanilla and lemon juice. Add to creamed mixture. Sift dry ingredients together and add to creamed mixture. Mix well. Add almonds and blend. Spray (or put in paper liner cups) 2 cupcake pans. Place 2 tablespoons of batter in each cup. Pat gently to cover bottom of each cup. Gently place 2 teaspoons of jam in the center of each tart. Bake at 350 for 15 minutes or until golden brown. Cool tarts in the pans for 1 hour. Remove and let cool completely.

PEANUT BUTTER CHOCOLATE TORTE

1-1/2 C. heavy cream
8 sq. semi-sweet chocolate, chopped
1/3 C. creamy peanut butter
4 C. round crisp cereal (plain, chocolate or peanut butter)
1-1/2 pkg. (8 oz. each) cream cheese
1-1/2 C. creamy peanut butter
1-1/2 C. powdered sugar
2 tsp. vanilla

Heat 1/2 C. cream until bubbles appear on edges. Remove from heat. Add chocolate and 1/3 C. peanut butter. Whisk. Stir in the cereal. Spread 1/2 on the bottom of a greased 9" pan. (About 2 cups). Beat together cream cheese, 1-1/2 C. peanut butter, sugar and vanilla until smooth. In a small bowl beat 1 cup cream until stiff peaks form. Fold onto cream cheese. Spread over cereal. Carefully spoon remaining chocolate cereal mixture over top. Refrigerate.

LEMON BLOSSOM TWIST

1 pkg. yeast
3 Tbs. sugar
1/4 C. warm water
1 egg
3/4 C. sour cream
2-2/3 flour
1 tsp. salt
1/8 baking soda

FILLING:

8 oz. pkg. cream cheese
1 pkg. lemon instant pudding
2 Tbs. water
2 Tbs. lemon juice
1 egg

FROSTING:

1-1/2 C. powdered sugar
2 Tbs. lemon juice
1 Tbs. margarine

Dissolve yeast and sugar in water. Add egg and sour cream. Mix well. Combine four, salt and baking soda. Add to the yeast mixture. Mix well. Turn dough onto a floured surface and roll to a 20 X 8 inch rectangle. Mix the filling ingredients together until smooth and spread over dough, lengthwise down center. Fold long sides to center, slightly overlapping edges. Cut into 4 X 1 inch strips. Twist and place on baking sheet. Bake at 375 for 12-15 minutes. Frost while warm. To make frosting: Combine all the ingredients until smooth.

EASY CHERRY GELATIN

1 large pkg. gelatin
2 C. boiling water
1 can cherry pie filling
whipped topping

Dissolve gelatin in water. Add 8-10 ice cubes, stirring until gelatin starts to thicken. Then add pie filling. Put in a pretty glass bowl and top with whipped topping.

PUMPKIN CAKE ROLL

3 eggs
1 C. sugar
2/3 C. pumpkin
1 tsp. lemon juice
3/4 C. flour
1 tsp. baking soda
1 tsp. cinnamon
1 tsp. ginger
2 tsp. nutmeg
1/2 tsp. salt

FILLING:

1 C. powdered sugar
6 oz. cream cheese
4 Tbs. margarine
1 tsp. vanilla

Beat eggs, gradually add the sugar. Stir in pumpkin and lemon juice. Sift the rest of the ingredients and fold into egg mixture. Pour into a greased and floured jelly roll pan. Bake at 375 for 15 minutes. When done sprinkle powdered sugar on a towel and lay the cake on it. Sprinkle with powdered sugar and roll up. Cool. Unroll and spread with filling. Filling: Mix all the ingredients well and spread on cake. Roll the cake back up and chill. Cut into slices to serve.

QUICK RICE PUDDING

1 pkg. instant vanilla pudding
2 C. milk
1 C cold cooked rice

Combine pudding mix and milk. Beat for 1-2 minutes. Stir in rice. Chill.

RICE PUDDING

1/2 C. water
1/2 C. uncooked instant rice
3 eggs, beaten
1/2 C. sugar
2 tsp. vanilla
1/4 tsp. salt
2-1/2 C. milk, scalded

Heat water to boiling. Add rice, stir and remove from heat. Cover and let stand 5 minutes. Blend eggs, sugar, vanilla and salt. Gradually stir in the milk, stir in the rice. Pour into a ungreased 1-1/2 qt. casserole. Place casserole in a square pan. Pour very hot water (1-1/4" deep) into pan. Bake at 350 for about 70 minutes. Or until a knife inserted in center comes out clean. Remove from water. Serve hot or cold. Keep refrigerated.

EASY RHUBARB DESSERT

1 pkg. yellow cake mix
5 C. diced rhubarb
1 C. sugar
1 C. heavy cream

Mix cake as directed on box. Pour batter into a 9X13 pan. Spread rhubarb over batter. Sprinkle with sugar. Pour cream over top. Do not mix. Bake at 350 for 35-40 minutes.

RHUBARB CRISP

3 C. rhubarb
3/4 C. sugar
2 tsp. cinnamon
1 C. flour
1 C. sugar
1/2 C. margarine

Mix rhubarb with sugar and cinnamon. Place in a 9" square pan. Place flour, sugar and margarine in a bowl. Blend until crumbly. Sprinkle over rhubarb. Bake at 375 for 25-30 minutes.

RHUBARB COCONUT BREAD PUDDING

1 C. sugar
3/4 C. water
2 Tbs. margarine
3 C. sliced rhubarb
1 egg, beaten
1/2 tsp. vanilla
4 C. bread, lightly toasted and cubed
1 C. shredded coconut, divided

Combine sugar and water. Bring to a boil. Remove from heat and add margarine and rhubarb. Cover and let stand 15 minutes. Drain, reserving liquid. Blend the liquid with egg and vanilla. Combine bread cubes, rhubarb mixture, egg mixture and 3/4 C. coconut. Place in a greased 1 qt. casserole. Sprinkle with remaining coconut. Bake at 325 for 45 minutes.

RHUBARB DELIGHT

3/4 C. sugar
3 Tbs. margarine
1 C. flour
1/2 C. milk
3 C. rhubarb
1 C. hot water
1 Tbs. cornstarch
1 C. sugar

Mix sugar and margarine together. Add flour and milk. Put the rhubarb in a greased square pan. Add the mixture to this. Mix together the hot water, cornstarch and sugar. Pour over the rhubarb mixture. Bake at 350 for 40 minutes.

RHUBARB SQUARES

1 C. flour
1/3 C. powdered sugar
1/3 C. margarine

FILLING:

1 C. sugar
1/4 C. flour
2 eggs, lightly beaten
1 tsp. vanilla
3 C. finely chopped rhubarb

Combine flour and powdered sugar. Cut in margarine until mixture resembles coarse crumbs. Press into a greased 9X13 pan. Bake at 350 for 12 minutes.

For filling: Combine the sugar, flour, eggs and vanilla. Stir in rhubarb. Pour over warm crust. Bake at 350 for 35-40 minutes.

RHUBARB DUMPLINGS

SAUCE:

1-1/2 C. sugar
1 Tbs. flour
1/2 tsp. cinnamon
1/4 tsp. salt
1-1/2 C. water
1/3 C. margarine
1 tsp. vanilla

DOUGH:

2 C. flour
2 Tbs. sugar
2 tsp. baking powder
1/4 tsp. salt
2-1/2 Tbs. margarine
3/4 C. milk

FILLING:

2 Tbs. margarine
2 C. finely chopped rhubarb
1/2 C. sugar

For sauce: In a saucepan, combine sugar, flour, cinnamon and salt. Stir in water. Add margarine. Bring to a boil. Cook and stir 1 minute. Remove from heat. Add vanilla. Set aside. For dough: Combine flour, sugar, baking powder and salt. Cut in the margarine. Add milk quickly. Do not over mix. Gather dough into a ball and roll out onto a floured surface into a 12X9 rectangle. Spread margarine on dough. Arrange rhubarb on top. Combine sugar and cinnamon. Sprinkle on rhubarb. Roll up from long side. Cut into 12 slices. Arrange in a greased 9X13 pan. Pour sauce over top. Bake at 350 for 35-40 minutes or until golden brown.

STRAWBERRY PIZZA

1 refrigerator sugar cookie dough, rolled out to size of pizza pan. Bake as directed.
8 oz. cream cheese
1 C. powdered sugar
1 C. whipped topping
1 qt. strawberries

Cream together cream cheese, sugar and whipped topping. Spread over cooled cookie crust. Top with strawberries. And any other fruit you would like. Kiwi....mandarin oranges....bananas...peaches...etc.

RHUBARB UPSIDE DOWN CAKE

TOPPING:

3 C. rhubarb, cut into 1/2" slices
1 C. sugar
2 Tbs. flour
1/4 tsp. nutmeg
1/4 C. margarine, melted

BATTER:

1-1/2 C. flour
3/4 C. sugar
2 tsp. baking powder
1/4 tsp. salt
1/2 tsp. nutmeg
1/4 C. margarine, melted
2/3 C. milk
1 egg
whipped topping

Sprinkle rhubarb in a greased 10" heavy skillet. Combine sugar, flour and nutmeg. Sprinkle over rhubarb. Drizzle with margarine. For batter, combine flour, sugar, baking powder, salt and nutmeg in a bowl. Add margarine, milk and egg. Beat until smooth. Spread over rhubarb. Bake at 350 for 35 minutes. Loosen edges immediately and invert onto a serving plate. Serve warm with whipped top.

CHERRY CHEWBILEES

1-1/4 C. flour
1/2 C. brown sugar
1/2 C. butter flavored shortening
1 C. chopped walnut, divided
1/2 C. flaked coconut

FILLING:

2 pkg. (8 oz. ea.) cream cheese
2/3 C. sugar
2 eggs
2 tsp. vanilla
2 cans cherry pie filling

Combine flour and brown sugar. Cut in shortening until fine crumbs form. Stir in 1/2 C. nuts and coconut. Reserve 1/2 C. crumbs for topping. Press remaining mixture into bottom of a greased 9X13 pan. Bake at 350 for 12-15 minutes. Beat cream cheese, sugar, eggs and vanilla until smooth. Spread over the hot crust. Bake 15 minutes. Spread pie filling over top. Combine remaining nuts and reserved crumbs. Sprinkle over cherries. Bake 15 minutes more. Cool. Refrigerate until serving.

TOFFEE CANDY BAR DESSERT

1ST LAYER:

18 graham crackers, crushed
18 soda crackers, crushed
1/2 C. margarine, melted
Mix and press into a 9X13 pan.

2ND LAYER:

2 pkg. instant vanilla pudding
2 C. milk
1 qt. butter brickle ice cream
Mix pudding and milk by hand until smooth. Mix in ice cream and pour over 1st layer.

3RD LAYER:

4 regular size toffee candy bars, frozen, chopped or crushed
1 container whipped topping
Spread the whipped topping over 2nd layer then sprinkle with the toffee candy.

FUDGE POPS

1 pkg. cook and serve chocolate pudding mix
2-1/2 C. milk
1/2 C. peanuts
1/2 C. chocolate chips
1/2 C. marshmallow cream
12 plastic cups (3 oz. each)
12 popsicle sticks

Combine pudding and milk. Microwave, uncovered on high for 6 to 7-1/2 minutes or until bubbly and slightly thick, stirring every 2 minutes. Cool for 20 minutes, stirring several times. Meanwhile, combine peanuts and chocolate chips. Place about 2 Tbs. in each cup. Stir marshmallow cream into pudding. Spoon into cups. Insert popsicle sticks. Freeze.

JOYCE'S ICE CREAM DESSERT

1 pkg. (12) ice cream sandwiches
1 jar caramel ice cream topping
1 pkg. toffee and chocolate chips
1 large container whipped topping

Unwrap the ice cream sandwiches and place in a 9X13 pan. Pour the caramel topping over the ice cream sandwiches. Sprinkle most of the toffee chips over the topping. Spread the whipped topping over that. Sprinkle with the remaining toffee chips. Freeze.

New found recipes

New found recipes

New found recipes

New found recipes

New found recipes

New found recipes

New found recipes

New found recipes

MAIN DISHES
&
CASSEROLES

MEATLOAF MINIATURES

1 C. ketchup
3-4 Tbs. brown sugar
1 tsp. ground mustard
2 eggs, beaten
4 Tbs. Worcestershire sauce
3 C. crispy square cereal (corn on one side rice on the other)
3 tsp. onion powder
1/2-1 tsp. seasoned salt
1/2 tsp. garlic powder
1/2 tsp. pepper
3 lbs. ground beef

Combine ketchup, brown sugar and mustard. Remove 1/2 cup for topping. Set aside. To the remaining ketchup mixture, add eggs, Worcestershire and seasonings. Crush the cereal and add. Mix well. Let stand 5 minutes. Add the beef and mix well. Press meat into muffin cups. Bake at 375 for 18-20 minutes. Drizzle reserved ketchup mixture on top and bake 10 minutes longer. These freeze well.

RED BURGERS

1-1/2 lbs. ground beef
salt
pepper
garlic powder
1 can tomato sauce
1/2 C. brown sugar
2 tbs. chili powder

Make patties with the beef. Season with salt, pepper and garlic. Cook through. Drain. Mix tomato sauce, brown sugar and chili powder. Pour over burgers. Simmer 10-15 minutes.

JANA'S SPAGHETTI RED

1 lb. hamburger
1/4 C. onion, chopped
1 pkg. chili seasoning
salt
pepper
2 cans tomato sauce
2 C. spaghetti or elbow macaroni

Brown hamburger and onion. Add the seasonings and tomato sauce. Simmer on low for 15 minutes. Cook spaghetti. Add to hamburger. Serve with chopped onion, dill pickles, shredded cheese and catsup.

STUFFED PEPPERS

6 green peppers
1-1/2 lb. hamburger
1/2 C. onion, chopped
1 can stewed tomatoes
1 can diced tomatoes
1 tsp. salt
1/2 tsp. pepper
1 tsp. garlic powder
3/4 C. uncooked instant rice
1-1/2 C. shredded cheese
1 (16 oz.) jar spaghetti sauce

Cut off the tops of the green peppers. Remove seeds and membrane. Precook green pepper cups in boiling salted water about 5 minutes. Drain. Sprinkle inside with salt. Brown the hamburger and onion. Drain. Add the tomatoes, rice and seasonings. Cover and simmer until rice is tender. About 5 minutes. Add 1 C. cheese. Stuff the peppers. Stand upright in a baking dish. Bake uncovered at 350 for 20 minutes. Remove from over and spread spaghetti sauce over top. Sprinkle a little cheese over the sauce. Return to the oven and bake another 10 minutes.

KOLETTE'S MEATLOAF

2 lbs. hamburger
1 pkg. dry onion mix
1 sleeve crackers, crushed
1 C. vegetable tomato juice
2 eggs
BBQ sauce

Mix all but the BBQ sauce together and place into a loaf pan. Pour the BBQ sauce over top. Bake at 350 for 1 hour.

HOBO CASSEROLE

1 lb. hamburger
1/4 C. milk
1 tsp. salt
1/4 tsp. pepper
sliced onion
sliced potatoes
sliced cheese
1 can mushroom soup

Press raw hamburger into a 2 Qt. casserole dish. Pour milk over meat. Add salt and pepper. Layer onion, potatoes and cheese. Pour soup over all. Cover and bake at 350 for 1 hour.

TRACY'S SWEDISH MEATBALL SOUP

1 egg
2 C. half & half
1 C. bread crumbs
1 small onion, finely chopped
1-3/4 tsp. salt, divided
1-1/2 lbs. ground beef
1 Tbs. margarine
3 Tbs. flour
3/4 tsp. beef bouillon granules
1/2 tsp. pepper
18 to 1/4 tsp. garlic salt
3 C. water
1 lb. red potatoes, cubed
1 can peas

In a bowl, beat egg. Add 1/3 C. cream, bread crumbs, onion and 1 tsp. salt. Add beef. Mix well. Shape into 1/2 inch balls. Brown meatballs in margarine, half at a time. Remove from pan. Set aside. Drain fat. To pan, add flour, bouillon, pepper, garlic salt and remaining salt. Stir until smooth. Gradually stir in water. Bring to a boil, stirring often. Add potatoes and meatballs. Reduce heat, cover and simmer for 25 minutes or until potatoes are tender. Stir in peas and remaining cream. Heat through.

TRACY'S HEAVENLY BEEF

1-lb. ground beef
2 tsp. minced garlic
1/2 tsp. salt
30 oz. can tomato sauce
8 oz. pkg. cream cheese
1 pt. sour cream
1 C. chopped onion
1 lb. egg noodles, cooked
1 lb. shredded Mozzarella cheese

Brown the beef. Add garlic, salt and tomato sauce. Simmer for 30 minutes. Mix together cream cheese, sour cream and onions. In a greased 9X13 pan layer:

1/3 sauce
1/2 noodles
1/2 cream cheese
1/2 Mozzarella
1/3 sauce

remaining noodles, cream cheese, Mozzarella and sauce. Bake at 350 for 30 minutes.

BURGER BEANS

1 lb. hamburger
1/4 C. onion, chopped
1 can pork & beans
1 can tomato soup
2 Tbs. brown sugar
salt
pepper
garlic powder

Brown hamburger and onions. Drain. Add the rest of the ingredients and simmer 20 minutes.

HAMBURGER CASSEROLE

1 lb. hamburger
1/4 C. onions, chopped
1 tsp. salt
1/2 tsp. pepper
1 tsp. garlic powder
1 small can tomato juice
1 can cream of mushroom soup
2 C. tri-color twirl macaroni
1-1/2 C. shredded cheese

Cook hamburger and onion. Add the seasonings. Add the tomato juice and cream of mushroom soup. Cook macaroni according to directions on package. Drain and add to hamburger mixture. Mix in 1 cup of cheese. Place into a casserole dish and sprinkle 1/2 cup cheese on top. Bake at 350 for 30 minutes.

SWEET AND SOUR MEATBALLS

2 lbs. hamburger
1/2 C. onions, chopped
1/2 C. green peppers, chopped
1 C. cracker crumbs
1/2 C. vinegar
1/4 C. Worcestershire sauce
1/2 C. catsup
3 Tbs. brown sugar

Mix the hamburger, onion, green pepper and cracker crumbs. Shape into balls. Place in a casserole dish. Mix the rest of the ingredients and pour over the meatballs. Bake at 350 for 1 hour.

PORCUPINE MEAT BALLS

1 lb. hamburger
1/2 C. uncooked rice
1 egg, slightly beaten
2 Tbs. onion, chopped
1/4 C. of can cream of mushroom soup
1/2 tsp. salt
dash of pepper

Sauce: Balance of can of soup
1/2 C. water
1 tsp. Worcestershire sauce

Combine the meat, rice, egg, salt, pepper and 1/4 cup soup. Mix and shape into balls, brown in pan. Mix the sauce ingredients and pour over meat balls and bring to a boil. Reduce heat, cover and simmer 40 minutes. Stir several times. Or can bake at 350 for 1 hour. Or place in crock pot and cook on low 4-6 hours.

MEATBALLS IN PLUM SAUCE

2 lbs. ground beef
1 egg, slightly beaten
1 onion, chopped
1 tsp. salt
1-18 oz. jar plum jelly
1-12 oz. jar chili sauce
2 tsp. salt

Mix the beef, onion, egg and salt. Make into balls. Combine the rest of the ingredients together and put in skillet. Cook, stirring constantly over low heat until sauce is smooth. Add the meatballs and simmer 1 hour. Or you can put them in a slow cooker for 4-6 hours. Or you can put them in the oven at 350 for 1 hour.

CAMP STEW

1-1/2 lb. hamburger
2 C. diced potatoes
1 can diced tomatoes
2 C. diced carrots, if using canned, drain
1 small onion, chopped
1/2 instant rice
1 can peas, not drained

Us a 4 qt. casserole. Layer in order given. Season each layer with salt and pepper as you go. Bake at 350 for 1-2 hours, depending on how many fresh vegetable you use.

BACON CHEESEBURGER WRAP

1 lb. hamburger
4 slices bacon, chopped
1/2 C. onion, chopped
1/2 lb. processed cheese, cut into 1/2 inch cubes
1 pkg. refrigerated pizza crust

Cook hamburger, bacon and onion until hamburger is evenly browned, stirring occasionally. Drain. Add cheese to the hamburger and cook until completely melted, stirring frequently. Remove from heat.

Unroll pizza dough onto a baking sheet sprayed with cooking spray. Press into a 15x8 inch rectangle. Top evenly with the meat mixture. Roll up dough, starting at one of the long sides. Lay seam side down. Bake at 400 for 20-25 minutes or until golden brown.

Serve with mustard, ketchup, sliced tomatoes, salsa, and or dill pickles.

SHEPHERDS PIE

1 lb. hamburger (or leftover roast or chicken or ham)
1 small onion, chopped
1 can crushed tomatoes
1 can green beans, drained
1 can cream corn
1 tsp. salt
1/2 tsp. pepper
2 C. leftover mashed potatoes
1 C. shredded cheddar cheese

Brown the hamburger. Add the onion and cook until tender. Add tomatoes, beans, corn, salt and pepper. Spread into a casserole dish. Cover with potatoes. Sprinkle cheese on top. Bake at 400 for 20 minutes or until cheese melts.

TATER TOT CASSEROLE

1 lb. hamburger
1 small onion, chopped
1 can cream of celery coup
1 pkg. tater tots, frozen
salt and pepper to taste

Brown beef and onion together. Place in casserole. Pour soup over this and top with tater tots. Bake at 350 for 30 minutes.

ZUCCHINI & BEEF CASSEROLE

1 zucchini, chopped
1 lb. hamburger, cooked and drained
1 small onion, chopped
1 green pepper, chopped
2 C. shell macaroni
1 pkg. spaghetti seasoning
1 can kidney beans
3 tomatoes, chopped
1 C. processed cheese, shredded

Put everything into a large casserole dish and bake at 350 for 1 hour.

VEGGIE HAMBURGER SKILLET

1 lb. hamburger
1/3 C. onion, chopped
1 C. water
1 C. uncooked instant rice
1 pkg. (16 oz.) frozen broccoli, carrot, water chestnut, red pepper mix.
1/2 tsp. garlic powder
1/2 tsp. seasoned salt
1 can cream of chicken soup
1 can tomato sauce
4 oz. shredded Cheddar cheese

Brown hamburger and onion. Add water, rice, vegetables, garlic and salt. Bring to a boil. Reduce heat and simmer, covered for 6-8 minutes. Stir in soup and tomato sauce. Cook 5 minutes longer or until heated through. Sprinkle with cheese. Cover and let stand 2-3 minutes or until cheese is melted.

BEEF BROCCOLI SUPPER

3/4 C. uncooked rice
1 lb. ground beef
1-1/2 C. fresh broccoli
1 can condensed broccoli cheese soup
1/2 C. milk
1 tsp. seasoned salt
1 tsp. salt
1/2 tsp. pepper
1/2 C. dry bread crumbs
2 Tbs. margarine, melted

Cook rice according to directions on pkg. Cook the beef until no longer pink. Drain. Add rice, broccoli, soup, milk and seasonings. Stir until combined. Transfer to a baking dish. Toss crumbs and margarine. Sprinkle over beef mixture. Cover and bake at 350 for 30 minutes. Uncover and bake 5-10 minutes longer.

INDIAN TACOS

FRY BREAD:

2 C. flour
2 tsp. baking powder
1 tsp. salt
1 rounded tsp. shortening
3/4 C. warm water
1/4 C. milk

TACO MEAT:

1-1/2 lb. ground beef
1 tsp. onion, chopped
1/4 pkg. taco seasoning
1/4 C. salsa
1 can kidney beans
lettuce, chopped
tomatoes, chopped
shredded cheese
salsa
sour cream

For the fry bread: Cut the shortening into the dry ingredients. Add the water and milk. Knead until elastic. If too sticky add a little more flour. Let rise 15 minutes. Divide into 8 equal parts. Roll out as pie dough. Fry in hot grease until medium brown. Turn and brown other side. For the meat: Mix and cook the beef, onion and seasoning. Add salsa and beans. Place taco meat on top of the fry bread. Add lettuce, tomatoes, cheese, sour cream, salsa or anything else you would like....jalapenos.... black olives...

MEXICAN GOULASH

1 lb. hamburger
2 cans chili pinto beans
1 can tomato sauce
1 can hot tomato sauce (optional)
1/8 tsp. garlic salt
1/4 tsp. oregano
1-2 tsp. chili powder

Brown the hamburger. Drain. Add the rest of the ingredients and simmer 30-40 minutes. Serve over corn chips. (Chili flavored are great!) Garnish with shredded cheese, chopped onions, tomatoes and lettuce. Serve with sour cream, salsa and guacamole.

TACO BAKE

1 lb. ground beef
1 small onion, chopped
3/4 C. water
1 pkg. taco seasoning
1 can tomato sauce
1 pkg. (8 oz.) shell macaroni
1 can chopped green chilies
2 C. shredded Cheddar cheese, divided

Brown beef and onion. Drain. Add water, taco seasoning and tomato sauce. Bring to a boil. Simmer 20 minutes. Stir in macaroni, chilies and 1-1/2 C. cheese. Pour into a greased 1-1/2 qt. baking dish. Sprinkle with the remaining cheese. Bake at 350 for 30 minutes.

SANTA FE CASSEROLE

1 lb. hamburger
1 pkg. taco seasoning
2 C. chicken broth
1/4 C. flour
1 container sour cream
1 can diced green chilies
1 pkg. (11 oz.) corn chips
2 C. shredded Cheddar cheese
1/2 C. sliced green onions

Brown meat and drain. Add taco seasoning. Blend well. Mix together the broth and flour. Add to the meat. Bring to a boil to thicken. Remove from heat. Stir in sour cream and chilies. Blend. In a 9X13 baking pan, greased, place 1/2 the chips, top with 1/2 the beef mixture, 1/2 the cheese and 1/2 the onions. Layer again. End with the onions. Bake uncovered at 375 for 30 minutes.

CHIMICHANGAS

1-1/2 lb. hamburger
1 C. onion, chopped
1 can refried beans
1 tomato, chopped
1/3 C. parsley, minced
2 Tbs. salsa
1-1/2 tsp. oregano
3/4 tsp. cumin
1/2 lb. Cheddar cheese, shredded
12 flour tortillas
1 container sour cream
lettuce, chopped
tomatoes, chopped
guacamole
salsa

Brown hamburger and onions. Drain. Add beans, tomato, parsley, oregano and cumin. Heat through. Soften tortillas in hot oil. Or wrap in a paper towel and microwave a few seconds. Put some hamburger mixture on one side of the tortillas and roll up like a burrito. Secure ends with toothpicks. Drop each roll in hot oil and fry until crisp. Sprinkle cheese over top. Serve with lettuce, sour cream, tomatoes, guacamole and salsa.

BEEF ENCHILADAS

2-1/2 lbs. ground beef
1 med. onion, chopped
2 cans enchilada sauce
1 can cream of mushroom soup
20 flour tortillas
1-1/2 C. shredded Cheddar cheese

Brown beef and onion. Drain. Combine enchilada sauce and soups. Stir 1-1/2 C. sauce into beef mixture. Spoon 1/4 C. beef down the center of each tortilla. Top with 2 Tbs. cheese. Roll up tightly. Place seam side down in a greased 9X13 pan. Top with remaining sauce. Cover and bake at 350 for 25-30 minutes. Uncover and sprinkle with cheese. Bake 5-10 minutes more.

ENCHILADA CASSEROLE

1-1/2 lb. ground beef
1 onion, chopped
1 C. water
2-3 Tbs. chili powder
1-1/2 tsp. salt
1/2 tsp. pepper
2 C. salsa, divided
10 flour tortillas (7 inch) cut into 3/4" strips
1 C. sour cream
2 cans corn, drained
4 C. shredded Mozzarella cheese

Cook beef and onion until done, drain. Stir in water, chili powder, salt, pepper and garlic powder. Bring to a boil. Reduce and simmer, uncovered for 10 minutes. Place 1/2 C. salsa in a greased 9X13 pan. Layer with half of the tortillas and another 1/2 C. salsa. Put the meat on top of this. Then layer the sour cream on top of the meat. Then the corn. Top with the remaining tortillas, salsa and cheese. Cover and bake at 350 for 35 minutes. Uncover and bake another 5-10 minutes.

ENCHILADA PIE

1 lb. ground beef
1 onion, chopped
2 garlic cloves, pressed
1/3 C. picante sauce
1-10 oz. can refried beans
1-10 oz. can enchilada sauce
1 tsp. salt
6 C. crushed corn chips
3 C. shredded Cheddar cheese
garnishes: sour cream
chopped tomatoes
lettuce
green onions

Cook beef, onion and garlic until browned. Add the picante, beans, enchilada sauce and salt. Stir and cook until combined and bubbly. Place 1 C. of the chips in the bottom of a greased 9X13 pan. Put half the beef mixture on top. Top with another cup of the cheese and 1-1/2 C. cheese. Put the rest of the beef mixture, then the rest of the chips, then the rest of the cheese. Bake at 375 for 30-40 minutes.

BEEFY JALAPENO BAKE

1 lb. ground beef
2 eggs
1 can cream style corn
1 C. milk
1/2 C. vegetable oil
1 C. cornmeal
3 Tbs. flour
1-1/2 tsp. baking powder
3/4 tsp. salt
4 C. shredded Cheddar cheese, divided
1 med. onion, chopped
1/4 C. sliced jalapeno peppers

Cook beef. Drain. In a bowl, beat eggs, corn, milk and oil. Combine the cornmeal, flour, baking powder and salt. Add to egg mixture. Mix well. Pour half the batter into a greased 9X13 pan. Sprinkle with 2 cups cheese, top with beef, onion and jalapenos. Sprinkle with the remaining cheese. Top with remaining batter. Bake uncovered at 350 for 1 hour.

CORN BREAD TACO BAKE

1-1/2 lbs. ground beef
1 pkg. taco seasoning
1/2 C. water
1 can corn, drained
1 can tomato sauce
1 pkg. corn muffin mix
1/3 C. shredded Cheddar cheese
1 can French fried onions

Brown meat and drain. Stir in taco seasoning, water, corn and tomato sauce. Pour into a 2 qt. casserole. In another bowl prepare corn muffin mix according to directions, add half can of onions. Spoon corn muffin mix around outer edge of casserole. Bake uncovered at 400 for 20 minutes. Top corn bread with cheese and remaining onions. Bake 3-5 minutes longer.

SOUTHWEST CASSEROLE

1 pkg. (7 oz.) elbow macaroni, cooked and drained
2 lbs. ground beef
1 small onion, chopped
2 garlic cloves, minced
2 cans diced tomatoes
1 can kidney beans, drained and rinsed
1 can tomato paste
1 can green chilies
1-1/2 tsp. salt
1 tsp. chili powder
1/2 tsp. cumin
1/2 tsp. pepper
2C. shredded Monterey Jack cheese
1/4 C. sliced jalapeno peppers

Cook beef, onion and garlic. Drain, Stir in tomatoes, beans, tomato paste, chilies and seasonings. Bring to a boil. Reduce heat and simmer uncovered for 10 minutes. Stir the macaroni into the meat mixture. Put into a greased 9x13 pan. Top with cheese and jalapenos. Cover and bake at 375 for 30 minutes. Uncover and bake 10 minutes.

SPANISH NOODLES & BEEF

1 lb. hamburger
1 small green pepper, chopped
1 small onion, chopped
3-1/4 C. uncooked egg noodles
1 can diced tomatoes
1 C. water
1/4 C. chili sauce
1 tsp. salt
1/8 tsp. pepper
4 bacon strips, cooked and crumbled

Brown the hamburger, peppers and onion. Drain. Stir in noodles, tomatoes, water, chili sauce, salt and pepper. Mix well. Cover and cook on low for 15-20 minutes or until noodles are tender, stirring frequently. Add the bacon and serve.

STEAK QUESADILLAS

3/4 lb. sirloin steak, cut into thin strips
1/8 tsp. salt
1/8 tsp. pepper
2-3 Tbs. olive oil
1-1/2 C. shredded pepper Jack cheese
4 flour tortillas

Sprinkle steak with salt and pepper. Sauté steak in 1 Tbs. oil until no longer pink. Sprinkle 1/4 C. cheese over one side of each tortilla. Top each with 1/3 cup steak. Sprinkle the remaining cheese over steak. Fold tortillas over. In a large skillet, add 1 Tbs. oil. Heat to medium and heat each quesadilla for 1-2 minutes on each side or until cheese is melted. Cut into wedges.

Serve with corn salsa, sour cream and guacamole.

FAJITAS

1/2 C. Italian dressing, divided
1/2 tsp. chili powder
1 lb. boneless sirloin steak, cut in 1/4" strips
1 med. green pepper, sliced
1 med. onion, sliced and separated
6 flour tortillas

In a large re-sealable bag combine 1/4 C. dressing and chili powder. Add steak. Coat steak. Refrigerate 30 minutes. In a skillet, sauté peppers and onion in remaining dressing until tender crisp. Remove and keep warm. Drain steak, discarding dressing. In skillet, sauté steak for 6-8 minutes or until no longer pink. Return vegetables to skillet. Heat through. Wrap tortillas in a paper towel and microwave for a few seconds to soften. Spoon meat down center of flour tortilla. Fold sides in. Serve with guacamole, sour cream and salsa.

SLOPPY JOES

2 lbs. hamburger
1 small onion, chopped
2 garlic cloves, minced
2 C. ketchup
1 C. bbq. sauce
1/4 C. brown sugar
1/4 C. vinegar
2 Tbs. mustard
1 tsp. Italian seasoning
1 tsp. onion powder

Cook beef, onion and garlic. Drain. Stir in the rest of the ingredients. Bring to a boil and simmer for 20 minutes. Serve on hamburger buns.

BBQ CUPS

1 lb. hamburger
1/2 C. shredded cheese
garlic, to taste
1/4 C. onion, chopped
1/2 C. barbecue sauce

BISCUIT CUPS:

2C. baking mix
1/2 C. water

Beat 20 strokes, drop into ungreased muffin tins, press into cup shape. Fill with meat mixture. (canned biscuits may be used).

Brown hamburger, onion and garlic. Drain. Add the barbecue sauce, heat through. Spoon into biscuit in muffin tin cups. Sprinkle with cheese. Bake 15 minutes at 400.

LASAGNA

1-1/2 lb. ground beef, browned
2 cloves garlic, minced
1 stalk celery, chopped
3 Tbs. olive oil
1/2 tsp. oregano
1 tsp. salt
1 tsp. pepper
1 can tomato paste
2 cans tomato sauce
1 pkg. lasagna noodles, cooked
1 carton cottage cheese
1 egg, beaten
2 C. Mozzarella cheese

Sauté celery and garlic in oil. Add meat, spices, tomato paste and tomato sauce. Simmer 45 minutes. Mix the egg with the cottage cheese. In a 9X13 pan, layer meat sauce, noodles, Mozzarella, noodles, cottage cheese, noodles and then end with the meat. Sprinkle parmesan cheese or mozzarella cheese on top. Bake at 350 for 1 hour.

LORI'S LASAGNA

1 lb. ground beef
3/4 C. chopped onion
1 clove garlic, crushed
1 (16 oz) can tomatoes
1-1/2 c. tomato paste (2-6 oz. cans)
2 tsp. basil
1 tsp. oregano
2 tsp. salt
8 oz lasagna noodles (not the precooked kind)
3 C. low fat cottage cheese
1 Tbs. parsley flakes
2 eggs, beaten
3/4 lb shredded Mozzarella cheese

Brown beef with onion and garlic; drain. Add tomato paste, tomatoes, basil, oregano and salt. Simmer, uncovered, for 30 minutes, stirring occasionally. Preheat oven to 350. Cook lasagna noodles according to instructions. Mix cottage cheese, parsley flakes and eggs. In greased 9x13 pan, layer 1/2 noodles, cottage cheese mixture, meat sauce and shredded cheese. Repeat layers with remaining ingredients ending with cheese. Bake for 45 minutes. Let stand for 10 minutes before cutting.

CINDY'S WHITE LASAGNA

1 lb. ground beef, cooked and drained
1 C. celery, chopped
1/3 C. onion, chopped
1 clove garlic, minced
2 tsp. dried basil, crushed
1 tsp. oregano
3/4 tsp. salt
1/8 tsp. Italian seasoning
1 C. cream
1-3 oz. pkg. cream cheese
1/2 C. dry white wine
2 C. shredded Cheddar cheese
1-1/2 C. shredded Gouda cheese
1 carton cottage cheese
1 egg, slightly beaten
12 oz. Mozzarella cheese
8 oz. lasagna noodles, cooked

Mix together the beef, celery, onion, garlic, basil, oregano, salt and Italian seasoning. Set aside. Mix all the rest of the ingredients together except the noodles. Layer these all in a large baking dish or pan. Start with the meat, then noodles, then the cheeses. Repeat. Bake at 350 for 1 hour.

MANICOTTI

1 lb. ground beef
1/2 C. green pepper, chopped
1/2 C. onion, chopped
2 cans tomato paste
2 cans water
2 tsp. oregano
2 tsp. salt
1/2 tsp. pepper
1 Tbs. sugar
1 pkg. manicotti shells
6 qt. boiling water
1 lb. cottage cheese
2 C. Mozzarella cheese
2 tsp. chopped parsley
1/2 C. Parmesan cheese

Cook beef, add peppers and onions. Cook until tender. Drain. Stir in tomato paste, water, salt, pepper, sugar and oregano. Bring to a boil. Cover and simmer 1 hour. Put manicotti shells in boiling water. Cook uncovered until barely tender. Drain. Keep shells in cold water. Combine cottage cheese, Mozzarella cheese and parsley. Fill shells with cheese mixture. Pour a thin layer of the meat sauce in the bottom of a shallow 9X13 pan. Arrange filled shells side by side in a single layer. Cover with remaining meat sauce. Sprinkle with Parmesan cheese. Bake at 350 for 30-40 minutes.

CAVATINI

1 lb. hamburger
1 clove garlic, minced
1 small onion, chopped
1 green pepper, chopped
1/2 lb. pepperoni
1 can mushrooms
1 can or jar spaghetti sauce (32 oz.)
1/4 lb. curly noodles, cooked and drained
1/4 lb. shell macaroni, cooked and drained
1/2 C. Mozzarella cheese

Brown hamburger. Add garlic, onion and green pepper. Cook until tender. Stir in pepperoni, mushroom and spaghetti sauce. Combine noodles and macaroni. Layer noodle mixture, cheese and hamburger in a greased 9X13 pan. Bake at 375 for 35-40 minutes. Remove from oven. Let stand 10 minutes.

JACQUI'S ITALIAN MEAT SAUCE

1/2 C. chopped onion
2 Tbs. olive oil
1 lb. Italian sausage
2 cloves garlic, minced
2-1 lb. cans (4 cups) tomatoes
2-8 oz. cans (2 cups) tomato sauce
4 to 8 oz. fresh slice mushrooms
1/4 C. chopped parsley
1-1/2 tsp. oregano
1 tsp. salt
1/4 tsp. thyme
1 bay leaf
1/2 C. water
1 C. red wine
1 pkg. spaghetti sauce seasoning

Brown and drain sausage. Cook onion in oil until tender. Add remaining ingredients except spaghetti seasoning. Simmer 3 hours. Add the seasoning and simmer another 30 minutes. Remove bay leaf.

SLOW COOKER SPAGHETTI SAUCE

2 lbs. hamburger
1 C. onion, chopped
2 cans tomato sauce (15 oz. each)
1 can diced tomatoes (28 oz)
1 can tomato paste (12 oz)
1/2 lb. fresh mushrooms, sliced
1 C. grated Parmesan cheese
1/2 C. dry wine or beef broth
1/4 cup dried parsley flakes
1-2 tsp. oregano
2 tsp. Italian seasoning
2 tsp. minced garlic
1 tsp. salt
1 tsp. pepper
hot cooked spaghetti

Brown the hamburger and onion together. Place in a slow cooker. Stir in all the rest of the ingredients except the spaghetti. Cook on low for 6-8 hours. Serve over spaghetti.

MEATBALLS

1 lb. hamburger
2/3 C. grated parmesan cheese
1/2 C. seasoned dry bread crumbs
1/2 C. milk
1 egg, slightly beaten

Mix all together and shape into balls. Cook in microwave, turning about every 5 minutes until done. Or place in oven and bake at 350 for about 45 minutes to an hour, depending upon the size of the meatballs.

MEATBALL & CHEESE RAVIOLI

1 can garlic & herb spaghetti sauce
16 cooked meatballs
1 pkg. frozen cheese ravioli, cooked according to pkg. directions and keep warm
1 C. shredded mozzarella cheese
basil

Heat spaghetti sauce and meat balls over medium heat until hot. Coat a 9X13 pan with cooking spray. Place ravioli in an even layer into pan. Ladle sauce and meatballs over top. Sprinkle with cheese. Cover with foil and bake at 350 for 20 minutes or until cheese melts. Garnish with basil.

MEATBALL SUB SANDWICHES

1-1/3 C. pizza sauce
4 submarine buns, split and toasted
1-1/3 C. shredded mozzarella cheese
20 slices pepperoni
1 pkg. (12 oz) frozen fully cooked meatballs, thawed
Italian seasoning to taste

Spread 1/3 cup pizza sauce on each bun. Top each with 1/3 cup cheese, five slices pepperoni and three meatballs. Sprinkle with Italian seasoning. Place top bun over toppings. Wrap each sandwich in foil. Bake at 400 for 10-12 minutes or until heated through.

ITALIAN CHEESE BAKE

1 pkg. macaroni and cheese
1 lb. hamburger
1 can Italian style stewed tomatoes
1/2 tsp. oregano
1 C. shredded Cheddar cheese

Prepare dinner as directed on box. Brown hamburger. Drain. Add tomatoes and oregano. Mix well. Bring to boil. Add meat to macaroni and cheese. Put in a 2 qt casserole dish. Sprinkle with cheese. Bake at 400 for 10 minutes.

EASY GOULASH

1 lb. hamburger
1/2 C. chopped onion
garlic salt to taste
1 can tomato sauce
2 cans water
1 C. elbow macaroni

Brown hamburger and onion. Add the rest of the ingredients and cook and stir. Cover and simmer for 20-30 minutes. Until macaroni is tender.

EASY DEEP DISH PIZZA

3 C. quick baking mix
3/4 C. water
1 lb. hamburger
1/2 C. onion, chopped
2 beef bouillon cubes
garlic powder to taste
1 can tomato sauce
1 tsp. oregano
1 can mushrooms
1/2 C. green peppers
2 C. shredded Mozzarella cheese

Lightly grease cookie sheet. Mix baking mix and water until a soft dough forms. Pat dough in bottom and sides of pan with well floured hands. Cook and stir hamburger, onion, bouillon and garlic until hamburger is browned and bouillon is dissolved. Mix tomato sauce and oregano. Spread evenly over dough. Spoon hamburger mixture over sauce. Top with mushrooms, peppers and cheese. Bake at 425 until crust is golden brown. About 20 minutes.

GARLIC CHUCK ROAST

1 boneless chuck roast (3 lbs.)
15 garlic cloves peeled
1 tsp. salt
1/4 tsp. pepper
2 Tbs. vegetable oil
1 large onion, sliced
2 Tbs. margarine, melted
1-1/2 C. water
1 lb. baby carrots
2 C. potatoes, peeled and chopped

With a sharp knife, cut 15 slits in the roast. Insert the garlic into slits. Sprinkle meat with the salt and pepper. Brown the roast in the oil. Place the roast in a roasting pan. Top with onion. Drizzle with margarine. Add the water. Cover and bake at 325 for 1-1/2 hours. Baste roast with juices, add the carrots and potatoes. Cover and bake 1 hour longer. Let roast stand 10 minutes before slicing. Thicken pan juices if desired for gravy. Use this with any roast. May have to adjust the cooking time. Or just stick it in the crock pot on low for 6-8 hours.

STANDING RIB ROAST

1 standing rib roast of beef (6-1/2 lbs, 3 ribs)
3-4 cloves garlic, thinly sliced
salt
pepper

With tip of a paring knife, make small slits all over the roast and insert garlic slivers. Rub the roast with salt and pepper. Place on a rack in a shallow pan. Roast for 25 minutes at 450. Reduce heat to 350 and roast the meat until an instant read thermometer registers 135 to 140 degrees for medium rare. About 1-1/2 hours. Let the meat rest before carving.

GRILLED ROAST BEEF SANDWICHES

1 small onion, sliced
1 green pepper, sliced
1/2 lb. fresh mushrooms, sliced
2 Tbs. vegetable oil
1/4 tsp. salt
1/8 tsp. pepper
8 slices sourdough bread
16 slices Colby-Monterey Jack cheese or Swiss cheese, divided
8 slices deli roast beef
1/2 C. margarine
garlic powder

Sauté the onion, green pepper and mushrooms in oil. Sprinkle with salt, pepper and garlic. On four slices of bread, layer two slices of cheese, two slices of beef and a fourth of the vegetable mixture. Top with remaining cheese and bread. Butter outsides of bread. On a hot griddle or skillet, toast sandwiches for 3-4 minutes on each side or until golden brown.

SKILLET HASH

2 C. chopped cooked beef
2 C. chopped cooked potatoes
1/2 C. chopped onion
dash of salt and pepper
1/4 C. shortening
2/3 C. water

Combine beef, potatoes, onion, salt and pepper. Melt shortening in skillet. Spread meat mixture in skillet. Brown hash 10-15 minutes. Reduce heat and cover. Cook 10 minutes or until crisp.

BEEF AND NOODLES

2 C. leftover roast beef
1 pkg. frozen noodles
4 C. water
salt
pepper
garlic powder

Shred the roast beef and place in a large pan. Add some of the water, noodles, salt, pepper and garlic powder. Bring to a boil. Cover and simmer. Watch and add more water as you need. Cook until the noodles are tender. Serve with mashed potatoes.

BAKED STEAK

1 lb. round steak, cut into serving pieces
1 tsp. salt
1/4 tsp. pepper
1 tsp. garlic powder
1/4 C. flour
1/2 C. water
2 Tbs. shortening
1 can cream of mushroom soup

Mix salt, pepper, garlic and flour. Roll steak in this mixture. Cook steak in the oil until nicely browned. Put steak in a casserole dish. Mix the soup and water together. Pour over steak. Cover and bake at 350 for 1 to 1-1/2 hours.

SWISS STEAK

1 C. flour
1-1/2 lb. steak
salt, pepper and garlic powder to taste
1 onion, sliced
1 Tbs. oil
1 large can diced tomatoes

Pound flour into steak using a meat mallet. Season both sides of meat. Sauté onion in hot oil. Add the steak. Brown on both sides. Add the tomatoes. Cover and cook in electric skillet for 3-4 hours at 250-300. Or put in a casserole and bake at 350 for 1 hour. Can also use your slow cooker on low for 6 hours.

BEEF STROGANOFF

1 lg. sirloin, cut in strips
1/4 C. oil
1/2 C. onion, chopped
1 can mushrooms
garlic powder
salt
pepper
paprika
1/2 C. tomato juice
1 can cream of mushroom soup
8 oz. sour cream

Brown steak, onion and mushrooms in oil. Add tomato juice and seasonings. Cover and simmer about 20 minutes. Stirring occasionally. Stir in soup and sour cream. Heat gently. Serve over cooked noodles.

BEEF STIR FRY

2 C. instant brown rice, uncooked
1 lb. sirloin steak, cut into strips
1/2 C. balsamic vinaigrette dressing
2 cloves garlic, minced
1 Tbs. cornstarch
5 C. mixed cut up fresh vegetables (red pepper, broccoli, green onions) or pkg. of frozen vegetables, thawed
2 Tbs. soy sauce
1 tsp. ginger
1/4 C. dry roasted peanuts, chopped

Cook rice as directed on package.

Toss steak with 1 Tbs. of the dressing and the garlic. Add cornstarch. Mix well. Heat large nonstick skillet sprayed with cooking spray on medium heat. Add steak mixture. Stir fry 3 minutes or until steak is cooked through. Remove from skillet and keep warm. Add the vegetables, soy sauce, ginger and remaining dressing to skillet and stir fry 5 minutes or until vegetables are tender-crisp. Return steak to skillet and stir fry 1 minute or until steak is heated through and sauce is thickened, stirring occasionally. Serve or the rice. Top with peanuts.

PEPPERS AND BEEF TIPS

1-1/2 lbs. tenderloin steak
2 Tbs. oil
1-1/2 C. beef broth
2 Tbs. ketchup
1 tsp. salt
1 small garlic clove, minced
1 small onion, chopped
1 small red pepper, sliced
1 small green pepper, sliced
3 Tbs. flour

Cut beef across grain into strips about 1-1/2 X 1/2 inch. Cook and stir in oil until browned. Reserve 1/3 C. of broth. Stir remaining broth, ketchup, salt and garlic into skillet. Heat to boiling. Reduce heat and simmer, covered until tender, about 10 minutes. Stir in onion and peppers, simmer, covered until tender. About 5 minutes. Shake reserved broth and flour in tightly covered container. Gradually stir into beef mixture. Heat to boiling, stirring constantly for 1 minute. Serve over rice or noodles.

HUNGARIAN GOULASH

3 Tbs. margarine
1 onion, chopped
2 Tbs. paprika
2 lbs. round steak, cut into 1-1/2" cubes
2 Tbs. flour
salt
3/4 tsp. marjoram
4 C. beef broth
1-1/2 C. potato cubes
1-1/2 Tbs. lemon juice

Melt margarine in a pan. Add onion, stir and cook until tender. Stir in paprika and cook slowly 1-2 minutes. Roll meat in flour. Add to the pan with onion. Cook only enough to brown lightly. Sprinkle with salt and add marjoram. Pour in the broth and bring to a boil. Cover and simmer 1 hour. Add potato cubes and cook another 20 minutes or until potatoes are done. Remove from heat and stir in lemon juice and a little more salt for flavor. Serve over noodles.

LORI'S ITALIAN TURKEY SANDWICH

Italian bread
smoked turkey, thinly sliced or shaved
creamy Italian dressing
sliced mozzarella cheese
sauerkraut, drained

Spread dressing on each slice of bread. Lay a couple of slices of turkey on top, add a slice of cheese and add some sauerkraut and another couple slices of turkey. Top with a slice of bread. Butter the outsides of the bread and grill in a skillet on both sides.

CHICKEN STRIPS

2 eggs
1 C. milk
1 C. cornflakes
1 C. flour
1 tsp. salt
1/4 tsp. pepper
1 tsp. garlic powder
4 boneless, skinless, chicken breasts

In a small bowl, beat eggs, add the milk and mix well. Crush the cornflakes. Put them in a bowl and add the flour, salt, pepper and garlic powder. Mix together. Cut the chicken in long strips. Dip each strip first in the egg mixture then the flour mixture. Coat each piece completely. Fry 5 minutes or until golden brown.

COCONUT CHICKEN STRIPS

1 lb. chicken breast, skinless, boneless, cut into strips
8 oz. shredded coconut
1 egg
3/4 C. milk
1/4 C. brown sugar
1-1/4 C. flour
oil for frying

Place coconut in shallow pan. Combine the milk, egg and sugar. Beat until well blended. Gradually blend in the flour. Beat with rotary beater until smooth. Dip each chicken strip in the egg mixture then roll in the coconut, coating each piece thoroughly. Drop into hot oil and fry for 5-7 minutes.

LEMON-BASIL STUFFED CHICKEN BREASTS

4 boneless, skinless chicken breasts
1 lemon, cut into 8 slices
2 Tbs. chopped, fresh basil
1/2 C. chopped spinach
1-1/2 Tbs. olive oil
1/4 C. balsamic vinegar
3/4 C. chicken broth

Cut a deep, horizontal pocket in the side of each chicken breast. Make the pocket as large as you can without piercing the top or bottom of the breast. Place 2 lemon wedges, 1/2 Tbs. of the basil and 1/4 of the spinach in the pocket of each chicken breast. Secure the pocket with toothpicks threading along the side to close. Heat the oil in a heavy skillet over medium high heat. Add the chicken to the skillet and cook on each side until golden brown, about 4 minutes per side. Add the vinegar and chicken broth and bring to a boil. Lower the heat and gently simmer the chicken for 4-6 minutes until cooked through.

ONION TOPPED CHICKEN

4 boneless skinless chicken breast halves
4 medium potatoes, peeled and halved
1 can cream of mushroom soup
1 C. sour cream
1 can French fried onions

Put chicken in a greased square pan. Arrange potatoes around chicken. Combine soup and sour cream. Spread over chicken and potatoes. Bake uncovered at 350 for 1 hour and 15 minutes. Sprinkle with onions. Bake 10 minutes longer.

SMOTHERED CHICKEN

4 boneless skinless chicken breast halves
garlic powder and seasoned salt to taste
1 Tbs. oil
1 can sliced mushrooms, drained
1 C. shredded cheese
1/2 C. chopped green onions
1/2 C. bacon bits

Flatten chicken to 1/4" thickness. Sprinkle with garlic powder and seasoned salt. Brown chicken in oil for 4 minutes. Turn. Top with the rest of the ingredients. Cover and cook until juices run clear. About 5-7 minutes.

MEDITERRANEAN CHICKEN

SAUCE:

1/2 C. olive oil, divided
3 medium onion, thinly sliced
6 garlic cloves, pressed
2 C. tomato juice
1 tsp. salt, divided
3/4 tsp. paprika

Heat 1/4 C. oil until it shimmer. Add onions and turn heat to low. Stir and cook 1 minute, then add the garlic. Stir and cook until the onions are soft and translucent. Add the juice, salt and paprika. Stir and cook until mixture bubbles. Cover and keep over low heat.

4 boneless, skinless chicken breasts
1/2 C. flour
1/4 tsp. pepper

Rinse the chicken breasts and dry with paper towels. Put the chicken between plastic wrap and with the flat side of a meat mallet pound the chicken to ½" thickness. Whisk flour and remaining salt and pepper. Dip chicken one at a time into the mixture. In a frying pan, heat the remaining 1/2 C. oil over medium heat. Place the chicken in the pan and cook until seared on both sides, about 3 minutes per side. Place the chicken in a greased 9X13 pan. Pour hot sauce over. Bake at 350 for 20-30 minutes.

CHICKEN BUNDLES

2 boneless skinless chicken breast halves
2 medium red potatoes, quartered and cut into 1/2" slices
1/4 C. chopped onion
1 med. carrot, cut into 1/4" slices
1/2 tsp. rubbed sage
salt and pepper to taste

Divide chicken and vegetables between 2 pieces of double-layered heavy duty foil. (About 18" square.) Sprinkle with sage, salt and pepper. Fold foil around the mixture and seal tightly. Grill, over medium heat for 30 minutes or until juices run clear and vegetables are tender.

BAKED CHICKEN

1 chicken, cut up
1 egg, beaten
2 Tbs. water
salt
pepper
garlic powder
1 C. instant potato flakes
1/4 C. margarine

Mix egg, water and seasonings. Dip each piece of chicken in egg mixture. Roll in potato flakes. Melt margarine in 9X13 baking pan. Place chicken on pan and bake at 375 for 1/2 hour. Turn the chicken and bake another 1/2 hour.

ROASTED CHICKEN DINNER

1 oven bag, large size
1 Tbs. flour
1 tsp. garlic salt, divided
1 lb. baby red potatoes
1 pkg. peeled baby carrots
2 stalks celery, cut into 1/2" slices
1 med. onion, cut into eighths
4-5 lb. chicken
1 Tbs. oil
1 tsp. paprika

Shake flour and 1/2 tsp. garlic salt in bag. Place in a 9X13 pan. Put vegetables in bag. Turn bag to mix ingredients. Push vegetables to outer edge of bag. Brush chicken with oil, sprinkle and rub chicken with remaining garlic salt and paprika. Place chicken in bag. Close the bag with nylon tie. Cut six slits in top of bag. Bake at 350 for 1-1/2 hours. Meat thermometer inserted should read 180.

ANGEL HAIR PASTA WITH CHICKEN

2 Tbs. oil
2 skinless, boneless chicken breast halves, cut into 1" cubes
1 carrot, sliced
1 (10 oz.) pkg. frozen broccoli florets, thawed
2 cloves garlic, minced
12 oz. angel hair pasta, cooked and drained
2/3 C. chicken broth
1 tsp. dried basil
1/2 C. grated Parmesan cheese

Heat 1 Tbs. oil in skillet. Add chicken. Cook, stirring until chicken is cook through. About 5 minutes. Remove from skillet. Heat remaining oil in the same skillet. Add carrots. Cook 5 minutes. Add broccoli and garlic. Cook 2 minutes. Add chicken broth, basil and cheese. Return chicken to skillet. Reduce heat and simmer 4 minutes. Place pasta in a large bowl. Top with chicken and vegetable mixture.

CHICKEN MARINARA

4 boneless, skinless chicken breast halves
2 C. sliced fresh mushrooms
3 garlic cloves, minced
1 tsp. dried basil
1/2 tsp. Italian seasoning
1 jar (28 oz) meatless spaghetti sauce
1/2 C. chicken broth
Hot cooked angel hair pasta or spaghetti

In a non stick skillet coated with nonstick cooking spray. Cook chicken for 6 minutes on each side. Remove and keep warm. Add mushrooms, garlic, basil and seasoning to skillet. Sauté until mushrooms are tender. Stir in spaghetti sauce and broth. Add the chicken and simmer for 10 minutes. Serve over pasta.

CHICKEN PASTA PRIMAVERA

2 C. uncooked spiral pasta
1 lb. boneless skinless chicken breast, cubed
2 garlic cloves, minced
2 Tbs. margarine
1 pkg. broccoli, cauliflower and carrots, thawed (16 oz.)
3/4 C. whipping cream
3/4 C. grated Parmesan cheese
1 tsp. salt
1/4 tsp. pepper

Cook pasta according to directions on pkg. Sauté chicken and garlic in margarine until done. Add the vegetables and cream. Cook until vegetables are tender. Drain pasta and add it to the chicken. Add the Parmesan cheese, salt and pepper. Cook and stir until heated through.

SLOW COOKER CHICKEN & DUMPLINGS

1-1/2 lb. boneless, skinless chicken breasts, cut into 1" pieces
2 medium potatoes, peeled and cut into 1" pieces
2 C. baby whole carrots
2 cans cream of chicken soup
1 C. water
1 tsp. thyme leaves, crushed
1/4 tsp. pepper
1 tsp. salt
2 C. all purpose baking mix
2/3 C. milk

Place chicken, potatoes & carrots in a 6-qt. slow cooker. Mix soup, water and seasonings. Pour over chicken and vegetables. Cover and cook on low for 7-8 hours or until chicken is done. (or you may cook on high for 4-5 hours.) Mix baking mix and milk. Spoon over chicken mixture. Tilt lid to vent and cook on high for 30 minutes or until dumplings are cooked in center.

LORI'S CHICKEN MANICOTTI

1 jar 26-30 oz. tomato pasta sauce
1 tsp. garlic salt
1-1/2 lbs. boneless, skinless chicken breasts, not cooked, cut into strips
12 uncooked manicotti shells
1 can sliced ripe black olives, drained
2 C. shredded mozzarella cheese

Spread about 1/3 of the pasta sauce in ungreased 9X13 pan. Sprinkle garlic salt on chicken. Insert chicken into uncooked manicotti shells. Stuffing from each end of shell to fill if necessary. Place shells on pasta sauce in pan. Pour remaining pasta sauce evenly over shells, covering completely. Sprinkle with olives and cheese. Cover and bake 1-1/2 hours at 350.

CHICKEN STRUDEL

2 Tbs. vegetable oil
3 C. tomatoes, chopped
2 garlic cloves
8 oz. (2 small cans) chopped green chilies
1-1/2 C. chopped onions
1/8 tsp. cumin
2 C. cooked, shredded chicken
1-1/4 C. shredded Cheddar cheese
1 C. sour cream
1 tsp. salt
1/2 lb. phyllo dough (or you may use pie crust)
1 stick butter, melted

Heat the oil and add the tomatoes, garlic, chilies, onions and cumin. Cook, uncovered, stirring occasionally, until the mixture is thick, about 30 minutes. Set aside to cool slightly. Combine the chicken, cheese, sour cream and salt. Stir in the tomato mixture. Pour into a buttered 9X13 pan. Place the phyllo dough or pie crust over this mixture. Brush all the melted butter over top. Bake at 400 for 20-30 minutes. Serve immediately.

CHICKEN RICE SKILLET

4 boneless, skinless chicken breast halves
2 Tbs. oil
2 celery ribs, chopped
4 green onions, thinly sliced
1/2 C. chopped red pepper
1/2 C. chopped yellow pepper
2 C. frozen green beans, thawed
1 can sliced mushrooms, drained
1 can chicken broth
1/2 C. water
3 garlic cloves, minced
1/2 tsp. salt
1/4 tsp. lemon pepper
1/8 tsp. garlic powder
1/8 tsp. pepper
2 C. uncooked instant rice

Brown chicken in oil for about 4 minutes on each side. Add the vegetables. Cook until tender and chicken juices run clear. Stir in the broth, water and seasonings. Bring to a boil. Stir in rice. Cover and remove from heat. Let stand for 5 minutes. Fluff with a fork.

CHICKEN BROCCOLI SUPPER

1/2 lb. boneless skinless chicken breasts, cubed
1-1/2 C. frozen broccoli florets
1/2 C. uncooked elbow macaroni
1/2 C. shredded Cheddar cheese
1 can cream of chicken soup
3/4 C. chicken broth
1/4 tsp. garlic powder
1/4 tsp. pepper

Combine chicken, broccoli, macaroni and cheese. Whisk the soup, broth, garlic powder and pepper. Stir into chicken mixture. Pour into a greased 1-1/2 qt. casserole dish. Bake, uncovered at 350 for 30 minutes, then stir and bake another 30 minutes.

CALIFORNIA CHICKEN CASSEROLE

1 can cream of mushroom soup
1/3 C. milk
1 pkg. frozen California blend vegetables, thawed
1-1/2 C. cubed cooked chicken
1-1/2 C. shredded Swiss cheese
salt and pepper to taste.

Combine soup and milk. Stir in vegetables, chicken, 1-1/4 C. cheese, salt and pepper. Transfer to a square pan. Cover and bake at 350 for 40 minutes. Uncover and top with remaining cheese. Bake 5-10 minutes longer. Let stand for 5 minutes. Serve over rice or noodles.

JALAPENO CHICKEN ENCHILADAS

1 cans tomato sauce, divided
2 cans cream of chicken soup
2 C. sour cream
1/4 C. sliced jalapenos
1/2 tsp. salt
1/4 tsp. onion powder
1/8 tsp. pepper
2 C. cubed cooked chicken
1-1/2 C. shredded Cheddar cheese, divided
10 flour tortillas

In a greased 9X13 pan, spread half of the tomato sauce. In a large bowl, combine the soup, sour cream, jalapenos, onion powder, salt and pepper. Stir in chicken and 1 C. cheese. Spread about 1/2 C. chicken mixture down the center of each tortilla. Roll up and place seam side down in pan. Top with remaining tomato sauce. Sprinkle with remaining cheese. Cover and bake at 350 for 45 minutes.

CHICKEN ENCHILADA CASSEROLE

1 chicken, cooked, boned and chopped, reserving broth
1 can cream of mushroom soup
1 can cream of chicken soup
1 small can diced green chilies
1 C. chicken broth
1 bag nacho cheese flavored tortilla chips, crushed
shredded longhorn cheese

Mix the above ingredients. In a greased casserole dish, put a layer of crushed chips. Then a layer of the chicken mixture. Sprinkle cheese over the top of that. Repeat, ending with chips and cheese. Refrigerate for an hour or over night. Bake at 350 for 45 minutes to 1 hour.

LORI'S SESAME CHICKEN

2/3 C. finely ground cracker crumbs
1/4 C. toasted sesame seeds*
2-3 boneless chicken breasts cut into pieces
1/3 C. evaporated milk
1/2 C. melted butter

Combine cracker crumbs and sesame seeds. Dip chicken pieces into evaporated milk, then roll into sesame seed mixture. Dip chicken piece in melted butter then arrange in a shallow baking dish (chicken should fit in one layer). Bake, uncovered at 350 for about 1-1/2 hours, or until chicken is done, turning chicken once. Cover with brown sauce and serve over rice.

To toast sesame seeds, spread out in a single layer on a baking sheet. Toast in a 350 oven, stirring occasionally for about 10 minutes. Or, toast in an ungreased skillet over medium heat, stirring, until golden brown.

BROWN SAUCE:

2 Tbs. butter
1 C. beef broth
1/4 tsp. salt
1/8 tsp. pepper
3 Tbs. flour

Cook and stir butter until brown. Add flour and seasonings. Stir and brown. Gradually add the stock until thickened.

BRENDA'S CHICKEN PASTA

1 chicken, boiled, boned and chopped
2 C. pasta, your choice, cooked in the chicken broth
1 stick margarine
1 bunch green onions, chopped
1 green pepper, chopped
8 oz. processed cheese
1 can Mexican style tomatoes
1 can cream of mushroom soup

Sauté onion and pepper in the margarine until tender. Add cheese, tomatoes and soup. Heat until cheese is melted. Mix with drained pasta and the chicken. Pour into a 9X13 pan. Bake at 350 for 30 minutes.

CHEESY CHICKEN ENCHILADAS

2 C. chopped chicken or turkey
1-8 oz. pkg. cream cheese
1 jar (8 oz.) salsa
8 (6 inch) flour tortillas
3/4 lb. processed cheese
1/4 C. milk

Stir chicken, cream cheese and 1/2 C. salsa in a pan on low. Heat until cream cheese is melted. Spoon 1/3 C. chicken mixture down center of each tortilla. Roll up, place seam side down in a greased 9X13 pan. Stir cheese and milk in a pan or microwave until smooth. Pour sauce over tortillas. Cover with foil that has been sprayed with cooking oil to keep from sticking. Bake at 350 for 20 minutes. Pour remaining salsa over tortillas.

CHICKEN CASSEROLE

1 chicken cooked, and boned
1/2 lb. macaroni, cooked in chicken broth
4 Tbs. margarine
4 Tbs. flour
2-1/2 C. milk
1 can cream of mushroom soup
1/2 lb. grated processed cheese
1 pkg. frozen peas

Melt margarine. Add flour. Mix and add milk and soup. Cook and stir until thick. Stir in the cheese until it melts. Combine chicken, macaroni and peas. Pour sauce over all. Bake at 350 for 1 hour.

CASHEW CHICKEN CASSEROLE

1 lb. boneless chicken breast, cut into 1" cubes
1 med. onion, chopped
2 C. frozen broccoli cuts
1-3/4 C. boiling water
1 C. uncooked rice
1 can sliced mushrooms
1 Tbs. chicken bouillon granules
1/2 tsp. ginger
pepper to taste
3/4 C. salted cashews, divided

Combine the first nine ingredients. Put into a greased shallow baking dish. Cover and bake at 350 for 45-50 minutes. Stir in 1/2 C. cashews. Sprinkle the remaining cashews on top.

SPRINGFIELD CASHEW CHICKEN

4 C. water
8 cubes chicken bouillon
3 Tbs. cornstarch
4 tsp. sugar
4 tsp/ soy sauce
1/2 lb. boneless, skinless chicken breast, cubed
1 C. flour
1 egg
1/4 C. milk
1 tsp. salt
1 tsp. pepper
1/2 C. cashew halves
1/4 C. green onion, chopped
4 C. cooked rice

To make Sauce: Bring water to a boil. Dissolve bouillon cubes in boiling water. Remove 1 cup and mix with cornstarch in a small bowl, then return to mixture in pan and let thicken. Stir in sugar and soy sauce. Cover, remove form heat and set aside.

To make chicken nuggets: In a shallow bowl flour cubed chicken well and let stand in flour for 15 minutes. In a small bowl, beat egg, milk, salt and pepper together. Remove chicken from flour, dip in egg mixture, roll in flour again and deep fry until golden brown.

Heat the sauce over low heat. Put rice on a platter, chicken nuggets on top and pour the sauce over the chicken and rice. Sprinkle cashew halves and green onions on top and serve.

CASHEW CHICKEN

2 C. chicken, cooked and diced
1 can cream of mushroom soup
1 soup can of milk
1/4 C. celery
1/4 C. green onion, chopped
1/2 C. cashews
1 tsp. salt
1/4 tsp. pepper
1 can chow Mein noodles

Combine all the ingredients except noodles in a 2 qt. casserole. Cover and place in microwave. Bake 5 minutes. Remove lid and stir. Sprinkle noodles on top and return to microwave and bake 5 minutes. Serve over rice.

CORNISH HENS WITH STUFFING

1 C. apple juice
4 Tbs. margarine
2 C. herb seasoned stuffing mix
6 Tbs. chopped pecans
2 Cornish hens, giblets removed
2 Tbs. apple juice
2 Tbs. instant minced onion
1/2 tsp. paprika
1/2 tsp. pepper

Combine apple juice and margarine. Microwave for 1 minute or until margarine is melted. Add stuffing mix and pecans. Mix well. Stuff the hens with stuffing mixture. Place hens in shallow roasting pan. Bake uncovered at 350 for 1-1/4 to 1-1/2 hours. Mix the rest of the ingredients together for sauce and brush with sauce halfway through cooking.

SPAGHETTI PEPPERONI PIE

1/2 lb. spaghetti, broken up and cooked
1/3 C. dry seasoned bread crumbs
2 C. chunky pasta sauce
1 C. shredded mozzarella cheese
4 oz. sliced pepperoni
4 eggs, beaten
3 Tbs. parmesan cheese

Spray a 10" pie plate with cooking spray. Coat with crumbs. Combine the pasta sauce, cheese and pepperoni. Add the eggs. Pour into the plate. Bake at 350 for 30 minutes. Sprinkle with parmesan cheese.

BROCCOLI HAM RING

2 tubes (8 oz. each) refrigerated crescent roll dough
1-1/2 C. shredded Swiss cheese
1/4 lb. cooked ham, diced (about 1/2 C.)
2-1/2 C. chopped fresh broccoli
1 small onion, chopped
1/4 C. minced parsley
2 Tbs. Dijon mustard
1 tsp. lemon juice

Unroll crescent roll dough and place triangles on a 12" pizza pan, forming a ring with pointed ends facing outer edge of pan and wide ends overlapping. Lightly press wide ends together. Combine remaining ingredients. Spoon over wide ends of rolls. Fold points over filling and tuck under wide ends. (Filling will be visible). Bake at 375 for 20-25 minutes.

BISCUIT WRAPPED HOT DOGS

1 pkg. hot dogs
1 can refrigerator biscuits
slices of processed cheese

Slit the hot dogs down the middle without cutting all the way through.
Place a slice of cheese in the slit. Wrap a biscuit around the hot dog and
cheese. The ends of the hot dogs will stick out some. Place on a cookie
sheet and bake at 400 10-13 minutes.

COUNTRY STYLE CASSEROLE

2 cans cream of chicken soup
3/4 C. mayonnaise
1/2 C. milk
3 Tbs. honey
2 Tbs. Dijon mustard
1 pkg. frozen shredded hash browns
4 C. cubed, cooked chicken or fully cooked ham
3 C. sliced carrots

Combine the first 5 ingredients. Stir in hash browns, chicken and
carrots. Put in a 9X13 greased pan. Cover and bake at 350 for 45-50
minutes. Uncover and bake 15-20 minutes longer.

RED BEANS & RICE

2 cloves garlic, minced
1/3 C. onion, diced
1/8 tsp. cayenne
1/8 tsp. cumin
1/8 tsp. chili powder
2 tsp. Tabasco sauce
2 C. brown rice, cooked
2 C. red beans, cooked
1 C. ham, cooked and diced (or smoked sausage)
1 lb. ground beef, cooked and drained
1 C. BBQ brisket

Sauté garlic and onion with seasonings. Add the rest of the ingredients. Cook over medium heat. Stir in approximately 1/4 C. water. Cook until heated through.

HAM AND CHEESE POTATO BAKE

1 pkg. frozen hash brown
2 C. cubed fully cooked ham
3/4 C. shredded cheese
1 small onion, chopped
2 C. sour cream
1 can Cheddar cheese soup
1 can cream of potato soup
1/4 tsp. pepper

Combine potatoes, ham, 1/2 C. cheese and the onion. In another bowl, combine sour cream, soups and pepper. Add to the potato mixture and mix well. Transfer to a greased 3 qt. baking dish. Sprinkle with remaining cheese. Bake uncovered at 350 for 1 hour or until potatoes are tender. Let stand 10 minutes before serving.

SLOW COOKER CASSEROLE

1 pkg. (16 oz.) frozen broccoli cuts, thawed and drained
3 C. cooked ham, cubed
1 can cream of mushroom soup
1/2 C. processed cheese, cubed
1 C. milk
1 C. uncooked instant rice
1 small onion chopped

In a slow cooker, combine broccoli and ham. Combine the soup, cheese, milk, rice and onion. Stir into broccoli mixture. Cover and cook on low for 4-5 hours or until rice is tender.

HAM & POTATO CASSEROLE

1/4 C. oil
1/2 C. chopped onion
1/4 C. flour
1 tsp. salt
2 C. milk
1 C. shredded processed cheese
1/2 lb. jam, cut into chunks or can use polish sausage
3 C. sliced potatoes

Cook onion in oil until tender. Stir in flour and salt. Add milk and cook over heat, stirring until thick and beginning to boil. Remove from heat, stir in cheese. Mix ham, potatoes and cheese sauce. Put in a greased casserole and bake at 325 for 1-1/4 hours. (I like to cook my potatoes before putting them in the casserole. Peel and chunk or slice your potatoes and put in a sauce pan of water and bring to boil and cook until almost tender. About 20 minutes.)

ZUCCHINI CASSEROLE

2 lbs. zucchini, peeled and chopped
1/2 lb. sausage
1/4 C. finely chopped onion
1/2 C. finely rolled cracker crumbs
2 eggs, well beaten
1/4 tsp. thyme
1/2 tsp. salt
1/2 C. shredded cheese

Put sausage and onion in skillet and cook until brown. Combine sausage, zucchini, crumbs, eggs, thyme, salt and half of the cheese. Put in a casserole dish and top with the rest of the cheese. Bake at 350 for 30-40 minutes.

HAM AND SWISS STROMBOLI

1 tube refrigerated French bread
6 oz. thinly sliced deli ham or beef
6 green onions, sliced
8 bacon strips, cooked and crumbled
1-1/2 C. shredded Swiss cheese

Unroll dough on a greased baking sheet. Place ham over dough to with in 1/2 inch of edges. Sprinkle with onions, bacon and cheese. Roll up jelly roll style, starting with long sides. Pinch seams to seal and tuck ends under. Place seam side down on baking sheet. With a sharp knife, cut several 1/4 inch deep slits on top of loaf. Bake at 350 for 25-30 minutes. Cool slightly before slicing. .

PORK CHOPS AND RICE

2 Tbs. oil
1 small onion, chopped
4 pork chops
dash of salt
dash of pepper
1-1/2 C. water
2 Tbs. brown sugar
1/2 tsp. salt
1/4 tsp. pepper
16 oz. can tomato sauce
1. C. uncooked rice

Sauté onion in oil. Sprinkle pork chops with salt and pepper. Add to the skillet and brown both sides. Remove chops. Add water, brown sugar, salt, pepper and tomato sauce. Stir and bring to a boil. Add rice and stir. Return chops to the skillet. Cover and simmer 30 minutes.

PORK CHOP SUPPER

1 Tbs. margarine
4 pork chops (1/2" thick)
3 medium red potatoes cut into small wedges
2 C. baby carrots
1 medium onion, quartered
1 can cream of mushroom soup
1/4 C. water

In a skillet, melt margarine. Brown pork chops for 3 minutes on each side. Add the potatoes, carrots and onion. Combine the soup and water. Pour over chops and vegetables. Cover and simmer for 20 minutes, or until vegetables are tender.

PORK CHOP BAKE

6 pork chops, 3/4" thick
1 tbs. oil
1 can cream of chicken soup
3 Tbs. ketchup
2 Tbs. Worcestershire sauce
1/2 tsp. salt
1/4 tsp. pepper
4 medium potatoes, cut into 1/2" wedges
1 medium onion, sliced into rings

Brown pork chops in oil. Transfer to a greased 9X13 pan. In a bowl, combine soup, ketchup, Worcestershire sauce, salt and pepper. Mix and add the potatoes and onion. Toss to coat. Pour over chops. Cover and bake at 350 for 1 hour or until potatoes are tender.

ROSEMARY PORK CHOPS

1-1/2 C. dry bread crumbs
1/2 C. flour
1-1/2 tsp. salt
1 tsp. dried rosemary, crushed
1 tsp. paprika
1/4 tsp. onion powder
3 Tbs. oil
6 bone in pork loin chops

In a bowl, combine the first 6 ingredients. Stir in oil until crumbly. Place 3/4 C. coating in a re-sealable plastic bag. Place a small amount of water in a shallow bowl. Dip pork chops in water. The place in the bag and shake until coated. In a skillet, cook chops in oil over medium heat for 4 minutes on each side or until juices run clear. The rest of the coating mix can be kept in the refrigerator to be used again.

PORK CHOP CASSEROLE

8 pork chops, 1/2" thick
1 tsp. seasoned salt
1 Tbs. oil
1 can cream of celery soup
2/3 C. milk
1/2 C. sour cream
1/2 tsp. salt
1/4 tsp. pepper
1 pkg. frozen shredded hash browns
1 can French fried onions
1-1/2 C. shredded Cheddar cheese

Sprinkle pork chops with seasoned salt. In skillet, brown chops on both sides in oil. In a bowl, combine soup, milk, sour cream, salt and pepper. Stir in the hash browns, 3/4 C. cheese and half the onions. Spread in a greased 9X13 pan. Arrange pork chops on top. Cover and bake at 350 for 40 minutes. Uncover. Sprinkle with remaining cheese and onions. Bake uncovered 5-10 minutes longer.

ZIPPY PORK CHOPS

4 tsp. chili powder
1-1/2 tsp. oregano
3/4 tsp. cumin
2 garlic cloves, minced
4-6 pork chops

Combine all the ingredients. Gently rub over both sides of pork chops. Cover and refrigerate for at least 2 hours. Grill covered, over medium, hot heat for 5-7 minutes on each side.

BBQ PORK CHOPS

4-6 pork chops
flour
oil
salt
pepper
garlic powder
BBQ sauce

Flour the pork chops and place in an electric skillet with the oil heated up. Season with salt, pepper and garlic powder. Brown both sides. Cover with BBQ sauce and turn on low or simmer for 3-4 hours. This is good using chicken also.

RUEBEN PIE

1 lb. hamburger
1/4 lb. ground pork
1/3 C. quick oats
1/4 C. Worcestershire sauce
1 egg
1/4 tsp. pepper
dash garlic powder
1-16 oz. can sauerkraut, drained
2 C. shredded Swiss cheese
1-1/2 tsp. caraway seeds
1-3 oz. can French fried onion rings

Mix the first 7 ingredients and pat into a 9" pie plate. Bake at 350 for 15 minutes. Remove from oven and drain. Add remaining ingredients and bake for 20 minutes more.

REUBEN SANDWICHES

2-1/4 C. sauerkraut, drained
1/4 C. onion
creamy Russian dressing
16 slices rye bread
3/4 lb. corned beef
3/4 lb. Swiss cheese
margarine

Combine sauerkraut and onion. Toss until well blended. Spread dressing on each slice of bread. Top 8 slices with corned beef, cheese and sauerkraut mixture. Top with remaining slices of bread. Spread both sides of sandwiches with margarine. Grill slowly until cheese melts and bread browns.

RAVIOLI AND BACON

2 pkg. (9 oz. each) cheese ravioli
1 C. milk
4 oz. cream cheese
1/3 C. grated Parmesan cheese
1/2 tsp. Italian seasoning
2 C. frozen broccoli florets
2 green onions, chopped
4 slices bacon, cooked, drained and crumbled

Cook ravioli as directed on package. Cook milk, cream cheese, Parmesan cheese and seasoning in a pan, 3-4 minutes or until cream cheese is melted. Stir frequently.

Drain ravioli. Add to pan. Add the broccoli. Mix together. Cover and reduce heat. Cook 5 minutes or until heated through. Add onion and bacon. Stir and cook 2 minutes or until heated through.

SAM'S EGGS & BACON SPAGHETTI

2 Tbs. olive oil
generous 1/2 C. bacon, cut into match sticks
1 clove garlic, crushed
1 lb. spaghetti
3 eggs, room temperature
3/4 C. freshly grated Parmesan cheese
salt & pepper

Bring a large pot of water to boil. In a frying pan, heat the oil and sauté the bacon and garlic until the bacon renders it's fat and starts to brown. Remove and discard the garlic. Keep the bacon and its fat hot until needed. Add salt and the spaghetti to the boiling water and cook until it is al dente. While paste is cooking, warm a large serving bowl and break the eggs into it. Beat in the cheese with a fork and season with salt and pepper. As soon as the paste is done, drain it quickly and mix it into the egg mixture. Pour on the hot bacon and it fat. Stir well. The heat from the pasta and bacon fat will cook the eggs. Serve immediately.

ITALIAN SAUSAGE SPAGHETTI

1 small onion, chopped
1 green pepper, chopped
3 garlic cloves, minced
2 tsp. oil
5 cooked Italian sausages, cut into ¼" strips
1 can diced tomatoes
1 can tomato paste
1/4 C. water
1 Tbs. Italian seasoning
1 tsp. sugar
1/2 tsp. salt
1/2 tsp. pepper
hot cooked spaghetti

Sauté onion, pepper and garlic in oil. Stir in the sausage, tomato, tomato paste, water and seasonings. Bring to boil. Reduce heat and simmer 15 minutes. Serve over spaghetti.

SLOW COOKER RIBS

2-1/2 lb. pork baby back ribs, cut into 8 pieces
2 tsp. Cajun seasoning
1 medium onion, sliced
1 C. ketchup
1/2 C. packed brown sugar
1/3 C. orange juice
1/3 C. vinegar
1/4 C. molasses
2 Tbs. Worcestershire sauce
1 Tbs. BBQ sauce
1 tsp. ground mustard
1 tsp. paprika
1/2 tsp. garlic powder
1/2 tsp. liquid smoke
dash of salt
5 tsp. cornstarch
1 Tbs. cold water

Rub ribs with Cajun seasoning. Layer ribs and onion in 5 qt. slow cooker. In a bowl combine all the rest of the ingredients except the cornstarch and water. Pour over ribs. Cook on low for 6 hours. Remove ribs and keep warm. Strain cooking juices and skim fat. Transfer the juices to a pan. Bring to boil. Mix the water with the cornstarch and add to the pan. Cook and stir for 2 minutes or until thickened. Serve with the ribs.

SUMMER SAUSAGE

2 lbs. hamburger
1 C. water
2 Tbs. tender quick salt
pinch of salt
1/4 tsp. garlic powder
1/8 tsp. onion powder
1-1/2 Tbs. liquid smoke

Combine ingredients and mix well. Shape into rolls 2 inches in diameter. About 6 inches long. This will make 2-3 rolls. Wrap rolls in foil, shiny side in. Refrigerate for 24 hours. On the following day, poke holes in the bottom of the foil and bake on broiler pan which has 1/2 c. water in the bottom. Bake at 325 for 90 minutes. Immediately after rolls are baked, open ends of the roll to let juices drain. When cool, re-wrap and refrigerate or serve. Rolls may be frozen or will keep in refrigerator for 7-10 days.

KENT'S SHRIMP SCAMPI

1/4 C. olive oil
1-lb. peeled and deveined large shrimp
4 large garlic cloves, minced
1/2 tsp. dried hot pepper flakes
1/2 C. dry white wine
1 tsp. salt
1/2 tsp. pepper
5 Tbs. unsalted butter
3/4 lb. angel hair pasta

Cook pasta in boiling water until tender, 8-10 minutes. Reserve 1 cup pasta water, then drain the pasta.

Heat oil in heavy skillet, until hot but not smoking. Sauté shrimp, turning over once until cooked through, 2-3 minutes. Transfer with slotted spoon to a large bowl. Add garlic to oil in skillet, along with red pepper flakes, wine, salt and pepper. Cook over high heat, stirring occasionally for 1 minute. Add butter, stirring until melted. Toss with pasta. Add the shrimp and toss again. Add some of the water if necessary to keep moist.

FISH CAKES

2 cans tuna
2 Tbs. sweet pickle relish
1 C. cheddar cheese, shredded
1/2 C. shredded carrots

---or---
2 cans crab
3 Tbs. tartar sauce
1/4 C. chopped celery

---or---
2 cans salmon
1 Tbs. lemon juice
1 C. mozzarella cheese, shredded
1/4 C. green onion, chopped

Pick one of the above combinations and add 1 pkg. (6 oz.) any flavor stuffing mix, 1/3 C. mayonnaise and 3/4 C. water. Make into patties and put into a skillet sprayed with cooking oil. Cook 3 minutes on each side.

TUNA CHEESE TWIST

2 cans chunk light tuna, drained
1/2 C. onion, chopped
1/2 C. green pepper, chopped
1/2 C. celery, chopped
1 can cream of mushroom soup
2 C. quick baking mix
1/2 C. cold water
1-1/2 C. shredded Cheddar cheese
1/4 C. milk
1 egg
1 Tbs. water

Lightly grease a cookie sheet. Mix tuna, onion, green pepper, celery and 1/2 cup of the soup. Mix baking mix and the 1/2 cup cold water until dough forms. Beat vigorously 20 strokes. Gently smooth dough into a ball on floured surface. Knead 5 times. Roll dough into a rectangle. Place on cookie sheet. Spoon tuna mixture lengthwise down center of rectangle. Sprinkle with 1 cup cheese. Make cuts 2-1/2 inches long at 1 inch intervals on long sides of rectangle. Fold strips over filling. Mix egg with 1 Tbs. water. Brush over dough. Bake at 350 until light brown, 15-20 minutes. Mix remaining soup, cheese and milk over medium heat, stirring until hot. Serve over slice of twist.

CORN SALMON CASSEROLE

2 C. cream style corn
1 can salmon
2 eggs
3 Tbs. margarine
1 C. bread crumbs
1 C. cream of mushroom soup

Combine all the ingredients and bake at 350 for 30 minutes.

NOVA'S SALMON CAKES

2 eggs
1/4 C. heavy cream
1/4 C. cornmeal
2 Tbs. sliced green onions
2 Tbs. flour
1/4 tsp. baking powder
dash of pepper
1/2 tsp. salt
1 can salmon, drained, skinned and boned
1-2 Tbs. margarine

Beat eggs, add cream, cornmeal, onions, flour, baking powder, pepper and salt. Flake salmon into a bowl. Blend salmon and egg mixture gently together. Melt margarine in a skillet. Drop salmon in skillet by 1/3 cup and fry for 5 minutes per side. Turn gently.

New found recipes

328

New found recipes

New found recipes

New found recipes

New found recipes

New found recipes

New found recipes

PIES

PIE CRUST

2 C. flour
pinch of salt
1/2 C. oil
5 Tbs. water

Mix flour and salt together. Mix oil and water together and add to flour with a fork. Roll out between wax paper. Makes 2 crusts. For a single bake pie crust, prick pie crust with fork. Bake at 425 for 10 minutes. For a fruit filled pie, prick bottom of pie crust, fill with fruit, place top crust on top, prick and bake at 425 for 10 minutes, then reduce heat to 350 for 40 minutes.

COLD WATER PIE CRUST

2 C. flour
1 tsp. salt
2 Tbs. sugar
1/2 C. cold unsalted butter, cut into small pieces
1/3 C. shortening
5-6 Tbs. ice cold water

Place the flour, salt and sugar in a food processor and pulse on and off to mix. Add the butter and shortening and pulse on and off until the mixture resembles coarse meal. Add the water through the tube, pulsing on and off until the dough gathers together in the side of the work bowl. Remove dough and form into a disk. Wrap it in plastic and chill for at least 1 hour.

Divide in half. Roll out on a floured surface or between 2 sheets of waxed paper into a 1/8 inch round large enough to fit your pie pan. Repeat with the other dough for a top crust.

For a single crust pie, prick the bottom of the crust and bake at 425 for 10 minutes.

For a 2 crust fruit pie, prick the bottom, add the fruit, place the second crust on top. Prick the top crust several times. Bake at 425 for 10 minutes, reduce heat to 350 and bake 40-45 minutes,

BANANA CREAM PIE

2 C. crushed vanilla wafers
1/3 C. margarine
1 pkg. cook type pudding
1-3/4 C. milk
1-1/2 C. miniature marshmallows
1 C. whipped topping
bananas

Mix the vanilla wafers and margarine. Press into a pie plate. Bake at 375 for 8 minutes. Prepare pudding with the milk as directed on package. Cover with plastic wrap and chill. Fold in the marshmallows and whipped topping. Slice bananas into crust. Pour pudding over the bananas. Chill.

CUSTARD PIE

1-9" pie crust, unbaked
4 eggs
2-1/2 C. milk
1/2 C. sugar
1 tsp. vanilla
1 tsp. salt
1 tsp. nutmeg

Put pie crust in pie plate. Bake at 400 for 10 minutes. Beat eggs. Add remaining ingredients. Mix well. Pour into crust. Cover edges with foil to prevent the crust from getting too dark. Bake at 400 for 35-40 minutes, or until knife inserted in center comes out clean.

CHERRY CUSTARD PIE

3 eggs
2 C. milk
1/2 C. sugar
2 Tbs. flour
1 tsp. vanilla
1 can sour cherries
1-9" unbaked pie crust

Scald milk. Beat eggs and add to scalded milk. Mix flour and sugar. Combine with milk and eggs. Beat well. Add vanilla and beat slightly. Thoroughly drain the cherries. Place the cherries in the bottom of the pie crust. Pour the egg and milk mixture over the cherries. Bake at 400 for 35-40 minutes.

WHITE CHRISTMAS PIE

1 Tbs. unflavored gelatin
1/4 C. water
1/2 C. sugar
4 Tbs. flour
1/2 tsp. salt
1-1/2 C. milk
1 tsp. vanilla
1/2 tsp. almond flavoring
1/2 tsp. coconut flavoring
1/2 C. whipping cream, whipped
3 egg whites
1/4 tsp. cream of tartar
1/2 C. sugar
1 C. coconut
1-10" pie shell, baked

Mix the gelatin and water. Set aside. Combine the sugar, flour, salt and milk. Boil 1 minute until thick. Add the gelatin mixture, the vanilla, almond flavoring and coconut flavoring. Fold in the whipped cream. Make a meringue with the egg whites, cream of tartar and sugar. Fold into the other mixture and then add the coconut. Pour into pie shell. Refrigerate over night.

CHILLY COCONUT PIE

1 pkg. cream cheese (3 oz)
2 tbs. sugar
1/2 C. milk
1/4 tsp. almond flavoring
1 C. coconut
1 carton(8 oz) whipped topping
1 graham cracker crust (9")

Beat cream cheese and sugar until smooth. Gradually beat in milk and almond flavoring. Fold in coconut and whipped topping. Spoon into crust. Cover and freeze for at least 4 hours. Remove from freezer 30 minutes before serving.

COCONUT CREAM PIE

1 pie crust, baked
1/2 C. sugar
4 Tbs. cornstarch
1/4 tsp. salt
2-1/2 C. scalded milk
4 egg yolks
1 tsp. vanilla
1-1/2 C. coconut
1 Tbs. margarine
1 C. heavy whipping cream, whipped
2 Tbs. powdered sugar

In a double boiler, mix sugar, cornstarch and salt. Stir in milk until smooth. Cook until mixture thickens. Beat egg yolks. Add 4 Tbs. of the hot milk mixture. Then stir egg mixture into milk mixture. Cook and stir until custard is smooth and thick. Remove from heat. Stir in vanilla, 1 C. of the coconut and margarine. Pour into pie shell. Refrigerate. Mix the whipped cream and powdered sugar. Stir in coconut and spread on pie. Chill.

IMPOSSIBLE PIE

2 C. milk
3/4 C. sugar
1/2 C. baking/biscuit mix
1/4 C. margarine
4 eggs
1-1/2 tsp. vanilla
1 C. coconut

Put all the ingredients in a blender or food processor. Blend on high for 1 minute. Pour into a greased pie plate. Bake at 350 for 50-55 minutes or until knife inserted comes out clean. Keep refrigerated.

For chocolate pie.......Add 2 tsp. cocoa
For fruit pie..............Spread pie filling over top.
For lemon pie...........Add 1/4 C. lemon juice
For custard pie..........Omit coconut and sprinkle about 1 tsp. of nutmeg on top of pie before baking.

PECAN PIE

1 C. brown sugar
3 eggs
1/2 C. butter, melted
1/2 tsp. salt
1 C. light corn syrup
1 tsp. vanilla
unbaked pie shell
1 C. pecans

Mix all the ingredients except the pecans together. Pour into pie crust. Sprinkle pecans on top. Bake at 350 for 45-50 minutes or until toothpick inserted comes out clean.

OATMEAL PIE

3 eggs
1 C. white syrup
3/4 stick margarine
1/4 tsp. salt
3/4 Tbs. lemon juice
1 C. sugar
1 C. oatmeal
3/4 tsp. vanilla
1/4 tsp. cinnamon
1-9" unbaked pie shell

Mix all the ingredients and pour into pie shell. Bake at 350 for 45 minutes.

DINNER HORN PIE

1 C. sugar
6 Tbs. margarine
2 eggs
1/2 tsp. vanilla
dash of salt
1/2 C. raisins
1/2 C. pecans
1/2 C. coconut
1 unbaked pie crust (9")

Cream sugar and margarine. Add eggs, vanilla and salt. Beat well. Add raisins, pecans and coconut. Mix well. Pour into pie crust and bake at 350 for 1 hour. This will freeze well.

CHOCOLATE CHIP PIE

2 eggs
1/2 C. flour
1/2 C. sugar
1/2 C. brown sugar
1 C. margarine
1 C. chocolate chips
1 C. chopped nuts
1-9" pie shell

Beat eggs until foamy. Add flour and sugars. Mix in margarine. Stir in chips and nuts. Pour into pie shell. Bake at 325 for 1 hour.

DECADENT CHOCOLATE PIE

3 sq. semi-sweet baking chocolate, melted
1/4 C. sweetened condensed milk
1 chocolate cookie pie crust
1/2 C. chopped pecans
2 C. milk
2 pkg. instant chocolate pudding
1-8 oz. container whipped topping

Mix the melted chocolate and condensed milk together. Pour into pie crust. Sprinkle with pecans. Pour milk into a large bowl. Add the pudding mixes. Beat 2 minutes. Spoon 1-1/2 cups over pecans. Add half the whipped topping to the remaining pudding. Stir until well blended. Spread over pudding layer in crust. Top with remaining whipped topping. Chill 3 hours.

GERMAN CHOCOLATE PIE

1 pkg. (4 oz.) German chocolate
1/4 C. margarine
1 can evaporated milk
1-1/2 C. sugar
3 Tbs. cornstarch
1/8 tsp. salt
2 eggs, lightly beaten
1 tsp. vanilla
1 unbaked deep dish pie shell
1/2 C. pecans, chopped
1-1/3 C. coconut

Melt chocolate and margarine. Gradually add milk. Set aside. Combine sugar, cornstarch and salt. Stir in eggs and vanilla. Gradually stir in the chocolate mixture. Pour into pie shell. Combine pecans and coconut. Sprinkle over filling. Bake at 375 for 45-50 minutes or until puffed and browned. Cool 4 hours. Chill. Mix all the ingredients in a pan and heat until hot. Pour into pie shell. Sprinkle chopped pecans on top if desired. Bake at 325 for 1 hour.

PEANUT BUTTER PIE

2 pkg. cook type vanilla pudding
4 C. milk
1/2 C. creamy peanut butter
3/4 C. powdered sugar
1 pie crust, baked
whipped topping

Cook pudding and milk until thick and bubbly. Remove from heat and cool slightly. Add the peanut butter and powdered sugar. Mix well. Pour into pie crust. Refrigerate. Serve with whipped topping.

PUMPKIN PIE

2 eggs, slightly beaten
1 can pumpkin
3/4 C. sugar
1/2 tsp. salt
1 tsp. cinnamon
1 tsp. ginger
1/4 tsp. cloves
1 can evaporated milk
1-9" unbaked pie shell
Whipped topping

Mix the first 8 ingredients together with a mixer. Pour into pie shell. Bake at 425 for 15 minutes. Reduce heat to 350 and bake 45 minutes. Cool. Serve with whipped topping.

LORI'S DOUBLE LAYER PUMPKIN PIE

4 oz. cream cheese, softened
1 Tbs. milk
1 Tbs. sugar
1-1/2 C. whipped topping
1 graham cracker crust
2 C. milk
2 pkg. vanilla instant pudding
1 can pumpkin (16 oz)
1 tsp. cinnamon
1/2 tsp. ginger
1/4 cloves

Mix cream cheese, 1 Tbs. milk and sugar with a wire whisk until smooth. Gently stir in whipped topping. Spread on bottom of crust. Pour 1 cup milk into another bowl. Add pudding mixes. Beat with wire whisk until well blended, 1-2 minutes. Stir in pumpkin and spices with whisk. Mix well. Spread over cream cheese layer. Refrigerate at least 3 hours.

CARAMEL CRUNCH PIE

1-9" pie crust, baked
1-1/4 C. heavy cream
1 bag (12 oz.) semi-sweet chocolate chips
3 C. corn flake cereal
1 C. chopped pecans
1 C. coconut
3/4 C. light corn syrup
3/4 C. brown sugar

Combine 1/2 C. cream and 1-1/2 C. chocolate chips. Microwave 1 minute. Stir until smooth. Spread over pie shell. Refrigerate. Stir together cereal, pecans and coconut. In a pan, stir together 3/4 C. cream, syrup and brown sugar. Bring to a boil. Cook about 20 minutes to soft ball stage, (240 degrees). Quickly pour caramel mixture over cereal mixture. Stir until coated. Spoon into pie crust, mounding slightly in center. Place remaining 1/2 C. chocolate over pie. Refrigerate overnight. Serve with whipped topping.

IMPOSSIBLE BROWNIE PIE

4 eggs
1 bar (4 oz.) sweet cooking chocolate, melted and cooled
1/2 C. baking/biscuit mix
1/2 C. brown sugar
1/2 C. sugar
1/4 C. margarine
3/4 C. nuts, chopped

Beat all the ingredients except nuts until smooth, 2 minutes in blender on high, stopping blender occasionally to stir. Or 2 minutes with hand beater. Pour into a greased 9" pie plate. Sprinkle with nuts. Bake at 350 for 30-35 minutes. Cool. Serve with ice cream.

PEACHES AND CREAM PIE

1/2 C. finely crushed vanilla wafer cookies
1/3 C. butter, melted
1 pkg. (4 oz.) orange gelatin
3/4 C. boiling water
2 C. ice cubes
1-1/2 C. whipped topping
1 C. chopped fresh peaches

Combine the crumbs and butter. Press into a pie plate. Stir gelatin into boiling water. Add the ice cubes. Stir until thick. Remove any un-melted ice cubes. Add the whipped topping. Blend. Stir in peaches. Chill 15 minutes. Spoon into crust and refrigerate for 3 hours.

TRACY'S PEACHES AND CREAM PIE

1 pkg. graham crackers, crushed
1/4 C. sugar
6 Tbs. margarine, melted
4 ounces cream cheese, softened
1/2 C. powdered sugar
1/2 C. whipped topping
1 pkg. (3 oz.) peach gelatin
1 pkg. (3 oz.) vanilla cook type pudding
1-1/4 C. water
2 C. fresh peaches or 1 can sliced cling peaches, drained

Combine the graham cracker crumbs, sugar and margarine. Press into a 9" pie plate. Bake at 375 for 6-9 minutes. Cool. Beat together the cream cheese and sugar. Stir in whipped topping. Spread over crust. Stir together the gelatin, pudding and water in a pan until smooth. Place over medium heat, stir constantly until mixture comes to a boil. Let cool 5 minutes. Arrange fruit in a pattern over top of pie. Spoon pudding mixture over pie. Refrigerate 4 hours or until set.

FRESH PEACH PIE

5-6 C. peeled, pitted & sliced peaches
5 Tbs. flour
3/4 C. sugar
1/4 tsp. salt
2 Tbs. lemon juice
2 Tbs. butter
2-9" pie crusts

Mix together the flour, sugar and salt. Pour over peaches along with the lemon juice and toss well. Pile the fruit into the bottom crust and dot with butter. Place the other crust on top of the peaches. Crimp or flute the edges. Bake at 425 for 25 minutes. Reduce heat to 350 and bake for 20-25 minutes. Put foil around edges to keep them from getting too brown.

APPLE PIE

8 or 9 tart cooking apples, peeled and sliced
3/4 C. sugar
6 Tbs. flour
1 tsp. cinnamon
1 tsp. nutmeg
2 Tbs. butter
2-9" pie crusts

In a small bowl, combine flour, sugar, cinnamon and nutmeg. Sprinkle about 1/4 C. of the mixture on the bottom of the pie crust and add the rest to the apples. Stir to coat the apples well. Fill pie crust heaping full of the apple mixture, dot with butter. Put top crust over filling. Flute the edges and cut slits in the top crust and sprinkle with a little sugar. Bake at 400 for about 50 minutes.

SUPER STRAWBERRY PIE

3/4 C. butter
1-1/2 C. flour
1 Tbs. powdered sugar
1/2 C. nuts, chopped
2 lbs. strawberries, divided
1/2 C. cold water
1 C. sugar
3 Tbs. cornstarch
1-1/4 C. whipped topping
1/4 lb. cream cheese
3/4 tsp. vanilla
1/2 C. powdered sugar

For crust, mix together the butter, flour, powdered sugar and nuts. Press into a 10" pie plate. Bake at 375 for 25 minutes. Cool.

Start topping by mashing enough strawberries to make 1 cup. Cut tops off the rest of the strawberries and set aside. Place mashed strawberries in a saucepan and add water. Mix sugar and cornstarch into crushed berry mixture and bring to a boil, stirring. Boil one minute or until clear and thickened. Set aside to cool.

For filling, beat cream cheese with vanilla and powdered sugar. Carefully fold in whipped topping. Spread onto crust. Stand the whole berries (or halved) on top of the cream cheese mixture, cut side down. When entire filling is covered with the berries, carefully spoon the crushed berry mixture all over. . Keep refrigerated.

STRAWBERRY PIE

1 C. water
1 qt. strawberries
4 Tbs. cornstarch
1 baked pie shell

Mix the water, strawberries and cornstarch. Bring to a boil. Boil until clear. Pour into pie shell. Refrigerate until set. About 3 hours.

MANDARIN PIE

1 pkg. (8 oz.) cream cheese
1 can sweetened condensed milk
1/2 C. orange juice concentrate
1/2 sour cream
1 carton (8 oz) whipped topping
1 chocolate crumb crust (9")
1 can mandarin oranges, drained
1 sq. unsweetened chocolate
1 tsp. shortening

Beat cream cheese until fluffy. Add the milk, orange juice and sour cream. Beat until smooth. Fold in the whipped topping. Spoon into crust. Set 8 mandarin orange segments aside. Fold the rest of the oranges in to filling. Arrange the set aside oranges on top of filling. In microwave, melt chocolate and shortening. Stir until smooth. Cool slightly and drizzle over pie. Chill for at least 4 hours.

RASPBERRY MOUSSE PIE

1-1/2 C. milk
1 pkg. instant vanilla pudding
1 chocolate crumb crust
1-1/2 tsp. unflavored gelatin
2 Tbs. cold water
1/2 C. seedless raspberry jam
1 tsp. lemon juice
1 carton (8 oz) whipped topping

Beat milk and pudding mix on low for 2 minutes. Pour into crust. Sprinkle gelatin over water. Let stand for 1 minute. Microwave for 20-30 seconds. Stir until dissolved. Gradually whisk in jam and lemon juice. Chill for 10 minutes, Fold in the whipped topping. Spread over pudding. Refrigerate for 2 hours or until set.

RHUBARB CHERRY PIE

3 C. sliced rhubarb
1 can pitted tart red cherries, drained
1-1/4 C. sugar
1/4 C. quick cooking tapioca
double pie crust

Combine the first 5 ingredients. Let stand 15 minutes. Put filling between pie shells. Prick top crust. Bake at 400 for 40-45 minutes.

CREAM CHEESE RHUBARB PIE

1/4 C. cornstarch
1 C. sugar
pinch of salt
1/2 C. water
3 C. chopped rhubarb
1 unbaked pie shell
1-8 oz. pkg. cream cheese
2 eggs
1/2 C. sugar
whipped cream
sliced almonds

Combine cornstarch, sugar and salt. Add water. Stir until thoroughly combined. Add the rhubarb. Cook, stirring often, until mixture boils and thickens. Pour into pie shell. Bake at 425 for 10 minutes. Beat cream cheese, eggs and sugar until smooth. Pour over pie. Return to oven. Reduce heat to 325. Bake for 35 minutes or until set. Cool. Chill several hours or over night. Serve with whipped cream and sliced almonds.

CHERRY RHUBARB COBBLER

1 can cherry pie filling
3 C. chopped rhubarb
1 C. sugar
4 Tbs. margarine
1/2 C. shortening
1 C. sugar
1 egg
1 C. flour
1 tsp. baking powder
1/2 C. milk

Spread fruit in a 9X13 pan. Sprinkle with sugar and dot with margarine. Cream shortening and sugar. Add egg and beat well. Combine flour and baking powder. Add alternately with milk to creamed mixture. Pour over fruit. Bake at 350 for 50-60 minutes.

GRANDMA MINNIE'S RHUBARB PIE

2 eggs
1-1/4 C. sugar
2/3 C. cream
1 Tbs. flour, heaping
1/2 C. water
2 C. rhubarb, cut into small pieces
1 unbaked pie shell

Beat eggs, sugar, cream and flour together. Add 1/2 C. water. Beat again. Place rhubarb in pie shell and pour filling over rhubarb. Bake at 325 for 1 hour or until set.

RHUBARB PIE

4 C. sliced rhubarb
4 C. boiling water
1-1/2 C. sugar
3 Tbs. flour
1 tsp. quick cooking tapioca
1 egg
2 tsp. water
pastry for double crust pie
1 Tbs. margarine

Place rhubarb in a colander and pour water over it. Set aside. Combine sugar, flour and tapioca. Mix well. Add rhubarb. Toss to coat. Let stand for 15 minutes. Beat eggs and water. Add to rhubarb mixture and mix well. Put mixture in pie shell. Dot with margarine. Cover with remaining crust. Cut slits in top. Bake at 400 for 15 minutes. Reduce heat to 350 and bake 40-45 minutes.

RHUBARB SURPRISE PIE

1 C. flour
1 tsp. baking powder
1/2 tsp. salt
2 Tbs. margarine
1 egg, beaten
2 Tbs. milk
3 C. rhubarb
1 pkg. strawberry gelatin
1/2 C. flour
1 C. sugar
1/2 tsp. cinnamon
1/2 C. margarine

Sift together flour baking powder and salt. Cut in margarine. Add the egg and milk. Mix and press into a 9" pie plate. Place rhubarb in pie shell. Sprinkle gelatin on top of rhubarb. Make a crumble mixture with the flour, sugar and cinnamon, cutting in the margarine. Crumble this over the top and bake at 350 fort 50 minutes.

GOOSEBERRY PIE

1-1lb. can gooseberries, drained
1 baked pie shell
2 eggs, separated
1 C. milk
1/2 C. sugar
2 Tbs. cornstarch
1/4 tsp. butter flavoring

Put gooseberries in bottom of crust. Make a custard using egg yolks, milk, sugar and cornstarch. Cook until thick. Pour custard over berries. Make a meringue using the egg whites and 4 Tbs. sugar. Brown in a 350 oven for 12-15 minutes.

KEY LIME PIE

1 Tbs. unflavored gelatin
1 C. sugar
1/4 tsp. salt
4 egg yolks
1/2 C. lime juice
1/4 C. water
A few drops of green food coloring
4 egg whites
1 C. whipped topping
1 baked 9" pie shell

Thoroughly mix gelatin, 1/2 C. sugar and salt in a pan. Beat together egg yolks, lime juice and water. Stir into gelatin mixture. Cook over medium heat, stirring constantly, just until mixture comes to a boil. Remove from heat and stir in the food coloring to give a pale green color. Chill, stirring occasionally, until the mixture mounds when dropped from a spoon. Beat egg whites until soft peaks form. Gradually add the remaining sugar and beat to stiff peaks. Fold gelatin mixture into egg whites. Fold in whipped topping. Pile into cooled shell and chill until firm.

APPLE TURNOVERS

3 C. flour
3 Tbs. sugar
1 tsp. salt
1/2 tsp. cinnamon
1-1/4 C. shortening
5-6 Tbs. water
1 can apple pie filling (or any kind you prefer)

Combine flour, sugar, salt and cinnamon. Cut in shortening. Sprinkle dough with water, adding 1 Tbs. at a time, stirring with a fork, until just enough has been added so the dough can be patted into a ball. Divide pastry in half. On a lightly floured surface, roll one of the halves into a 10X15 rectangle. Cut into 6 squares, 5" each. Repeat with the other half of the dough. Place 2 Tbs. of the fruit in the center of each square. Moisten edges with water. Fold over 1/2 the square to form a triangle. Seal edges by going around the edges with a fork. Prick top for steam. Bake at 425 for 12-15 minutes. Drizzle a glaze made with powdered sugar, water and vanilla while hot.

New found recipes

New found recipes

New found recipes

New found recipes

New found recipes

New found recipes

New found recipes

New found recipes

SALADS

ORIENTAL CHICKEN SALAD

DRESSING:

3/4 C. honey
1/4 C. + 2 Tbs. rice wine vinegar
1 C. mayonnaise
4 tsp. Dijon mustard
1/2 tsp. sesame oil

CHICKEN STRIPS:

2 eggs
1 C. milk
1 C. cornflakes
1 C. flour
1 tsp. salt
1/4 tsp. pepper
1 tsp. garlic powder
4 boneless, skinless, chicken breasts

SALAD:

6 C. chopped romaine lettuce
2 C. shredded red cabbage
4 C. chopped Napa cabbage
2 carrots. shredded
3 green onions, chopped
sliced almonds
chow Mein noodles

For the dressing: blend together all the ingredients with a mixer. Put in refrigerator to chill while preparing the salad and chicken. For the salad: Toss the lettuce, cabbages, onions and carrots. Refrigerate while preparing chicken. For chicken: In a small bowl, beat eggs, add the milk and mix well. Crush the cornflakes. Put them in a bowl and add the flour, salt, pepper and garlic powder. Mix together. Cut the chicken in long strips. Dip each strip first in the egg mixture then the flour mixture. Coat each piece completely. Fry 5 minutes or until golden brown. To serve: Put the salad in individual bowls. Top with the almonds and chow mien noodles. Cut the chicken into bite size pieces and place on top of that. Serve with the dressing.

LORI'S NAPA SALAD

1 head Napa cabbage (sometimes called Chinese lettuce)
2 bunches green onions, chopped
2 pkg. ramen noodles
4 Tbs. margarine
1 small container sesame seeds
1 pkg. slivered almonds
1/4 C. vinegar
3/4 C. oil
1/2 C. sugar
2 Tbs. soy sauce

Chop and toss cabbage and onions. Brown noodles in margarine. Watch carefully. Add sesame seeds and almonds. Let cool. Combine the rest of the ingredients in a saucepan and bring to a boil. Boil 1 minute. Cool. Toss with the noodle mixture. Pour over cabbage and onions. Toss well. Serve immediately.

ANITA'S FESTIVE SALAD

1/2 C. sugar
1/3 C. red wine vinegar
2 Tbs. lemon juice
2 Tbs. finely chopped onion
1/2 tsp. salt
2/3 C. canola oil
3 Tsp. poppy seeds
10 C. Romaine lettuce (or 2 bags)
1 C. shredded Swiss cheese
1 medium apple, cored and cubed
1 medium pear, cored and cubed
1/4 C. dried cranberries
1/2 to 1 C. chopped cashews

Put first 7 ingredients into a blender and blend well.

Toss the rest of the ingredients together and pour dressing over and toss again.

VEGETABLE SALAD

1 can French green beans
1 can corn
1 can peas
1 green pepper, chopped
1/2 C. onion, chopped
1 C. carrot, shredded
2/3 oil
1 tsp. salt
2/3 C. vinegar
2/3 C. sugar
1 Tbs. water
dash of pepper

Drain the beans, corn and peas. Mix together and add the pepper, onion and carrot. Mix the rest of the ingredients in a pan and bring to a boil. Boil 1 minute. Cool. Pour over vegetables and refrigerate overnight.

CRUNCHY VEGETABLE SALAD

2 C. cauliflower
2 C. broccoli florets
2 carrots, thinly sliced
1 small zucchini, sliced
1 small onion, sliced
1 to 1-1/2 C. Italian salad dressing

Combine vegetables. Pour dressing over. Toss well. Refrigerate.

BROCCOLI CASHEW SALAD

6 C. broccoli florets
2 med. tomatoes, cut into chunks
3 Tbs. red onion, chopped
1 C. mayonnaise
1 Tbs. soy sauce
2 Tbs. lemon juice
1-1/2 tsp. seasoned salt
1/8 tsp. pepper
1/2 C. cashews
lettuce

Cook broccoli in a small amount of water until crisp tender. 5-8 minutes. Rinse in cold water and drain. Place in a bowl. Add tomatoes and onion. Combine mayonnaise, soy sauce, lemon juice, seasoned salt and pepper. Mix well. Pour over broccoli mixture and toss to coat. Stir in cashew. Serve on a bed of lettuce.

BROCCOLI & CAULIFLOWER SALAD

2 C. broccoli florets
2 C. cauliflower
4 large mushrooms, sliced
1 med. green or red pepper, diced
1 celery rib, sliced
1/4 onion, chopped
1/3 C. oil
1/4 C. sugar
1/4 C. vinegar
1/4 tsp. salt
1-1/2 tsp. poppy seed

Combine all the vegetables. Combine remaining ingredients in a jar and shake well. Pour over vegetables and toss. Cover and chill 6-8 hours.

SUNFLOWER SALAD

2 bunches broccoli, chopped
1 small red onion, chopped
1 C. sunflower seeds
12 slices, bacon, cooked and crumbled
1 C. mayonnaise or salad dressing
1/2 C. sugar
2 Tbs. vinegar

Mix the broccoli, onion, sunflower seeds and bacon together. Mix the rest of the ingredients together and blend well. Pour over vegetables and toss. Refrigerate.

GARDEN SALAD

1 head cauliflower
1 bunch broccoli
1 red onion
1 C. mayonnaise
1/2 C. sugar
1/3 C. vinegar
1/2 tsp. prepared mustard
salt
pepper

Chop all the vegetables fine. (Works great in a food processor). Place in a bowl. Mix the rest of the ingredients together and pour over vegetables. Stir and refrigerate.

CREAMY CORN SALAD

1 can whole kernel corn, drained
1 med. tomato, diced
2 Tbs. green onion, chopped
1/2 C. mayonnaise
1/4 C. sugar
2 Tbs. vinegar

Combine all the vegetables and mix well. Put the mayonnaise, sugar and vinegar in a container and shake well. Pour over vegetables and stir well. Cover and refrigerate until serving.

POTATO SALAD

12-14 potatoes. peeled, chopped and cooked
or can use leftover mashed potatoes
1/4 C. onion, chopped
1/2 C. pickles, chopped (sweet or dill)
5 eggs, cooked and chopped
3/4 C. salad dressing
1/3 C. mustard
1/4 C. vinegar
1/3 C. sugar
1/2 tsp. salt
1/8 tsp. pepper

Toss the potatoes, onions, pickles and eggs. Add the rest of the ingredients. Mix well. Refrigerate.

TANGY POTATO SALAD

6 potatoes, peeled, boiled & diced
1/4 C. chopped onion
1 tsp. salt
1/8 tsp. pepper
1/4 C. vinegar
3 Tbs. oil
1/2 tsp garlic salt

Mix and marinated over night.

RUTH'S POTATO SALAD

Sliced cooked potatoes
Cottage cheese
Chopped green onions
Pinch of MSG flavor enhancer per layer
Mayonnaise

Start with a potato layer, then cottage cheese, onion, flavor enhancer and finish with mayo. Repeat layers ending with mayo.

3 BEAN SALAD

1 can cut green beans, drained
1 can wax beans, drained
1 can kidney beans, drained and rinsed
1 small onion, chopped
3/4 C. sugar
2/3 C. vinegar
1/2 C. salad oil
1 tsp. salt
1/2 tsp. pepper

Combine beans and onion. Combine the rest of the ingredients and mix well. Toss with the beans. Refrigerate overnight.

PEA SALAD

2 cans peas, drained
1/4 C. green onions, chopped
1/2 C. cheddar cheese, cubed
1/2 C. mayonnaise
1/4 C. sugar
2 Tbs. vinegar

Mix together the peas, onions and cheese. Mix together the mayonnaise, sugar and vinegar. Pour the dressing over the vegetables and refrigerate.

MOM'S BEAN SALAD

2 cans kidney beans, drained and rinsed
1/4 C. chopped sweet or dill pickles (or use relish)
1/4 C. onion, chopped
2 eggs, cooked, peeled and chopped
1/2 C. salad dressing or mayonnaise
1/4 C. vinegar
1/4 C. sugar
1/4 tsp. salt
dash pepper

Mix the beans, pickles, onion and eggs together. Mix the salad dressing, vinegar, sugar, salt and pepper together in a jar or container and shake until well mixed. Pour over bean mixture. Chill at least 1 hour.

COPPER PENNY SALAD

1 can sliced carrots
1 green pepper, chopped
1 onion, chopped
1 can tomato soup
3/4 C. vinegar
1 C. sugar
1/2 C. oil
1 Tbs. Worcestershire sauce

Stir together soup, vinegar, sugar, oil and Worcestershire sauce. Drain carrots and mix with the peppers and onions. Pour sauce over and let set overnight.

TOMATO SALAD

8 qts. tomatoes, peeled and chopped
2 C. onion, sliced
2 C. sugar
2 tsp. salt
1/2 tsp. mustard seed
2 C. vinegar

Mix all but the tomatoes and onion together. Then add the tomatoes and onions. This will keep quite a long time in the refrigerator. Just keep adding more tomatoes and onions. Can also add other vegetables that you like....peppers....cucumbers...etc.

GERMAN SLAW

1 med. head of cabbage, shredded
1 C. sugar
1 small onion, chopped fine
1 Tbs. celery seed
3/4 C. oil
1 C. vinegar
1 tsp. dry mustard
1 tsp. salt

Mix oil, sugar, salt, celery seed, vinegar and mustard together. Bring to a boil. Boil 1 minute. Mix cabbage and onion together. Pour dressing over and let set overnight in refrigerator.

48 HOUR SLAW

1 med. head of cabbage, shredded
1 onion, sliced thin
3/4 C. sugar
1 C. oil
1 C. vinegar
1 tsp. celery seed
1 tsp. dry mustard
1 tsp. sugar
3/4 tsp. salt
dash of pepper

Alternate layers of cabbage and onion. Sprinkle with 3/4 C. sugar over top. Cover and refrigerate 1 hour. Bring the rest of the ingredients together and bring to a boil. Cool. Pour over cabbage and onions. Stir. Refrigerate overnight.

CREAMY COLESLAW

1/2 head of cabbage, shredded
1 C. salad dressing or mayonnaise
1/3 C. vinegar
1/3 C. sugar
1 C. milk
1/2 tsp. salt
dash of pepper

Place all the ingredients except the cabbage in a jar with a lid and shake until well blended. Pour over cabbage. Stir well. Refrigerate.

DIJON PASTA SALAD

1 lb. tri-colored rotini pasta
2/3 C. corn oil
2 Tbs. cider vinegar
2 tsp. Dijon style mustard
2/3 C. mayonnaise
1/2 C. sugar
6 bacon slices, chopped and cooked crisp
2 hard cooked eggs, chopped
2 green onions, chopped
1/2-1 tsp. salt
paprika

Cook pasta in boiling water just until done, about 11-13 minutes. Drain. Run cold water over pasta until completely cool. Whisk together the oil, vinegar, mustard, sugar and mayonnaise. Add the pasta and the rest of the ingredients. Mix carefully. Chill.

PASTA VEGETABLE SALAD

1-1/2 C. uncooked tricolor spiral pasta
1/2 C. fresh broccoli florets
1/2 C. cauliflowerets
1/3 C. sliced carrots
1/4 C. chopped tomato
1/3 C. ranch salad dressing

Cook pasta according to directions on package. Drain and rinse in cold water. Place in a large bowl. Add the vegetables. Drizzle with dressing. Toss. Cover and refrigerate for 1-2 hours.

PASTA SALAD

16 oz. zesty Italian dressing
2 C. fresh broccoli florets
2 C. chopped cauliflower
1-1/2 C cherry tomatoes, halved
1/2 C. green onions
1 lb. spiral macaroni, cooked and drained

Mix all together and toss well. Refrigerate.

EGG SALAD

6 hard cooked eggs, chopped
1/4 C. mayonnaise
1/4 C. mustard
1/4 C. sugar
2 Tbs. vinegar
1/4 tsp. salt
1/8 tsp. pepper

Mix all together and serve on slices of bread or toast.

TUNA SALAD

1 can tuna, packed in water, drained well
1 Tbs. chopped onion
1 Tbs. pickle relish
1-2 Tbs. mayonnaise
1 tsp. sugar
salt

Mix all together and spread on bread or toast.

SAUERKRAUT SALAD

1 can sauerkraut, drained
1 C. carrots, grated
1 C. green peppers, chopped
1 C. onions, chopped
3/4 C. sugar
1/2 C. oil

Mix all the vegetables together. In a jar, combine the sugar and oil. Shake well to mix. Pour over vegetables. Refrigerate overnight.

MEXICAN SALAD

1 lb. ground beef
1/2 C. onion, chopped
1 can kidney beans, rinsed
1/2 C. Catalina French dressing
1/2 C. water
1 tsp. chili pepper
4 C. shredded cheese
1/2 C. green onions
1-1/2 C. shredded cheddar cheese
tomatoes, chopped

Cook beef and onions. Stir in beans, water and chili powder. Simmer 15 minutes. Combine lettuce and green onions. Add the beef and cheese. Add the dressing. Toss lightly. Top with tomatoes.

FRUIT SALAD

2 C. cubed cantaloupe
2 large red apples, chopped
1 C. grapes
1 firm bananas, sliced
1/2 C. yogurt
1 Tbs. orange juice concentrate

Combine fruit. Combine yogurt and orange juice, drizzle over the fruit.

FLUFFY GELATIN SALAD

1-10 oz. carton cottage cheese
1 container whipped topping
1-3 oz. pkg. orange gelatin
1-11 oz. can mandarin oranges, drained

Mix all the ingredients together. May serve immediately or refrigerate overnight. Can use any flavor gelatin and fruit.

FROG EYE SALAD

1 C. soup macaroni (BB size)
2 small cans mandarin oranges
1-1/2 C. miniature marshmallows
3 eggs
1 C. sugar
3 Tbs. flour
1-9 oz. container whipped topping

Cook macaroni in boiling water 30 minutes. Drain. Drain fruit, saving juice. Add eggs, sugar and flour to juice. Mix well and cook over medium heat until thick. Cool. Add macaroni and let set in refrigerator overnight. Add the fruit, whipped topping and marshmallows.

ITALIAN DRESSING

1/2 C. sugar
1/2 C. vinegar
1 pkg. dry Italian seasoning packet
1/2 C. oil

Put in a jar with a lid, the sugar, vinegar and seasoning mix. Shake. Add the oil and shake well. Serve with tossed salad.

SPECIAL ITALIAN SALAD DRESSING

1/2 C. mayonnaise
1/3 C. white vinegar
1 tsp. vegetable oil
2 Tbs. corn syrup
2 Tbs. Parmesan cheese
2 Tbs. Romano cheese
1/4 tsp. garlic salt (or one clove garlic, minced)
1/2 tsp. Italian seasoning
1/2 tsp. parsley flakes
1 Tbs. lemon juice
1 tsp. sugar

Mix all the ingredients in a blender until well mixed. Serve over salad.

BALSAMIC SALAD DRESSING

3/4 C. tomato juice
1/4 C. balsamic or red wine vinegar
1 envelope Italian dressing mix
2 tsp. sugar

In a jar with a lid, combine all the ingredients and shake well. Store in refrigerator.

New found recipes

New found recipes

New found recipes

New found recipes

New found recipes

New found recipes

New found recipes

New found recipes

SOUPS, SAUCES & GRAVIES

CALICO BEANS

1 lb. hamburger
3/4 lb. bacon cut into pieces
1 C. onion, chopped
2 can pork 'n' beans
1 can kidney beans
2 cans pinto beans
2 cans green beans
1 C. ketchup
1/4 C. brown sugar
3 Tbs. vinegar
1 Tbs. liquid smoke

Brown the hamburger and drain. Brown the bacon and onion. Drain. Put all the ingredients in a crock pot and cook on low for 4-6 hours.

CHICKEN SOUP

2 fresh mushrooms, sliced
2 Tbs. butter
2 green onions, chopped
1 carrot, diced
1 celery rib, diced
2 boneless, skinless chicken breast halves
2 Tbs. flour
4 C. chicken stock, divided
1 C. sour cream
1 C. fine cut noodles
salt and pepper

Melt the butter and add the mushrooms, onion, carrot, celery and chicken. Cover and cook over low heat for 5 minutes. Stir and turn the chicken. Cover and cook for another 5 minutes or until the chicken is done. Remove the chicken and set aside to cool. Sprinkle flour into the pan and stir to cook over low heat for 2 minutes. Slowly add 2 cups of broth. Stir and cook until bubbly and thick. Add the sour cream very slowly and allow to cook gently while you slice the chicken into thin, bite size pieces. In another pan, bring the rest of the broth to a boil and add the noodles. Cook 4 minutes or until done. Slowly add the noodle mixture to the hot vegetables and sour cream mixture. Add the chicken and bring back to a boil. Serve immediately.

PAPRIKA CHICKEN AND PIEROGIE STEW

1/2 lb. bacon, chopped into half inch pieces
3 Tbs. olive oil
3-1/2 lbs. boneless, skinless chicken breast and thighs, cut into chunks
salt and pepper to taste
1 onion, chopped
4 carrots, peeled and chopped
4 cloves garlic, minced
2 Tbs. flour
2 tsp. paprika
1 Tbs. cumin
1/2 tsp. marjoram
2 bay leaves
1/2 C. white wine
2-1/2 C. chicken stock
1-28 oz can crushed tomatoes
4 Tbs. butter
24 potato pierogies (or you can serve over buttered noodles)
1/2 C. sour cream

Cook the pierogies as directed on package.
In a large pan place 1 Tbs. oil and add the bacon and cook until brown and crisp. Season chicken with salt and pepper, add to the pot with the bacon and brown all sides. About 5 minutes. Add onions, carrots, garlic, paprika, cumin, marjoram and bay leaves and cook for 5 minutes, or until vegetables are tender. Make a well in the center of the pan and add 2 Tbs. oil and add the flour and mix to form a paste. Add the wine, scrapping up all the brown bits on the bottom of the pan. Add the chicken stock and tomatoes and cook about 20 minutes until the stew has thickened.

Remove the pierogies from the water, drain and coat with olive oil so they won't stick together. Heat a skillet and add the butter, place the pierogies in the butter and cook until slightly browned on both sides, about 1-2 minutes per side.

Place stew in a large soup bowl, place 3-4 pierogies on top and a dollop of sour cream in the center.

CHEESE SOUP

2 C. chicken broth
2 C. potatoes, cooked and chopped
2 C. carrots, cooked and chopped
2 C. chicken, cooked and chopped
1-lb processed cheese
salt and pepper

Put all the ingredients in a pan and bring to a boil. Simmer until cheese is melted.

CREAMY CHICKEN STEW

3/4 lb. small red potatoes (about 8) quartered
2 Tbs. water
1 Tbs. oil
1 lb. boneless skinless chicken breasts, cut into bite-size chunks
1 can cream of mushroom soup
1/4 C. zesty Italian dressing
1 can peas
1 can carrots
1/2 C. sour cream

Place potatoes and water in microwave. Cover and cook on HIGH 7 minutes or until fork tender. Heat oil in saucepan and add chicken. Cook 7 minutes or until brown, stirring occasionally. Add potatoes, soup, dressing and vegetables to pan. Bring to boil. Cover, reduce heat and simmer 3 minutes or until chicken is cooked through and vegetables are heated through. Stir in sour cream. Cook 1 minute or until heated through.

POTATO SOUP

4 C. cooked and diced potatoes
1 stick margarine
1/2 C. onions, chopped
6 C. milk
salt
pepper
garlic powder

Sauté the onions in the margarine until tender. Add the rest of the ingredients and heat until hot.

SAUSAGE POTATO SOUP

1/2 lb. fully cooked kielbasa, diced
6 med. potatoes, peeled and cubed
2 C. frozen corn
1-1/2 C. chicken broth
1/4 C. carrots, sliced
1/2 tsp. garlic powder
1/2 tsp. onion powder
1/2 tsp. salt
1/4 tsp. pepper
1-1/2 C. milk
2/3 C. shredded cheddar cheese

In a large saucepan, brown sausage. Drain. Set aside. In the same pan, combine potatoes, corn, broth, carrots and seasonings. Bring to a boil. Reduce heat and simmer 15 minutes or until vegetables are tender. Add milk, cheese and sausage. Cook until cheese is melted and soup is heated through.

TRACY'S SWEDISH MEATBALL SOUP

1 egg
2 C. half & half
1 C. bread crumbs
1 small onion, finely chopped
1-3/4 tsp. salt, divided
1-1/2 lbs. ground beef
1 Tbs. margarine
3 Tbs. flour
3/4 tsp. beef bouillon granules
1/2 tsp. pepper
1/8 to 1/4 tsp. garlic salt
3 C. water
1 lb. red potatoes, cubed
1 can peas

In a bowl, beat egg. Add 1/3 C. cream, bread crumbs, onion and 1 tsp. salt. Add beef. Mix well. Shape into 1/2 inch balls. Brown meatballs in margarine, half at a time. Remove from pan. Set aside. Drain fat. To pan, add flour, bouillon, pepper, garlic salt and remaining salt. Stir until smooth. Gradually stir in water. Bring to a boil, stirring often. Add potatoes and meatballs. Reduce heat, cover and simmer for 25 minutes or until potatoes are tender. Stir in peas and remaining cream. Heat through.

CORN CHOWDER

2 C. potatoes, chopped
1/2 C. onions, chopped
1/2 lb. bacon, cut into small pieces
1 can cream of mushroom soup
1 can corn
2 C. milk
salt
pepper

Fry together the potatoes, onion and bacon. Add the rest of the ingredients and cook until hot.

OYSTER STEW

1 can oysters
2 tbs. margarine
2 C. milk
1 tsp. salt
1/2 tsp. pepper

Drain the oysters, reserving liquid. Sauté the oysters in the margarine until edges curl. Add the milk, salt, pepper and the reserved liquid. Heat through and serve.

CHILI

1 lb. suet
4 lbs. hamburger
1 C. onion, chopped
1 tsp. cumin
1 tsp. garlic powder
1 tsp. salt
2 pkg. chili seasoning
2 cans diced tomatoes
4 cans pinto beans

Put suet in a pan and let simmer until all the fat is out. (Melted) About 3 hours. Add the meat and onion. Brown. Add the seasonings, tomatoes and beans. Bring to a boil. Simmer. Add water if necessary to keep from getting too dry.

CINDY'S CROCK POT CHILI

2 lbs. hamburger
1-1/2 C. onion, chopped
1 green pepper, chopped
2 garlic cloves, minced
1-28 oz. can whole tomatoes
2-16 oz. cans kidney beans
2 tsp. salt
2 Tbs. chili powder
1 tsp. cumin
1 Tbs. crushed red pepper

Brown the hamburger. Drain. Put in a crock pot and add the rest of the ingredients. Cook on low for 7-10 hours. This freezes well.

BAKED BEAN CHILI

2 lbs. hamburger
3 cans (28 oz. each) baked beans
1 can tomato juice
1 can tomato vegetable juice
1 envelope chili seasoning

Brown hamburger. Drain. Stir in remaining ingredients. Bring to a boil. Reduce heat and simmer, uncovered for 10 minutes.

BEEF STEW

2 lbs. stew meat, cut into 1" squares
2 Tbs. oil
1 C. onion, chopped
3 potatoes, peeled and chopped
6 carrots, chopped
1 can chopped tomatoes
1 can beef broth
1 tsp. garlic powder
1 tsp. salt
1/4 tsp. pepper

In a large pan, brown the meat in oil. Drain and add the remaining ingredients. Bring to a boil. Turn heat down and simmer 2 hours.

VEGETABLE SOUP

Put 2 lbs. stew meat or soup bone in a 6-quart pan. Cover with water and cook 2-3 hours until meat falls from the bone. Remove bone, leave water in broth. Add salt & pepper to taste. (Or use left over roast meat, cut into small pieces.)

Add: 2 C. diced potatoes
1 C. onion, chopped
2 C. peas
1 qt. canned tomatoes
2 C. green beans
2 C. corn

Cook one hour, serve hot.

HAMBURGER SOUP

1 lb. hamburger
1/2 C. onion, chopped
1 pkg. frozen (or a large can) mixed vegetables
1 can tomato soup
1/2 C. rice or pasta
1/2 tsp. sugar
1 tsp. salt
1/2 tsp. pepper
dash of Worcestershire sauce
3 C. water

Brown the hamburger and onions. Add the rest of the ingredients and bring to a boil Simmer until vegetables are tender.

TRACY'S CHICKEN TORTILLA SOUP

3-4 C. cooked chicken, boned
2 cans cream of chicken soup
2 cans cream of mushroom soup
2 cans spicy tomatoes (Mexican style)
2 C. milk
4 C. chicken broth
3-4 flour tortillas, cut into 1/2" strips, about 3" long
2 C. shredded cheddar cheese

Boil chicken, remove from bone, reserve 4 C. broth. Mix soups, tomatoes, milk, broth and chicken in a pot. Heat until boiling. Add the tortilla strips. Cook until puffy. Add cheese and serve.

LORI'S TACO SOUP

2 lbs. ground round
1 sm. chopped onion
1 small can chopped green chilies
1 pkg. taco seasoning
1 pkg. ranch dressing
1 tsp. salt
1/2 tsp. pepper
1 can pinto beans with juice
1 can pinto beans with jalapenos with juice
1 can yellow hominy with juice
1 can corn, drained
3 cans stewed tomatoes or diced tomatoes
Corn Chips or Tortilla Chips

Brown meat and onion. Add all the rest of the ingredients except the chips and simmer 30 minutes. Serve with chopped tomatoes, olives, shredded cheese, lettuce, sour cream, green onions, etc. Serve over tortilla chips or corn chips.

SPICY POTATO SOUP

1 lb. ground beef
4 C. potatoes, peeled and cubed
1 small onion, chopped
3 cans tomato sauce
4 C. water
2 tsp. salt
1 tsp. pepper
1/2 tsp. 1 tsp. hot pepper sauce

Brown ground beef. Drain. Add onion, potatoes and tomato sauce. Stir in water, salt, pepper and hot pepper sauce. Bring to a boil. Reduce heat and simmer for 1 hour or until potatoes are tender.

TOMATO SOUP

1/2 pint canned tomatoes
1/4 tsp. baking soda
3 C. milk
1/2 stick margarine

Put tomatoes in a pan. Bring to a boil. Quickly stir in the soda. Pour in milk. Season with salt and pepper. Add the margarine. Heat until hot.

SPICY CHICKEN TOMATO SOUP

2 cans chicken broth
3 C. cubed, cooked chicken
2 C. frozen corn
1 can tomato paste
1 can diced tomatoes and green chilies
1 onion, finely chopped
2 garlic cloves, minced
1 bay leaf
1-2 tsp. cumin
1 tsp. salt
1/8 tsp. pepper
1/8 tsp. cayenne pepper

In a slow cooker, combine all the ingredients. Cover and cook on low for 4 hours. Discard bay leaf and serve.

RATATOUILLE

3 Tbs. oil
3 medium zucchini, cut into 1/2" slices
2 large tomatoes, peeled and chopped
1 onion, chopped
1 green pepper, chopped
1/4 C. minced fresh parsley
1 tsp. basil
1/2 tsp. salt
1/4 tsp. pepper

Heat oil. Sauté all the ingredients for 5 minutes. Cover and simmer, stirring occasionally for 15 minutes or until vegetables are tender.

CHILI VERDE

2 C. cooked pork, chopped fine
1 can stewed tomatoes
1-1/2 C. green salsa
1 onion, chopped fine
2 cans chopped green chilies
2 garlic cloves, minced
1 Tbs. minced cilantro
2 tsp. cumin
1 C. processed cheese, shredded

In a large saucepan, combine all the ingredients. Bring to a boil. Reduce heat and simmer uncovered for 10 minutes. Serve with any Mexican dish. Burritos, quesadillas, and tortilla chips as a dip.

BASIC TOMATO SAUCE

1/4 C, extra virgin olive oil
1 onion, chopped
4 garlic cloves, minced
1 Tbs. thyme
1/2 medium carrot, finely chopped
2 (28 oz.) cans peeled whole tomatoes, crushed by hand
salt to taste

In a 3 qt. saucepan, heat oil over medium heat. add the onion and garlic and cook until soft and light golden brown, about 8 minutes. Add the thyme and carrot. Cook 5 minutes more, until carrot is quite soft. Add the tomatoes and bring to a boil, stirring often. Lower heat and simmer 30 minutes. Season with salt and serve over tortellini or spaghetti. This sauce will keep up to 1 week in refrigerator or up to 6 months in the freezer.

TARTAR SAUCE

1 C. mayonnaise
1 Tbs. pickle relish

Stir the ingredients together. Serve with fish.

BASIC WHITE SAUCE

2 Tbs. margarine
2 Tbs. flour
1/2 tsp. salt
dash of pepper
1 C. milk

Place the margarine, flour, salt and pepper in a bowl. Place in the microwave for 2 minutes. Stir until well mixed. Add the milk and whisk. Put back in microwave and cook for 3 minutes or until thick, stirring about every minute.

TO MAKE CHEESE SAUCE: Add 1 C. diced processed cheese. Stir well. Cook in microwave for 1 minute. Stir until the cheese is melted. Pour over vegetables or macaroni.

CHEESE SAUCE

2 Tbs. margarine
2 Tbs. flour
1/2 tsp. salt
dash of pepper
1 C. milk
1 C. diced processed cheese

Place the margarine, flour, salt and pepper in a bowl. Place in the microwave for 2 minutes. Stir until well mixed. Add the milk and whisk. Put back in microwave and cook for 3 minutes or until thick, stirring about every minute. Add the cheese and stir well. Microwave for 1 minute. Stir until cheese is melted. Pour over vegetables or macaroni.

BROWN GRAVY

3 Tbs. fat from roast beef
3 Tbs. flour
1-1/2 C. water
salt and pepper

After cooking a roast, use the fat left in the pan. Add the flour and stir until well browned. Gradually add the water and seasonings. Bring to a boil and cook and stir until thick.

WHITE GRAVY

2-3 Tbs. meat drippings
2-3 Tbs. flour
2-3 C. milk
salt and pepper

Using the drippings after frying meat, stir in the flour, while the heat is still on. Stirring constantly, until it is bubbly, add milk and seasonings. Bring back to a boil. Stir until thick. May need more or less milk to get the right consistency.

TURKEY GRAVY

6 Tbs. turkey fat
6 Tbs. flour
3 C. turkey stock
salt and pepper

Pour off liquid in pan which turkey has been roasted. From liquid, skim off the fat. Return fat to a pan and add the flour. Gradually pour the stock into the pan. Add the seasonings. If you don't have enough stock, add water. Bring to a boil and cook until thick.

HAM GRAVY

1 C. ham drippings
1 C. water
2 heaping Tbs. cornstarch

Bring drippings to a boil. Add the water to the cornstarch. Add the water and cornstarch mixture to the drippings. Stir or whisk continually until it thickens to gravy consistency.

New found recipes

New found recipes

New found recipes

New found recipes

New found recipes

New found recipes

New found recipes

VEGETABLES
&
SIDE DISHES

CAJUN POTATOES

8 potatoes, cleaned, not peeled and chopped
1 small onion, chopped
1/2 lb. bacon, cut into pieces
1 stick margarine
salt
pepper
garlic powder
1-2 tsp. Cajun seasoning or cayenne pepper

Put the potatoes, onion and bacon in a 9X13 pan. Slice the margarine over top. Add the seasonings. Bake at 350 for 1 hour.

CORN

1 can corn
2 Tbs. margarine
1 Tbs. sugar
salt
pepper

Put all in a pan and bring to a boil. Simmer a couple of minutes.

CUSTARD CORN CASSEROLE

2 cans corn, drained
4 eggs
1/2 C. sugar
2 C. milk

Beat eggs. Add remaining ingredients. Pour into a greased baking dish. Bake at 400 for 45 minutes to an hour. Check for doneness by inserting knife in center and it comes out clean.

GREEN BEANS

1 can green beans
1 Tbs. bacon grease
1/2 tsp. salt
1/4 tsp. pepper

Put all in a pan and bring to a boil. Simmer for a couple of minutes.

GREEN BEAN CASSEROLE

1 can cream of mushroom soup
1/2 can milk
1 can French fried onions
dash of pepper
4 C. green beans

In a 1-1/2 qt. casserole, mix soup, milk, pepper, beans and 1/2 can onions. Bake at 350 for 25 minutes. Stir. Sprinkle remaining onions over top. Bake 5 minutes longer.

CHEESY RICE AND PEAS

2-1/2 C. cooked rice
1 pkg. (10 oz.) frozen peas, thawed
2 can mushrooms, drained
6 oz. processed cheese, cubed

Combine all the ingredients. Put in a greased 1-1/2 qt. baking dish. Cover and bake at 350 for 20 minutes. Stir before serving.

CHEESY GREEN BEANS

10 slices bacon
2 cans green beans, drained
1 can sliced mushrooms
3/4 C. onion, chopped
1/2 tsp. pepper
1 C. processed cheese, melted

Chop the bacon and cook until crisp. Reserve drippings. Add mushrooms and onion to bacon drippings. Cook and stir for 10 minutes. Drain. Add the bacon (save about 2 Tbs. for topping), green beans and pepper. Mix lightly. Put into a 2 qt. serving dish. Pour melted cheese over top. Sprinkle with bacon.

HOLLI'S STIR FRY GREEN BEANS

1 ½ pounds green beans, trimmed
3 tablespoons soy sauce
1 tablespoon sesame oil
1 teaspoon sugar
6 garlic cloves, minced

In large pot of water, boil green beans approx. 5 minutes, just until tender. In a small bowl, combine soy sauce, oil, and sugar; set aside. Drain beans and set aside. Spray wok or skillet with nonstick cooking spray and heat to medium-high. Add garlic; cook, stirring constantly, until softened. Add green beans; cook, stirring constantly about 2 minutes (more or less to your desired doneness). Add soy sauce mixture; continue to stir until most of the liquid is absorbed, 1-2 minutes.

You can actually use olive or canola oil.

CREAMY VEGETABLES

1 can mixed vegetables
1/8 tsp. garlic salt
2 tsp. milk
3 oz. pkg. cream cheese

Drain the vegetables. Add the rest of the ingredients and cook until cheese melts.

GREEN RICE CASSEROLE

2 C. instant rice
1 box frozen broccoli
1 stick margarine
1/2 C. water
1 can cream of mushroom soup
1 small onion, chopped fine
1 C. shredded cheese

Put rice and broccoli in a casserole dish. Heat margarine, water, soup and onion until hot. Pour over rice and mix. Stir in cheese. Bake at 350 for 30-45 minutes.

HASH BROWN POTATOES

4 medium potatoes
1/4 C. onion, finely chopped
1/2 med. red pepper, cut into 1" strips
2 Tbs. flour
1/4 C. milk
1/4 tsp. salt
pepper to taste
1/4 C. margarine

Pierce potatoes. Cook in microwave on high for 12-14 minutes. Cool. Peel and cube. Place potatoes in a bowl. Add onion and red pepper. In another bowl combine flour, milk, salt and pepper until smooth. Pour over potatoes. Mix and toss. In a large skillet, melt margarine. Add potato mixture. Cook over medium heat for 15 minutes or until golden brown.

JACQUI'S MASHED POTATO CASSEROLE

4 lbs. baking potatoes
1-8 oz. pkg. cream cheese
1-9 oz. carton sour cream
1/2 C. butter or margarine
1-1/2 tsp. salt
1/2 tsp. pepper
melted butter
chopped fresh parsley, opt.

Cook and drain potatoes. Return to pot and mash with the remaining ingredients. Serve with drizzled butter and sprinkle with parsley.

SCALLOPED POTATOES

4 potatoes, peeled and sliced
salt
pepper
3 Tbs. flour
4 Tbs. butter
1-1/2 C. milk

Cover the bottom of a casserole with a single layer of potatoes. Sprinkle with salt, pepper, flour and a few dots of butter. Repeat until all the potatoes are used. Pour milk over until the potatoes are covered. Dot with the remaining butter. Bake at 350 for 1-1/2 HR. until potatoes are tender. I like my potatoes really done, so I sometimes will cook them before putting them in this dish.

CHEESY POTATOES

1 pkg. (2 lb.) frozen hash browns, thawed
1 can cream of chicken soup
2 C. sour cream
2 C. processed cheese, cubed
2 Tbs. butter
bacon bits

Combine hash browns, soup and sour cream. Mix well. Put the cheese and butter in a bowl and microwave until smooth, stirring after every 30 seconds. Add to the hash brown mixture. Pour into a casserole dish. Sprinkle with bacon bits. Bake at 350 for 1 hour.

POTATO CASSEROLE

1 bag hash brown potatoes, thawed
1 onion, chopped
1 stick margarine, melted
1 small carton sour cream
1 can cream of mushroom soup
1 C. corn flakes
1/2 stick margarine

Mix margarine and sour cream. Stir in soup. Put the hash browns and onion in a large casserole dish. Pour margarine mixture over top. Mix the margarine and corn flakes together and sprinkle on top. Bake at 350 for 25 minutes.

TWICE BAKED POTATO CASSEROLE

6 medium potatoes, unpeeled and baked
1/4 tsp. salt
1/4 tsp. pepper
1 lb. bacon, cooked and crumbled
3 C. sour cream
2 C. shredded Mozzarella cheese
2 C. shredded Cheddar cheese
2 green onions, chopped

Cut baked potatoes into 1" cubes. Place half in a greased 9X13 pan. Sprinkle with half the salt, pepper and bacon. Top with half the sour cream and cheeses. Repeat layers. Bake uncovered at 350 for 20 minutes or until cheese is melted. Sprinkle with onions.

LORI'S TWICE BAKED POTATOES

4 left over baked potatoes
1/4 C. margarine, softened
1/4-1/2 C. milk
1/2 C. sour cream
1/4 C. bacon bits
1 C. shredded cheese
1 tsp. salt
1/2 tsp. pepper

Scoop the potatoes out of the skins. Put the potatoes, margarine and milk in a bowl and mash. Add the rest of the ingredients and mix well. Put into greased muffin tins. Bake at 400 for 30 minutes. Sprinkle a little cheese over top and bake another 5 minutes.

FRIED POTATOES

8 potatoes, peeled and sliced thin
1/2 onion, chopped
1/4 C. oil
1/4 C. butter
salt
pepper
garlic powder

Heat oil and butter together in a skillet. Add the potatoes and onions. Add seasonings. Let the potatoes get browned on one side and turn and brown the other side and cook until potatoes are tender.

CREAMED PEAS AND POTATOES

4 med. red potatoes, cubed and cooked
1 pkg. (10 oz.) frozen peas, cooked
2 Tbs. margarine
2 Tbs. flour
1/2 tsp. salt
1/4 tsp. pepper
1-1/2 C. milk

Melt margarine. Add flour, salt and pepper. Bring to a boil. Gradually stir in milk. Boil 1 minute. Drain potatoes and peas. Place in a serving bowl and pour sauce over and stir to coat.

VEGETABLE CASSEROLE

1 C. sour cream
1 can cream of celery soup
1 C. Cheddar cheese
1 can green beans, drained
1 can corn, drained
1/2 C. onion, chopped
1 can water chestnuts, drained
1 roll snack crackers, crushed
1 stick margarine, melted
sliced almonds

Mix together the sour cream, soup and cheese. Add the beans, corn, onion and water chestnuts. Pour into a greased casserole dish or 9X13 pan. Mix the crackers with the margarine. Sprinkle on top. Sprinkle almonds on top of that. Bake at 350 for 40 minutes.

VEGETABLE MEDLEY

4 C. diced, peeled potatoes
1-1/2 C. frozen corn
4 med. tomatoes, diced
1 C. sliced carrots
1/2 C. onion, chopped
3/4 tsp. salt
1/2 tsp. sugar
1/2 tsp. dill weed
1/8 tsp. pepper

Put all the ingredients in a slow cooker and cook for 5-6 hours on low.

WINTER VEGETABLE MEDLEY

1/2 lb. brussel sprouts, halved
1/2 lb. fresh baby carrots
2 medium red potatoes, cut into 1/2" cubes
2 medium white potatoes, cut into 1/2" cubes
1/2 C. margarine, melted
1-1/2 tsp. rubbed sage
2 garlic cloves, minced

Place vegetables in a greased baking dish. Combine the rest of the ingredients. Drizzle over vegetables. Cover and bake at 375 for 45-50 minutes.

BAKED MACARONI & CHEESE

8 oz. shell macaroni
4 Tbs. butter
4 Tbs. flour
3 C. milk
2-1/2 C. shredded Cheddar cheese
1 tsp. dry mustard
1 tsp. salt
1/4 tsp. pepper

Prepare macaroni according to directions on package. Drain. In saucepan, melt butter. Add flour, stirring constantly for 2 minutes. Stir in milk, cheese, mustard, salt & pepper. Cook until cheese is melted. Mix with shells in a 3 qt. casserole. Bake at 350 for 30 minutes.

KOLETTE'S MACARONI & CHEESE

2 C. elbow macaroni
1 C. processed cheese, chopped or shredded

Cook the macaroni in boiling water until done. About 10-12 minutes. Drain. Add the cheese and stir until melted. Can add a little milk if too thick.

BAKED BEANS

2 cans pork n beans
1/3 C. brown sugar
1/3 C. ketchup
1/2 tsp. salt
1/2 tsp. garlic powder
1/4 C. onion, finely chopped
2 slices bacon

Mix the beans, sugar, ketchup, salt, pepper, garlic powder and onion.
Either chop up the bacon and mix it in the beans or lay over the top of
the beans. Bake at 350 for 45 minutes to an hour.

MACARONI & TOMATO

1 can crushed tomatoes
2 C. cooked elbow macaroni
4 Tbs. margarine
1/3 C. sugar
salt
pepper

Cook the macaroni according to directions on package. Drain. Add
the rest of the ingredients and bring to a boil. Reduce heat and simmer
until margarine is melted.

BREADED TOMATOES

1 can crushed tomatoes
3 slices of bread, cubed
2 Tbs. margarine
1/4 C. sugar
salt
pepper

Put all the ingredients in a pan and bring to a boil. Reduce heat and simmer until margarine is melted.

DEVILED EGGS

6 eggs
2 Tbs. mayonnaise
1 tsp. mustard
1 tsp. sugar
1 tsp. vinegar
salt
paprika

Bring the eggs to a boil. Boil 10 minutes. Put in cold water until cool to touch. Peel eggs. Cut in half lengthwise. Scoop out the yolk. Mash with a fork until smooth. Add the rest of the ingredients except for the paprika and mix well. Spoon the yolk mixture back into the whites and sprinkle paprika on top. Refrigerate.

RICE PILAF

1 2/3 C. water
1/2 tsp. salt
1 1/3 C. instant brown rice
3 Tbs. butter
1/2 C. onion, chopped
1 clove garlic, minced
2 carrots, sliced
2 C. mushrooms, sliced
1 can peas
2 eggs, beaten
pepper
1/4 C. chopped cashews

Bring water to a boil. Add the rice and cook according to directions. Put butter in pan and add the onion and sauté. Add garlic and carrots. Cook 10 minutes. Add the mushrooms and peas. Scramble the egg in a little oil in a pan and add to the rice. Add the pepper and cashews. Mix well.

MEXICAN RICE

1/2 C. tomato sauce
2 C. water
1/4 tsp. cumin
1/2 tsp. salt
1 C. long grain rice
1 Tbs. margarine

Bring tomato sauce, water, cumin and salt to a boil. Add rice and margarine. Stir. Cover and reduce heat to a simmer and cook for 20 minutes. Remove from heat. Let stand 5 minutes. Fluff with fork.

FAST MEXICAN RICE

1 C. salsa
1 C. water
2 Tbs. margarine
2 C. uncooked instant rice

Combine salsa, water and margarine. Bring to a boil. Stir in rice. Remove from heat. Cover and let stand 5-7 minutes. Fluff with fork.

FRIED RICE

1/3 C. chopped onion
1/4 C. margarine
4 C. uncooked instant rice
3 Tbs. soy sauce
2 Tbs. minced parsley
1 tsp. garlic powder
1/8 tsp. pepper
1 egg, lightly beaten

Sauté onion and margarine until tender. Stir in the rice, soy sauce, parsley, garlic and pepper. Cook for 5 minutes, stirring occasionally. Add the egg, cook and stir until egg is completely set, about 5 minutes.

SPINACH RICE

1/2 C. onion, chopped
2 Tbs. margarine
1 pkg. (10 oz.) frozen chopped spinach, thawed & drained
1 C. cooked rice
1 can cream of mushroom soup
1/4 C. milk
2 jalapeno peppers, seeded and chopped
1/2 tsp. salt
1/4 tsp. pepper
4 oz. processed cheese, cubed

Sauté the onion in the margarine. Stir in the spinach and rice. Combine the soup, milk, jalapenos, salt and pepper. Add to the spinach mixture and heat through. Stir in the cheese. Pour into a 1-1/2 qt. baking dish. Bake, uncovered, at 350 for 30 minutes.

ZUCCHINI FRIES

1 med. zucchini
1/2 C. flour
1 tsp. onion salt
1 tsp. oregano
1/2 tsp. garlic powder
1 egg, slightly beaten
1/3 C. milk
1 tsp. oil
4 C. crispy corn cereal squares

Cut zucchini in half widthwise, then cut each half lengthwise into eight wedges. Set aside. Combine flour, onion salt, oregano and garlic powder. Combine egg, milk and oil. Stir into dry ingredients just until moistened. Crush the corn cereal. Dip zucchini wedges in batter, then roll into crushed cereal. Deep fry at 375 for 3-4 minutes.

ONION RINGS

1 C. flour
1/4 tsp. salt
1/2 C. milk
2 Tbs. oil
1 egg
1/3 C. water
2-3 large onions

Combine flour, salt, milk, oil, egg and water and beat until smooth.
Cut onions into 1/4 inch slices. Separate into rings. Dip in the batter
and let drain slightly on a cake rack placed over a plate to catch the
drippings. Fry in deep, hot fat. Drain on paper towels. Serve hot.

New found recipes

New found recipes

New found recipes

New found recipes

New found recipes

New found recipes

New found recipes

MISC.
&
HELPFUL
HINTS

ANNIVERSARY GIFT BASKET

picture frame
champagne glasses
napkins in napkin rings
heart shaped pie plate
cheese
crackers
nuts
mints
juice or champagne
chocolates
candy bars with anniversary message
votive candle

You can put as many of these items as you would like into a basket, planter or gift box.

CHEER UP BASKET

3 different kinds of baked goods:
muffins, cookies, cake, bread, etc
2 kinds of fresh fruit
2 kinds of fancy cheese
soup, casserole or salad
bouquet of flowers

Place all of these items in a basket and take to someone that needs some cheering up!

GARDNER'S GIFT BASKET

gardening gloves
garden tools
kneeling pad
hat
outside thermometer
bottled water
fruit
banana chips
cookies
rain gage

Choose any of the items and put into a toy wheel barrel.

GIFT BASKET

cheese
crackers
nuts
fruit
coffee
tea
cocoa
chocolates
cookies
snack mix
popcorn
hard candies
chewy candies
jelly
candy bars
summer sausage
beef jerky
pretzels
mints
gum
tortillas chips
salsa
water
pop
wine
juice
marinara pasta sauce
extra virgin olive oil
Parmesan cheese
chicken soup
spices
dip mixes

champagne glasses
napkins
napkin rings
picture frame
candle
room freshener
cookbook
mug
tea pot
colander
kitchen towel
table cloth
kitchen utensils
glycerin soap
hand lotion
body wash
facial scrub
lip balm
body brush
sponge
brush
comb
hand held games
stuffed animals
t-shirts
magnets
CD's
word search
book
pen
note pad
address book
playing cards

Choose any and as many items as you want. Place them in any kind of container. Basket....clay pot....gift basket.... planter....large bowl........platter.....decorative trash can......horn of plenty...... use your imagination!

MEN'S GIFT BASKET

chamois
brush
car air freshener
outside thermometer
mitt
car shampoo
banana chips
chocolate soda
soft drinks
gloves
garden tools
peanuts mitt
car shampoo
banana chips
chocolate soda
soft drinks
gloves
garden tools
cookies
pretzels

Put the items in a bucket.

MOVIE NIGHT GIFT BASKET

movie gift card
popcorn
tortilla chips
salsa
pretzels
chocolate chips cookies
chocolates
red licorice
6 pack of pop

Place the items in a large bowl. Wrap with clear cellophane.

SPORTS GIFT BASKET

note pad
pen
hand lotion
snack mix
bottled water
cheese & crackers
chewy candies
fruit
nuts
golf balls
towel
any sports item
water bottle

Choose which items you would like to give and place in a basket or

CANDY TREE

1 package of small candy bars
cone shaped Styrofoam
flower

Starting at the bottom of the cone, start hot gluing the candy bars all around, working your way to the top. Glue the flower on the top.

CHRISTMAS POTPOURRI

1 grapefruit
2 oranges
2 lemons
4 C. water
2 sticks cinnamon
1 Tbs. cloves
1 Tbs. allspice

Peel the grapefruit, oranges and lemons. Use only the peels. Add the rest of the ingredients. Bring to a boil in a kettle and let simmer as long as you like. Add more water as needed.

BUBBLES

Fast bubbles:
3 parts water
2 parts dish soap
1/2 part white syrup
Big bubbles:
4 parts water
1 part dish soap
1 Tbs. glycerin

For fast bubbles, mix together and use with a bubble wand. For big bubbles, mix together and let set for 1 week. Use with the bubble wands.

PLAY DOUGH

2 C. flour
2 tsp. cream of tartar
1 Tbs. oil
1 C. salt

1 C. water, add a few drops of food coloring to the water

Mix and cook, stirring constantly until it forms a mass. (3-5 minutes.)
Knead to a smooth consistency.

MEASUREMENTS AND EQUIVALENTS

3 tsp.	1 Tbs.
4 Tbs.	1/4 C.
5-1/3 Tbs	1/3 C.
8 Tbs.	1/2 C.
16 Tbs	1 C.
2 C.	1 pint
4 C.	1 quart
4 quarts	1 gallon
8 quarts	1 peck
4 pecks	1 bushel
1 fluid oz.	2 Tbs.
8 fluid oz.	1 C.
16 fluid oz.	2 C. or 1 pint
32 fluid oz.	4 C. or 1 quart
2 fluid pints	1 quart
16 dry oz.	1 LB.
baking powder	1 C. = 5-1/2 OZ.
American cheese	1 LB. =2-2/3 C. cubed
Cocoa	1 LB. =4 C. ground
Coffee	1 LB. = 5 C. ground
Cornmeal	1 LB. = 3 C.
Cornstarch	1 LB. = 3 C.
Eggs	1 egg = 4 Tbs. liquid
	4-5 whole = 1 C.
	7-9 whites = 1 C.
	12-14 yolks = 1 C.
Flour	1 LB. all purpose = 4 C.
	1 Lb. cake = 4-1/2 C.
Lemons	1 medium = 2-3 Tbs.
	¾ medium = 1 C.
lemon rind	1 lemon = 1 Tbs. grated
shortening or butter	1 LB. = 2 C.
	1 stick = 1/2 C.
	4 sticks = 2 C.
onion	1 medium = 1/2 C. chopped

sugar .... 1 LB. granulated = 2 C.
.... 1 LB. brown = 2-1/2 C.
.... 1 LB. powdered = 3-1/2 C.
macaroni cooked .....4 oz. (1 -1-1/4 C.) uncooked = 2-1/4 C. cooked
spaghetti...7 oz. uncooked = 4 C. cooked
noodles..................... 4 oz. (1-1/2 to 2 C.) uncooked = 2 C. cooked

SUBSTITUTIONS

Ricotta ....cottage cheese
1 C. sifted all purpose flour .... 1 C. less 2 Tbs. flour
1 C. cake flour.. 1 C. less 2 Tbs. flour
1 Tbs. cornstarch.. 2 Tbs. flour
1 C. buttermilk .... 1 C. plain yogurt
.... or add 1 Tbs. lemon juice or vinegar
to enough milk to make 1 C. Let stand 5 minutes
1 C. heavy cream.............................. 7/8 C. milk + 3 Tbs. butter
1 C. light cream ....7/8 C. milk + 1-1/2 Tbs. butter
1 C. milk.............................. 1/2 C. evaporated milk + 1/2 C. water
peanut oil................................... vegetable oil + a splash of sesame oil
1 oz. unsweetened chocolate.. 3 Tbs. cocoa
....+ 1 Tbs. butter, oil or shortening
1 sq. or oz. semi-sweet chocolate .... 3 Tbs. chocolate chips
1 pkg. dry yeast .... 1/2 cake compressed yeast
1 Tbs. lemon juice................................1/2 Tbs. cider vinegar
1 C. chopped apples ....1 C. chopped pears +
.... 1 Tbs. lemon juice or 1 C. chopped zucchini
1 C. dry bread crumbs flakes .... 3/4 C. cracker
....crumbs or 1 C. cornflakes
1 C. butter .... 1 C. margarine
.... or 7/8 C. vegetable oil
1 C. dark syrup ....3/4 C. light corn syrup +
.... 1/4 C. molasses
1 C. light corn syrup ....1 C. maple syrup or
.... 1 C. sugar + 1 C. water
1 C. molasses.. 1 C. honey

1 C. honey	1-1/4 C. sugar + 1/4 C. liquid
1 whole egg	2 egg yolks for custard
1 small onion, chopped	1 Tbs. minced dry onion
1 clove garlic	1/8 tsp. garlic powder
1 C. broth	1 C. hot water + 1 tsp. bouillon granules or 1 bouillon cube
1 tsp. Cajun seasoning	1/2 tsp. hot pepper sauce, 1/2 tsp. thyme, 1/4 tsp. basil & 1 minced garlic clove
1 C. tomato juice	1/2 C. tomato sauce + 1/2 C. water
2 C. tomato sauce	3/4 C. tomato paste + 1 C. water

QUANTITIES TO SERVE 100 PEOPLE

Coffee	3 lbs.
loaf sugar	3 lbs.
cream	3 qt.
whipping cream	4 pints
milk	6 gallons
fruit cocktail	2-1/2 gallons
fruit juice	4 #10 cans or 26 lbs.
tomato juice	4 # 10 cans or 26 lbs.
soup	5 gallons
oysters	18 qt.
wieners	25 lbs.
meat loaf	24 lbs.
ham	40 lbs.
beef	40 lbs.
roast pork	40 lbs.
hamburger	30-36 lbs.
chicken for chicken pie	40 lbs.
potatoes	35 lbs.
scalloped potatoes	5 gallons
vegetables	4 # 10 cans or 26 lbs.
baked beans	5 gallons

```
beets..............................................................30 lbs.
cauliflower...................................................18 lbs.
cabbage for slaw .......................................20 lbs.
carrots ..........................................................33 lbs.
bread .......................................................10 loaves
rolls ................................................................. 200
butter ............................................................3 lbs.
potato salad ............................................... 12 qt.
fruit salad .................................................. 20 qt.
vegetable salad ......................................... 20 qt.
lettuce ....................................................20 heads
salad dressing...............................................3 qt.
pie...................................................................... 18
cake..................................................................... 8
ice cream ..............................................4 gallons
olives .................................................... 1-3/4 lbs.
cheese ...........................................................3 lbs.
pickles ...........................................................2 qt.
nuts................................................................3 lbs.
```

To serve 50, divide by 2
To serve 25 divide by 4

HELPFUL HINTS

Wipe your TV screen and computer screen with a used fabric softener sheet. This will help cut down on static electricity, which attracts dust.

Apply mineral oil to fiberglass shower doors to quickly remove soap scum and make it easier to clean next time. About twice a year, wax your shower with car wax after it has been thoroughly cleaned. This will keep soap scum from sticking.

Spray the inside of your microwave with a plant mister. Then turn on high for a few seconds. Allow it to sit a minute or two. Wipe with a clean cloth. You can also nuke a few tablespoons of baking soda in a cup of water and then wipe up the mist with a paper towel. For stubborn stains, scrub with a toothbrush.

Spray your cheese grater with a non stick cooking spray. The cheese slides right off.

Put your orange in the freezer the night before you want to grate it.

When making crispy rice treats run your hands under cold water before pressing then into the pan. The marshmallow won't stick to your hands.

Use wax paper to press marshmallow treats into a pan.

Bury an avocado in flour overnight to ripen.

For cut out cookies, try rolling the dough out on the greased cookie sheet, cutting them and pulling the outline off, leaving the cut out cookie on the pan.

Need to check to see if cake's done, but no toothpick? Use an uncooked spaghetti noodle.

Sprinkle rice or oyster crackers in you salt shaker to keep it running freely.

Place your hand in a sandwich bag and dip in the shortening to grease a pan.

To soften brown sugar, microwave it for a few seconds.

Freeze leftover waffles or pancakes, Microwave them later.

Keeping staples such as flour, sugar brown sugar, powdered sugar, graham crackers, chocolate chips, marshmallows, popcorn, etc. in the freezer is a great idea. Keeps them fresh for whenever you need them. Fresh eggs....stale ones float in water.

Add a little vinegar to the water when boiling eggs. This will seal the eggs while boiling.

When you want to crush graham crackers for crumbs, use a zip lock bag. Use a rolling pin to smash them. Then put the bag in the box with the rest of the crackers to use next time.

After frying steak, pork chops, etc. Put a little water in the pan and turn on the burner for a few minutes. Let it set for a few more minutes and then it will clean right up.

To remove candle wax, scrap up as much as you can with a knife. Put 3 layers of paper towels on top of the spill.
Take a hot iron and place on top of the paper towels. Allow them to absorb the wax. You may need to do this several times.

To get chewing gum out of anything, put some peanut butter on a rub in. Then clean with soap and water.

To get ink out use some hair spray on the spot and blot.

To remove rust get some navel jelly in the automotive department, works fine on clothes.

WHAT'S FOR DINNER??

MEAT.. SIDES

GROUND BEEF

Meat loaf....................................mashed potatoes & green beans
Shepherds pie ....tossed salad or slaw
Stuffed peppers................................cheesy potatoes & corn salad
Lasagna .... tossed salad & batter bread rolls
Cavatini .... corn salad & cheese bread
Spaghetti .... corn, tossed salad & garlic bread
Hobo casserole .... crunchy vegetable salad
Hamburger casserole ....vegetable salad

ROAST

Garlic chuck roast .... in crock pot with potatoes,
    carrots and onions. And slaw. Left over roast:
Beef & noodles........................mashed potatoes, slaw or corn salad
    or pea salad
Vegetable soup... batter bread rolls
    BBQ beef....shred beef and add BBQ sauce. Heat and serve on
    buns. Potato salad.
Shepherds pie .... festive salad, cottage cheese

ROUND STEAK OR SIRLOIN STEAK

Baked steak .... mashed potatoes or noodles, corn and
    Napa salad
Swiss steak............................ mashed potatoes or rice, green beans
Peppers & beef tips......................... rice, stir fry green beans
Beef stroganoff .... noodles, garden salad
Hungarian goulash .... noodles, peas or green beans, festive
    salad

CHICKEN

Smothered chicken .... rice pilaf, vegetable salad or green
    beans
Lemon basil chicken .... rice pilaf, corn salad
Chicken enchilada casserole .... Napa salad

HAM

Stromboli .... Cajun potatoes, broccoli salad,
Ham & potato casserole .... 3 bean salad or garden salad

PORK CHOPS

BBQ pork chops .... macaroni & cheese,
    baked beans, garden salad
Rosemary pork chops .... macaroni & tomato,
    crunchy vegetable salad
Zippy pork chops .... cheesy potatoes,
    slaw or pea salad, corn fritters
Pork chops & rice .... cheesy green beans
RIBS .... baked beans,
    potato salad, deviled eggs

SALMON

Salmon cakes .... creamed peas & potatoes,
    or fried potatoes, baked beans, Dijon pasta salad

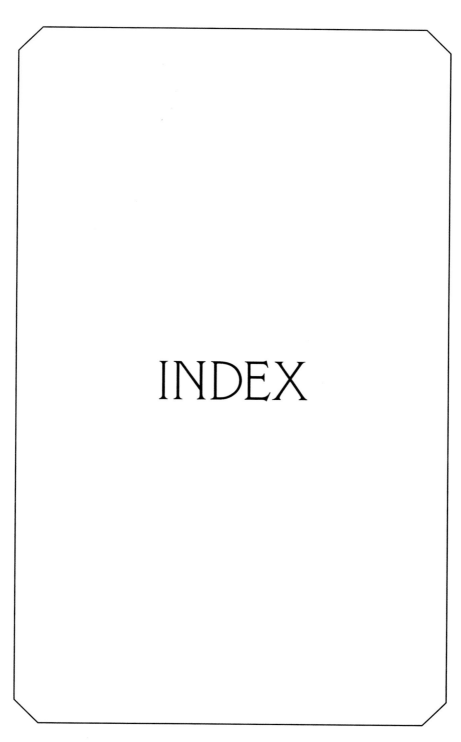

INDEX

3 BEAN SALAD 373
48 HOUR SLAW 376

A

ANGEL HAIR PASTA WITH CHICKEN 298
ANITA'S FESTIVE SALAD 368
ANNIVERSARY GIFT BASKET 445
ANTIPASTO 17
APPLE CAKE 128
APPLE CHEESE QUESADILLA 20
APPLE DIP 25
APPLE FRITTERS 62
APPLE PIE 348
APPLE TURNOVERS 232
APPLE TURNOVERS 356

B

BACON CHEESEBURGER WRAP 263
BACON IN THE OVEN 75
BAKED BEANS 430
BAKED BEAN CHILI 401
BAKED CHICKEN 297
BAKED FRUIT FRENCH TOAST 85
BAKED MACARONI & CHEESE 429
BAKED STEAK 288
BALSAMIC SALAD DRESSING 382
BANANA CAKE 128
BANANA CREAM PIE 338
BANANA NUT BREAD 50
BASIC TOMATO SAUCE 406
BASIC WHITE SAUCE 407
BBQ CUPS 276
BBQ PORK CHOPS 318
BEEFY JALAPENO BAKE 272

BEEF AND NOODLES   288
BEEF BROCCOLI SUPPER   265
BEEF ENCHILADAS   270
BEEF STEW   401
BEEF STIR FRY   290
BEEF STROGANOFF   289
BERRY DELIGHT   228
BEST CHOCOLATE CHIP COOKIES   179
BISCUIT WRAPPED HOT DOGS   311
BLACK AND WHITE BARS   200
BLUEBERRY CREAM MUFFINS   57
BRAIDED COFFEE CAKE   54
BREADED TOMATOES   431
BREAD MACHINE GARLIC BREAD   46
BREAD MACHINE WHITE BREAD   45
BREAD PUDDING   223
BREAKFAST BAKE   79
BREAKFAST BURRITOS   76
BREAKFAST CASSEROLE   79
BREAKFAST FRUIT PARFAIT   91
BREAKFAST FRUIT SALAD   91
BREAKFAST PIZZA   88
BRENDA'S BATTER BREAD   44
BRENDA'S CHICKEN PASTA   306
BROCCOLI & CAULIFLOWER SALAD   370
BROCCOLI CASHEW SALAD   370
BROCCOLI HAM RING   310
BROWN GRAVY   408
BUBBLES   450
BURGER BEANS   260
BUTTERSCOTCH HAYSTACKS   166
BUTTER CREAM FROSTING   143

C

CAJUN POTATOES	419
CALICO BEANS	393
CALIFORNIA CHICKEN CASSEROLE	303
CAMP STEW	262
CANDY BAR COOKIES	182
CANDY BAR QUESADILLA	20
CANDY TREE	449
CARAMEL APPLE CAKE	130
CARAMEL CRUNCH PIE	346
CARAMEL DELIGHTS	156
CARAMEL OATMEAL BAR COOKIES	199
CARROT CAKE	135
CASHEW CHICKEN	309
CASHEW CHICKEN CASSEROLE	307
CAVATINI	280
CHAMPAGNE CAKE	122
CHEER UP BASKET	445
CHEESE BALL	5
CHEESE BREAD	46
CHEESE CAKE	220
CHEESE DIP	5
CHEESE SAUCE	407
CHEESE SOUP	396
CHEESY CHICKEN ENCHILADAS	306
CHEESY GREEN BEANS	421
CHEESY POTATOES	424
CHEESY RICE AND PEAS	420
CHERRY ANGEL DELIGHT	229
CHERRY BARS	203
CHERRY CHEESE CAKE	217
CHERRY CHEWBILEES	242
CHERRY COFFEE CAKE	54
CHERRY CUSTARD PIE	339
CHERRY ENCHILADAS	231
CHERRY MUFFINS	58

CHERRY RHUBARB COBBLER 353
CHEWY, FUDGY TRIPLE CHOCOLATE BROWNIES 195
CHICKEN ALMOND SPREAD 8
CHICKEN BROCCOLI SUPPER 303
CHICKEN BUNDLES 297
CHICKEN CASSEROLE 307
CHICKEN ENCHILADA CASSEROLE 304
CHICKEN MARINARA 299
CHICKEN PASTA PRIMAVERA 299
CHICKEN QUESADILLAS 11
CHICKEN RICE SKILLET 302
CHICKEN SOUP 394
CHICKEN STRIPS 293
CHICKEN STRUDEL 301
CHILI 400
CHILI CHEESE MUFFINS 48
CHILI VERDE 406
CHILLY COCONUT PIE 340
CHIMICHANGAS 269
CHIPS GALORE COOKIES 180
CHOCOLATE CAKE 106
CHOCOLATE CARAMEL FONDUE 26
CHOCOLATE CHERRY BALLS 165
CHOCOLATE CHIP CHEESECAKE 220
CHOCOLATE CHIP CHEESE BARS 202
CHOCOLATE CHIP COOKIES 179
CHOCOLATE CHIP PIE 343
CHOCOLATE COCONUT BALLS 157
CHOCOLATE COOKIES 184
CHOCOLATE COOKIE DESSERT 221
CHOCOLATE CREAM FRUIT DIP 25
CHOCOLATE CRINKLES 188
CHOCOLATE DESSERT WRAPS 233
CHOCOLATE FROSTING 144
CHOCOLATE KISS COOKIES 182
CHOCOLATE MACAROON CAKE 116
CHOCOLATE NO BAKE COOKIES 181

CHOCOLATE PEANUT BARS	202
CHOCOLATE PEANUT BUTTER BARS	201
CHOCOLATE PEANUT SUPREME	226
CHOCOLATE PECAN BARS	200
CHOCOLATE PIZELLES	192
CHOCOLATE SAUCE BROWNIES	197
CHOCOLATE SHEET CAKE	111
CHOCOLATE STREUSEL COFFEE CAKE	53
CHOCOLATE TRUFFLES	157
CHOCOLATE ZUCCHINI CAKE	110
CHOW CHOW	30
CHOW MEIN NOODLE CLUSTERS	165
CHRISTMAS BARK CANDY	163
CHRISTMAS POTPOURRI	450
CINDY'S CROCK POT CHILI	400
CINDY'S WHITE LASAGNA	278
CINNAMON FLOP CAKE	140
CINNAMON ROCK CANDY	163
CINNAMON ROLLS	43
COCONUT CHICKEN STRIPS	293
COCONUT CREAM CAKE	105
COCONUT CREAM PIE	340
COCONUT MACAROONS	191
COLD WATER PIE CRUST	337
CONFETTI COOKIES	204
COOKIE DOUGH CHEESE BALL	24
COPPER PENNY SALAD	375
CORN	419
CORNISH HENS WITH STUFFING	309
CORN BREAD TACO BAKE	272
CORN CHOWDER	399
CORN FRITTERS	48
CORN RELISH	31
CORN SALMON CASSEROLE	326
CORN SALSA	3
CORUM'S ORANGE SCONES WITH ORANGE BUTTER	60
CORUM'S ORANGE SCONES WITH ORANGE BUTTER	90

COTTAGE CHEESE MUFFINS 47
COTTAGE CHEESE PANCAKES 86
COUNTRY STYLE CASSEROLE 311
COWBOY COOKIES 186
CREAMED PEAS AND POTATOES 427
CREAMY CHICKEN STEW 396
CREAMY CHOCOLATE CAKES 106
CREAMY COLESLAW 377
CREAMY CORN SALAD 372
CREAMY FROSTING 144
CREAMY ORANGE DRINK 33
CREAMY SPINACH DIP 7
CREAMY VEGETABLES 422
CREAM CHEESE BALL 6
CREAM CHEESE BITES 15
CREAM CHEESE FROSTING 144
CREAM CHEESE MINTS 155
CREAM CHEESE RHUBARB PIE 352
CREAM FROSTING 143
CREAM WAFERS 187
CRISPY CEREAL MIX 18
CRISPY PRETZEL BARS 205
CRISPY RICE CEREAL BARS 205
CRUNCHY TRAIL MIX 19
CRUNCHY VEGETABLE SALAD 369
CRUSTLESS QUICHE 82
CUSTARD CORN CASSEROLE 419
CUSTARD PIE 338

D

DARK CHOCOLATE FUDGE 160
DECADENT CHOCOLATE PIE 343
DELMA'S ALMOND BARK CANDY 167
DEVILED EGGS 431
DIJON CHEESE SPREAD 8
DIJON PASTA SALAD 377

DILLY DIP 6
DILL JAR 28
DINNER HORN PIE 342
DISHPAN COOKIES 186
DIVINITY 164
DOUBLE DECKER BROWNIES 196
DREAM CAKE 124

E

EASY CHERRY GELATIN 236
EASY CHOCOLATE TRUFFLES 158
EASY DEEP DISH PIZZA 285
EASY GOULASH 284
EASY PUNCH 32
EASY RHUBARB DESSERT 237
EASY TURTLE CANDY 161
EGG ROLLS 13
EGG SALAD 378
ENCHILADA CASSEROLE 270
ENCHILADA PIE 271

F

FAIRY'S DELIGHT 227
FAJITAS 275
FANCY CRESCENTS 14
FARMERS BREAKFAST 78
FASTEST CAKE IN THE WEST 131
FAST MEXICAN RICE 433
FEATHER LIGHT SCONES 59
FESTIVE CAKE 138
FISH CAKES 325
FLOURLESS CHOCOLATE CAKE 114
FLUFFY GELATIN SALAD 381
FOUR LAYER DESSERT 217

FRENCH COOKIES 192
FRENCH TOAST 84
FRENCH TOAST BAKE 83
FRESH FRUIT DIP 24
FRESH PEACH PIE 348
FRIED POTATOES 426
FRIED RICE 433
FROG EYE SALAD 381
FROSTED BANANA BARS 203
FROSTED PEANUT BUTTER FINGERS 207
FRUIT COBBLER 230
FRUIT DIP 25
FRUIT FILLED QUESADILLA 19
FRUIT SALAD 380
FRUIT SMOOTHIE 33
FUDGE 159
FUDGE BROWNIES 194
FUDGE CRISPIES 160
FUDGE POPS 244
FUNNEL CAKES 61

G

GARDEN SALAD 371
GARDNER'S GIFT BASKET 446
GARLIC CHUCK ROAST 286
GARLIC BUTTER 64
GELATIN CAKE 127
GELATIN COOKIES 188
GERMAN APPLE CAKE 129
GERMAN CHOCOLATE CAKE 113
GERMAN CHOCOLATE COOKIES 189
GERMAN CHOCOLATE PIE 344
GERMAN SLAW 376
GIFT BASKET 447
GOOEY BUTTER CAKE 120
GOOSEBERRY PIE 355

GRANDMA MINNIE'S RHUBARB PIE 353
GREEN BEANS 420
GREEN BEAN CASSEROLE 420
GREEN RICE CASSEROLE 422
GRIDDLE SCONES 58
GRILLED ROAST BEEF SANDWICHES 287

H

HAMBURGER CASSEROLE 260
HAMBURGER SOUP 402
HAM & EGG SKILLET 77
HAM & POTATO CASSEROLE 313
HAM AND CHEESE POTATO BAKE 312
HAM AND SWISS STROMBOLI 314
HAM GRAVY 409
HASH BROWN POTATOES 423
HEARTY EGG SCRAMBLE 77
HEARTY QUICHE 81
HELPFUL HINTS 456
HOBO CASSEROLE 257
HOLLI'S STIR FRY GREEN BEANS 421
HOT CRAB DIP 8
HOT FUDGE CAKE 112
HUNGARIAN GOULASH 292

I

IMPOSSIBLE BROWNIE PIE 346
IMPOSSIBLE PIE 341
INDIAN TACOS 266
ITALIAN CHEESE BAKE 284
ITALIAN DRESSING 381
ITALIAN SAUSAGE SPAGHETTI 321

J

JACQUI'S ITALIAN MEAT SAUCE   281
JACQUI'S MASHED POTATO CASSEROLE   423
JALAPENO CHICKEN ENCHILADAS   304
JANA'S SPAGHETTI RED   256
JOYCE'S ICE CREAM DESSERT   244

K

KENT'S SHRIMP SCAMPI   324
KEY LIME PIE   355
KIDS GELATIN   24
KOLETTE'S MACARONI & CHEESE   429
KOLETTE'S MEATLOAF   257
KOLETTE'S VEGGIE PIZZA   16

L

LASAGNA   276
LAYERED TACO DIP   5
LEMON-BASIL STUFFED CHICKEN BREASTS   294
LEMON BAR COOKIES   204
LEMON BLOSSOM TWIST   235
LEMON FUDGE   164
LOCO MOCO   80
LONG JOHNS   63
LORI'S CHICKEN MANICOTTI   300
LORI'S DOUBLE LAYER PUMPKIN PIE   345
LORI'S ITALIAN TURKEY SANDWICH   292
LORI'S LASAGNA   277
LORI'S NAPA SALAD   368
LORI'S SESAME CHICKEN   305
LORI'S TACO SOUP   403
LORI'S TWICE BAKED POTATOES   426

M

MACADAMIA NUT COOKIES	189
MACARONI & TOMATO	430
MACAROONS	190
MAGIC COOKIE BARS	197
MANDARIN PIE	350
MANGO MOUSSE IN CRISPY CUPS	230
MANICOTTI	279
MEASUREMENTS AND EQUIVALENTS	452
MEATBALLS	282
MEATBALLS IN PLUM SAUCE	262
MEATBALL & CHEESE RAVIOLI	283
MEATBALL SUB SANDWICHES	283
MEATLOAF MINIATURES	255
MEDITERRANEAN CHICKEN	296
MEN'S GIFT BASKET	448
MENDI'S OCTOBERFEST WINE CAKE	119
MEXICAN CREAM CHEESE DIP	4
MEXICAN EGG ROLLS	12
MEXICAN GOULASH	267
MEXICAN RICE	432
MEXICAN SALAD	380
MICROWAVE PEANUT BRITTLE	156
MINIATURE CHERRY CHEESECAKES	22
MISSISSIPPI MUD CAKE	107
MOM'S BEAN SALAD	374
MOM'S CHERRY DELIGHT	225
MOM'S FRUIT COCKTAIL CAKE	134
MONKEY BREAD	52
MONSTER COOKIES	185
MOVIE NIGHT GIFT BASKET	448
MOZZARELLA CRACKERS	15
MULTIPLE CHOICE BARS	198
MY POPPY SEED CAKE RECIPE	102

N

NOVA'S ANGEL FOOD CAKE 121
NOVA'S SALMON CAKES 327
NO COOK CANDY 165

O

OATMEAL BAR COOKIES 199
OATMEAL CAKE 132
OATMEAL CHOCOLATE CHIP COOKIES 181
OATMEAL COOKIES 177
OATMEAL PIE 342
OMELET 83
ONION RINGS 435
ONION TOPPED CHICKEN 294
ORANGE FROSTING 143
ORANGE SCONES 89
ORIENTAL CHICKEN SALAD 367
OYSTER STEW 399

P

PANCAKES 86
PAPRIKA CHICKEN AND PIEROGIE STEW 395
PASTA SALAD 378
PASTA VEGETABLE SALAD 378
PEACHES AND CREAM DESSERT 223
PEACHES AND CREAM PIE 347
PEACH POUND CAKE 138
PEACH PUDDING 228
PEANUT BANANA MUFFINS 56
PEANUT BUTTER BARS 205
PEANUT BUTTER CAKE 104
PEANUT BUTTER CANDY 166

PEANUT BUTTER CHOCOLATE BALLS	162
PEANUT BUTTER CHOCOLATE QUESADILLA	21
PEANUT BUTTER CHOCOLATE TORTE	234
PEANUT BUTTER COOKIES	177
PEANUT BUTTER CRISPY RICE BARS	206
PEANUT BUTTER DESSERT	222
PEANUT BUTTER PIE	344
PEANUT BUTTER SHEET CAKE	103
PEANUT BUTTER SNOWBALLS	162
PEANUT CLUSTERS	155
PEANUT MALLOW BARS	201
PEAR CAKE	139
PEA SALAD	374
PECAN PIE	341
PECAN TARTS	22
PEPPERS AND BEEF TIPS	291
PERFECT DINNER ROLLS	45
PICCALILLI	30
PICKLED BEETS	26
PICKLE BITES	18
PIE CRUST	337
PISTACHIO CAKE	127
PISTACHIO DESSERT	222
PIZELLES	193
PIZELLES 2	193
PIZZA ENGLISH MUFFINS	16
PLAY DOUGH	451
PLUM CAKE	139
POPPY SEED CAKE	102
PORCUPINE MEAT BALLS	261
PORK CHOPS AND RICE	315
PORK CHOP BAKE	316
PORK CHOP CASSEROLE	317
PORK CHOP SUPPER	315
POTATO & CHEESE QUESADILLAS	87
POTATO AND CHEESE QUESADILLA	10
POTATO AND EGG CASSEROLE	80

POTATO CASSEROLE 425
POTATO SALAD 372
POTATO SOUP 397
PUDDING CAKE 125
PUMPKIN CAKE 136
PUMPKIN CAKE ROLL 236
PUMPKIN CHEESE CAKE 221
PUMPKIN DESSERT 225
PUMPKIN PIE 345
PUMPKIN SEEDS 19
PUMPKIN SHEET CAKE 137

Q

QUANTITIES TO SERVE 100 PEOPLE 454
QUESADILLA 9
QUICK CHERRY TURNOVERS 232
QUICK FRUIT DIP 25
QUICK MONKEY BREAD 52
QUICK ONION BREAD 47
QUICK RICE PUDDING 237

R

RASPBERRY CHOCOLATE CUPCAKES 109
RASPBERRY FUDGE CAKE 115
RASPBERRY MOUSSE PIE 351
RASPBERRY SWIRL CHEESECAKE 218
RASPBERRY TARTS 233
RASPBERRY TEA 32
RATATOUILLE 405
RAVIOLI AND BACON 319
RED BEANS & RICE 312
RED BURGERS 255
RED HOT APPLESAUCE HEARTS 23
RED HOT PUNCH 33

RED PICKLES   27
RED VELVET CAKE   101
REUBEN SANDWICHES   319
REUBEN SPREAD   9
RHUBARB CAKE   142
RHUBARB CHERRY PIE   351
RHUBARB COCONUT BREAD PUDDING   238
RHUBARB CRISP   238
RHUBARB DELIGHT   239
RHUBARB DUMPLINGS   240
RHUBARB MUFFINS   55
RHUBARB PIE   354
RHUBARB PUDDING CAKE   140
RHUBARB SQUARES   239
RHUBARB SURPRISE PIE   354
RHUBARB UPSIDE DOWN CAKE   141
RHUBARB UPSIDE DOWN CAKE   241
RICE PILAF   432
RICE PUDDING   237
ROASTED CHICKEN DINNER   298
ROSEMARY PORK CHOPS   316
RUEBEN PIE   318
RUSTIC PIZZA   88
RUTH'S POTATO SALAD   373

S

SALSA   3
SAM'S EGGS & BACON SPAGHETTI   320
SANTA FE CASSEROLE   268
SAUERKRAUT SALAD   379
SAUSAGE APPLE BRAID   89
SAUSAGE GRAVY   75
SAUSAGE POTATO SOUP   397
SCALLOPED POTATOES   424
SCRAMBLED EGG MUFFINS   81
SHEPHERDS PIE   263

SHERBET PUNCH	32
SIMPLE GUACAMOLE	3
SKILLET HASH	287
SKY HIGH BISCUITS	44
SKY HIGH BISCUITS	75
SLOPPY JOES	275
SLOW COOKER CASSEROLE	313
SLOW COOKER CHICKEN & DUMPLINGS	300
SLOW COOKER RIBS	322
SLOW COOKER SPAGHETTI SAUCE	282
SMOKEY CHEESE BALL	6
SMOTHERED CHICKEN	295
SNICKERDOOLES	178
SOPAIPILLAS	62
SOUTHWEST CASSEROLE	273
SPAGHETTI PEPPERONI PIE	310
SPANISH NOODLES & BEEF	274
SPECIAL ITALIAN SALAD DRESSING	382
SPICY CHICKEN TOMATO SOUP	405
SPICY POTATO SOUP	404
SPICY RED APPLESAUCE	23
SPINACH DIP	7
SPINACH RICE	434
SPORTS GIFT BASKET	449
SPRINGFIELD CASHEW CHICKEN	308
STANDING RIB ROAST	286
STEAK QUESADILLAS	274
STRAWBERRIES 'N' CREAM BREAD	51
STRAWBERRY BUTTER	64
STRAWBERRY CAKE	133
STRAWBERRY COOKIES	191
STRAWBERRY CREPES	231
STRAWBERRY DESSERT	229
STRAWBERRY MUFFINS	56
STRAWBERRY PIE	350
STRAWBERRY PIZZA	21
STRAWBERRY PIZZA	241

STUFFED MUSHROOMS 14
STUFFED PEPPERS 256
SUBSTITUTIONS 453
SUGAR COOKIES 183
SUMMER SAUSAGE 323
SUNFLOWER SALAD 371
SUNSET COOLER 32
SUPER STRAWBERRY PIE 349
SWEET AND SOUR MEATBALLS 261
SWEET TOMATO RELISH 29
SWISS STEAK 289

T

TACO BAKE 267
TACO DIP 4
TANGY POTATO SALAD 373
TARTAR SAUCE 407
TATER TOT CASSEROLE 264
TEA 31
TERESA'S BROWNIES 195
TEX-MEX DIP 4
TEXAS BRUNCH 76
TOFFEE BARS 161
TOFFEE CANDY BAR DESSERT 243
TOFFEE PECAN BARS 206
TOMATO SALAD 375
TOMATO SOUP 404
TRACY'S CHICKEN TORTILLA SOUP 403
TRACY'S CHOCOLATE CHIP COOKIES 178
TRACY'S COCONUT CAKE 104
TRACY'S HEAVENLY BEEF 259
TRACY'S PEACHES AND CREAM PIE 347
TRACY'S SWEDISH MEATBALL SOUP 258
TRACY'S SWEDISH MEATBALL SOUP 398
TRIPLE BLISS BUNDT CAKE 108
TRUFFLES 159

TUNA CHEESE TWIST   326
TUNA SALAD   379
TUNNEL OF FUDGE CAKE   108
TURKEY GRAVY   408
TWICE BAKED POTATO CASSEROLE   425

V

VALENTINE CUTOUTS   23
VANILLA WAFER CAKE   126
VANILLA WAFER COOKIES   190
VEGETABLE CASSEROLE   427
VEGETABLE MEDLEY   428
VEGETABLE SALAD   369
VEGETABLE SOUP   402
VEGGIE HAMBURGER SKILLET   265

W

WAKE-UP CASSEROLE   78
WHAT'S FOR DINNER??   458
WHIPPED CREAM FROSTING   145
WHITE CAKE   120
WHITE CHOCOLATE BREAD PUDDING   224
WHITE CHOCOLATE CHEESECAKE   219
WHITE CHOCOLATE FUDGE CAKE   118
WHITE CHRISTMAS PIE   339
WHITE GRAVY   408
WINTER VEGETABLE MEDLEY   428
WON TONS   13

Y

YUMMY BROWNIES   194

Z

ZIPPY PORK CHOPS   317
ZUCCHINI & BEEF CASSEROLE   264
ZUCCHINI BREAD   50
ZUCCHINI CAKE   110
ZUCCHINI CASSEROLE   314
ZUCCHINI FRIES   434
ZUCCHINI FRITTERS   49
ZUCCHINI RELISH   29
ZUCCHINI WEDGES   49

About the Author

Kathy Thornton was born and raised in southwest Missouri. Her mother and grandmothers were all great cooks and at an early age she started learning to cook. She loved 4-H and Home Ec and still has the recipes she used while in grade school and high school. Trying new recipes was a favorite thing to do and still is!

She and her husband of 34 years live in the same southwest Missouri area. They have 2 married daughters, Tracy to Sam and Lori to Danny. And one fabulous granddaughter, Morgan! During the time her girls were growing up she was a housewife and mother. Now she is a housewife, mother, Nana and business owner of KT Concepts.

Kathy loves to cook and give out recipes. This is the best way to give them out all at once!

Printed in the United States
126879LV00007B/1/P